Ex Libris Allison Cicenia
8/18/73

BY R. F. DELDERFIELD

For My Own Amusement

{ *Theirs Was the Kingdom*
  God Is an Englishman }

Mr. Sermon

The Avenue

{ *The Green Gauntlet*
  A Horseman Riding By }

R. F. DELDERFIELD

For My Own Amusement

SIMON AND SCHUSTER
NEW YORK

Contents

5

CONTENTS

CONTENTS

PART FIVE
The Uncertain Trumpet

A Wand'ring Minstrel I...

This volume of autobiographical stories has been assembled from two books containing nearly sixty essays. Each book had an introduction or, as I originally entitled it, "an apologia for so much rambling."

The American edition was compiled at the request of my American publishers, Simon and Schuster, who were responsible for introducing me (admittedly a very English writer) to the American scene with the publication of my long English sagas.

Since then I have made hundreds of American friends and taken part in a nonstop two-way correspondence across the Atlantic, so that I hope my publishers' view, that these linked fragments of autobiography will be acceptable, proves justified.

There was no plan about the original books. One was called *For My Own Amusement*, its successor *Overture for Beginners*. The titles tell their own story. I wrote them, unashamedly, for fun between acres of more organized material. Looking at them now, I am reminded of Nanki-Poo's song in *The Mikado* that begins:

> A wand'ring minstrel I, a thing of shreds and patches,
> Of ballads, songs and snatches . . .

For I have always seen myself as a lineal descendant of the medieval minstrel who trudged from castle to castle telling tales for his supper. Not that I am complaining. I am a compulsive teller of tales, a really chronic case. Give me a pen and some blank sheets of paper, and I am content to ply my craft in a hogshead, of the kind Huck Finn inhabited. Deny me the privilege and I would die of boredom and frustration in the Palace of the Doge set in the Garden of Eden.

So here they are—a ragbag of ballads, songs and snatches about a man who never had the slightest inclination to do anything other than write, a child who exchanged all toys for books, a boy who never once saw himself as an engine driver or a deep-sea diver or, indeed, anything but a professional minstrel.

I have made some attempt to arrange the stories chronologically. Part I concerns my childhood from, say, 1917 to 1925. Part II deals with my adolescence, between the years 1926 and 1932. Part III covers the period 1929 to 1939, when I was a reporter and editor on a weekly newspaper. Part IV is about my sources and methods as a professional writer. Part V deals mostly with World War II as I saw it in the R.A.F. between 1940 and 1945.

There are, however, two odd men out in this verbal striptease act. One is the introduction, called "The Character Farms," dealing with sectors of my life that have contributed to everything I have written for stage, screen or publisher. The other is a new chapter that seems to me obligatory in an American edition —my reactions, at the ripe old age of fifty-eight, to America and the Americans, after my first visit in the summer of 1970. Now—if you have any curiosity left—read on. . . .

PART ONE

*Another Place,
Another Time*

The Character Farms

The most popular question a professional novelist has to answer
and one which is certain to be asked whenever he addresses an
audience on the subject of his craft, is the old chestnut, "Do you
invent characters or do you take them from life?"

Having been a writer by trade for nearly forty years, I have
been asked this question, couched in those deceivingly simple
terms, about twice a week over three decades—that is to say, ever
since my friends and neighbors came to terms with the fact that
people who earn a living by writing about imaginary men and
women do actually exist.

It is a question I often shirk; for, however simple it sounds, it
has no short answer. Somerset Maugham, who was asked this
question *ad nauseam*, sometimes made a tetchy response to it,
once retorting that the man who had invented a character had
yet to be born. But this is not the whole truth. It is well known
that Maugham, once he had set to work to create a character,
could be merciless to friends and acquaintances. Dickens always
liked to tell himself that he invented characters. On one occasion,
drawn to his study threshold by a cacophony of groans, yells and
thuds, his children peeped through the keyhole and saw what
they took to be the victim of an epileptic fit. When they rushed
in, however, he said there was nothing the matter with him. He
was "inventing" Quilp. In later life he was more honest, admitting that Micawber owed much to his father and that many of

his characters were based upon men who were elderly when he was young.

Every professional author has his own sources of character, areas in his experience to which he returns, time and again, for raw material, and it is my belief that the majority do very little initial prospecting after the age of about twenty-five. Dickens, I would say, is an example of this withering of the feelers a creative artist puts out to restock his imagination. He lived throughout the development and high tide of railways, but his characters, almost to a man, used the stagecoach of his boyhood. He very rarely drew upon the contemporary scene. Judged on his writings, he might have died in 1840 instead of thirty years later. Similarly the best of Galsworthy's work portrays the customs, manners and social values of the author's youth. So does the work of Hardy, Arnold Bennett, D. H. Lawrence and a thousand others. Nearer our own day, popular novelists like J. B. Priestly, A. J. Cronin and Howard Spring go some way toward proving this petrification theory. Spring, in fact, wrote what was virtually the same book over and over again, whisking his characters from the north of England to Cornwall and back again between about 1880 and 1910, when he was an observant young man.

Perhaps character sources can be discovered and tapped only by the young. I know that this is so in my particular case. I write of the twenties with zest, of the thirties with enthusiasm, of the early forties with mild excitement. From then on my inventiveness diminishes with every day of the century. When I get to the fifties I am falteringly uncertain of my facts, whereas to begin a contemporary novel at all is to rob me of all the pleasure I derive from writing. Maybe it has something to do with the processes of mental digestion and I wouldn't care to be didactic on the subject. I was born two months before the *Titanic* sank, and possibly there is significance in this fact. It was the death-dive of the *Titanic*, and not the Great War, that marked the end of one era and the birth pangs of its successor.

One could call these areas of inspiration character farms, that is to say, fenced-off acres of personal experience both emotional and actual, sown in childhood, adolescence and early manhood, and reaped in middle age. I have at least six such farms, three of which have broad acres and three smaller ones with thinnish soil. Large or small, each farm is neatly fenced by the years. Rarely do they poach one another's preserves.

The richest but not the largest of these is the period between 1918 and 1923, the former date being the year I was transported from Thames-side to the rural outer suburb of Addiscombe, on the Kent-Surrey border. Then followed a second period, brief but emotionally enriching, covering some five years spent at a co-ed grammar school and a small public school at Exmoor. It was after that, in the spring of 1929, that I took possession of a much larger farm and went in for a wider variety of crops. I became a reporter on a weekly newspaper and worked this territory for eleven years. The harvests of character and situation reaped between the ages of seventeen and twenty-eight have kept me fed into my mid-fifties, although I continue to draw modest dividends from the smaller farms of childhood and adolescence.

As I say, the antennae of authors seem to grow less sensitive once they enter their twenty-fifth year. Like an ageing dog's, an author's scenting apparatus is impaired, although my own perked up and served me well enough under the special circumstances of the years I spent in the Royal Air Force. After 1945, however, the labor on the farms became steadily more irksome, and sometimes I have had to work hard to coax a crop above ground. Fortunately I was able to change my ground. Successively I was a dramatist, in the late evening of the Who's-for-tennis era, a countryman concerned with country pursuits, and finally an antique dealer. Each field, in its own way, contributed something to my stock in trade, but not enough to encourage me to abandon the richer soil of my youth. This essay is an attempt to introduce the fiction addict to a few of the products that have resulted from my slapdash labor in the fields.

2

"Inspiration" is a word to conjure with. The layman, who reads and enjoys but does not write books, should be wary of it. In the minds of those who browse along the shelves of the public library there is a fallacious notion of what the word "inspiration" means to the novelist, and how he applies it to his craft. Most fiction readers see the writer against two backgrounds, a Cowardesque-Maughamish figure on the Riviera, wearing a natty dressing gown and holding a long cigarette holder clenched between his teeth, or a forlorn and desperate social reject, wrestling with his soul in a fireless attic. They cannot or will not conceive of an author as a man or woman who goes to work very much like a bank clerk or an estate agent, who labors set hours, husbands his material, plans his endeavors and is deeply concerned with paying his rates and feeding his wife and children. Their interpretation of the word "inspiration" is therefore distorted from the outset by this bifocal view of the professional, for they not unnaturally assume that he is entirely dependent upon "inspiration" and that everything he sets down on paper is the direct result of a Road-to-Damascus revelation.

It saddens me to disillusion them, for I too am a romantic, but there are few professional authors who owe much to inspiration in this sense. What inspiration is to a man who sits doggedly at his typewriter each day is no more than a small, sputtering spark that ignites a portion of the lumber that has accumulated in the attics of his brain. If the flame burns up then he blows on it, hoping to enlarge it until his mind is on fire. But all too often, alas, it sinks and dies, leaving him to fill his ashtray with half-smoked cigarettes and hope that a more rewarding conflagration will start after dark.

I have never been the kind of author who looks for his materials in terms of plot or even person. I have never once had an *idea*, in the sense that some thrillers spring from ideas. Neither do I assemble a character, or group of characters, from a hotch-potch of living people on a ratio of about three to one in flesh and blood, and then cause certain things to happen to them, thus constructing a plot. For better or worse I am far more deeply concerned with backgrounds. With me it is the canvas on which I am going to paint that is the essential piece of apparatus, and the bigger it is the more hopeful I am of filling it profitably. It was the teeming canvas of my adolescence that prescribed my material and now it is too late to change course and attempt to write fashionably.

The impact of my transition from central London to what was then a semi-rural suburb was considerable. All my very earliest impressions were of drab streets, strident Cockney voices, khaki, naphtha flares, Zeppelin raids and fog, of maroons exploding neighbors into panic, of pinched, wartime expressions in butter queues and of the firelit security of a home dominated by a noisy, extrovert father. But on a showery day in April, 1918, all this disappeared as though banished by a fairy godmother's wand and in its place were rows of trim terrace houses lurking behind hedges of clipped privet, flocks of rosy-faced children who inhabited them, clumps of towering elms and meadows bordered by flowering hawthorn but, above all, acres of buttercups and daisies, with here a rash of bluebells and there a rank of foxglove.

In those days the tide of London had rolled no more than twelve miles from Temple Bar. On the country border the city ended so abruptly that it was possible to imagine there had once been a Hadrian's Wall running through places like Elmer's End and Purley. Within this wall were miles of streets and shops, patrolled by squadrons of singing trams and red Tilling buses. Just outside it, where I was privileged to live, were quiet avenues, farms, cottages and half-explored woods hiding crumbling Georgian houses surrounded by terraces of the kind made familiar to me by the steel engravings that hung in so many parlors of that era. It was Betjeman country before Betjeman wrote about it.

The freshness, color and variety of the scene enchanted me;

but what, I think, made an even deeper impression was the *tone* of the suburb, with its city clerks mowing their tiny lawns at weekends and the sound of their children "practicing" behind neatly gathered curtains, its ancillaries of private school and tennis court, its scents of autumn bonfire and clay-nurtured roses, its building sites and unadopted roads, some of them impassable sloughs in winter, its dwarf pillars and looped chains proclaiming the intense privacy of each householder and its over-all air of hard-won, desperately maintained gentility that was the dominant feature of all suburbs in the early years of the century. This was the backdrop that remained in my mind like the fairyglen scene of the first pantomime I attended. This was my promised land, my personal Avalon and has remained so, long after the bulldozers and speculators have marched across it like an army of savage mercenaries. Nearly forty years were to pass before I used it and coaxed it to earn its keep but it remained alive to me in every particular so that I could write of it with joy.

3

Between 1917 and 1929 I was enrolled at six schools and one commercial college. Each has shown me a modest profit, although not in the way my parents intended when they were scratching round to pay the modest fees charged for attendance at these establishments.

From the infant school in Bermondsey I passed into a private school that called itself a college, and at the time I must admit to being completely hoodwinked by the term, as indeed were all of us, parents and scholars. There were thousands of such establishments in those days, when a private education (inferior in every way to a state education) was reckoned the only reliable passport to a white-collar occupation. My "college" was as seedy and pretentious as most such schools—seventy boys and four underpaid ushers, presided over by a jovial gentleman who wore blue serge and sang "When you come to the end of a perfect day" at the annual prizegiving. Everything about that school was dog-eared, even the split-bamboo cane the Head used on occasion, but for me it was as rich in character as Tom Brown's Rugby.

I see them all now across a gap of half a century, the Headmaster, the comfortably built junior mistress who rewarded good and bad scholars with colored scraps, the one-eyed boy, pitilessly dubbed One-Eyed Winkle, who sat behind me and posed the never-to-be-solved riddle of whether his glass eye was fixed on me or elsewhere, the boy who wore a woolen cap because his head had been shaved for ringworm, and a score of others; but it was not so much the masters and scholars who lingered in the memory as the air of decay about those uncarpeted stairs, the shredded wallpaper, the spotted laurels in the yard and the impression that this large, four-storied house, with its gilded board proclaiming educational impossibilities, was once the home of some prosperous merchant whose son or grandson had died at Passchendaele or the Somme.

In spite of its seediness I was very happy at the College, far happier than at my next billet, a Council school that qualified as an early concentration camp. As cheerless as a vast public lavatory, it was fenced in by acres of iron railings and ruled by an unsmiling sadist for whom, I trust, the realm of Lucifer has since proved as merciless as his regime. Thank God I was his subject for but one, endless term and I had my revenge on him although it had to wait half a lifetime. He was the prototype for Mr. Short, the bullying headmaster in *The Avenue Story*, and herein lies one of the hidden rewards of the novelist. He can nurse his brickbats for years and then hurl them from ambush. In addition to an odious personality I invented for Mr. Short severe stomach cramps. I hope they frightened him as much as he frightened me when he prowled along the glass partitions of that terrible place and whipped a lithe cane from his trousers like a trained bravo forcing a duel upon a succession of weaker opponents. Schools like his, and disciplines such as his, have almost (although not quite, it seems) disappeared from the British scene. The certainty of their elimination is one of the worthwhile products of the

Welfare State. The few short months I spent there yielded one
or two unexpectedly pleasant by-products. It was here one of
the kindlier masters introduced me to George Eliot's *Silas Marner*
and Tennyson's *Idylls of the King*.

From here I moved to a grammar school where, for the first
time, I met a few schoolmasters who were neither clowns nor
bullies but men with a genuine interest in the practice of their
profession. I have used them all at one time or another, sometimes
compounding three or four into a single character—the mild and
courteous Bentley, who ruled like a cultured King Réné of the
Two Sicilies, the informative Scott, who had a way of making
English words perform the tricks of circus dogs, the grave and
kindly Parkinson, the ironic and candid Barlow, and above all, the
tempestuous Mr. Ferguson, who taught French and would leap
into the room, jab his forefinger at the nearest boy and roar, in
counterfeit fury, *"De quelle couleur est la fenêtre? Est-ce qu'elle
est blanche ou verte, garçon?"* I learned more French from
Ferguson in six months than from a succession of other teachers
in ten years, and when adrift in France in 1944 and thrown upon
my own inadequate resources, I often summoned his spirit to my
side.

But these schools were mere curtain-raisers. The one that convinced me there was a living to be made from the study and
practice of romanticism was the co-ed school I attended for a
period after I went to live in the West. Here, praise God, sun-
beams stole through the windows of Nissen huts and alighted not
upon the snub noses and inky fingers of bullet-headed boys but
the stray tendrils of a hundred Margerys and Sybils, Catherines
and Joyces, an audience awaiting diversion and sly courtship in
a garden populated by houris in gym slips, light-blue blouses
and dark-blue regulation knickers. Here were endless opportunities to indulge in an exchange of sighing glances, fingertip pressures and love-notes written on squared geometry paper. Here
was a whole production line of heroines, the pert, the demure,
the bold and the blushing, girls who, in a year or so, would step
into the frames of Burne-Jones and Rosetti, and others who

might have been serving an apprenticeship for attendance at the court of Louis XV. There were girls who typified the ukelele age into which they had been born and others (and these were they who beguiled) whom I could identify with Little Em'ly, Jane Eyre, Alice and Silas Marner's Eppie. Who could trifle with common factors and irregular verbs in such enchanting company?

Alas, I was soon drummed out of it. Whoever was acting as my unseen agent in the occupation of character farms saw to it that I was offered plenty of variety. From here I went, long-trousered, heavy-booted and mildly apprehensive, to the seclusion of an exceptionally isolated boarding school, where feminine company was limited to that of North Devon farmers' wives who spoke almost unintelligible English as they baked pasties to supplement our diet of porridge and stewed prunes. Yet the change had tremendous compensations, for here I was actually sharing the adventures of Tom Brown, those of the heroes of *Vice Versa* and *The Hill*, and (what was more immediate at that time) the jolly japes of Bob Cherry and Harry Wharton at Greyfriars.

It is a thankless task to discourage the professional romantic from seeing life as he would prefer to see it. Nobody ever had much success in this direction with me, but they showered me with raw material for fiction in the process of trying. This final attempt on the part of my parents to equip me with a formal education achieved no more than any previous attempt. Grounded on simple fractions and elementary declensions, I was only confirmed in my determination to raise and sell the crops at my disposal, and tested seed was available in large quantities at that school on the moor!

Here was a Reverend Headmaster playing rugby and losing his false teeth in his sixty-third year. Here was "Judy" Taylor, domed, walrus-mustached, and so lovably pedantic that he would reward a boy with the wrong answer who had neatly underlined his sum rather than put his tick against a correct total emphasized with a blot. Here were masters with Churchillian voices and masters with a Quasimodo gait, high-minded prefects, new-boy-baiting prefects and fifth-formers who studied *La Vie Parisienne* when they should have been thinking of isotherms, boys who walked alone and boys whose natural grace and good looks carried them effortlessly through every trial, boys who wrote despondent letters home and boys who punched them for bringing such shame upon British manhood. All manner of boys and all manner of masters, and again that inescapable schooly smell of chalk, dust, apple cores, boiling greens, steam heat and damp flannel. What was Greyfriars or St. Jim's to this? Who envied Tom Brown his triumph in the scrum, when I had so much served on a platter, with Gilbert and Sullivan and the Officers' Training Corps thrown in for good measure? This was the only educational establishment I left with regret, and the time there passed too quickly, the days were so short and so full. But sometimes I return and not only in the flesh. Anyone who can remember this school in the mid-twenties might equate it with Barrowdene in *The Spring Madness of Mr. Sermon*, Hearthover in *The Avenue Story* and High Wood in *A Horseman Riding By*. It has earned its fees three times over.

Time was running on. I had been sowing for ten or more years and was now impatient to reap. I took a diligent look at the short-skirted students at my next port of call, a commercial college, and then set to work. It seemed to me at that time that I had absorbed not only a sufficiency but more than I could comfortably digest. I would have been surprised and disconcerted if someone older and wiser in the art of crystallizing and then selling human experience had warned me that seventeen is time to start writing, but not, perhaps, with an eye to offering what emerges for public sale. The era of teen-age triumph and overnight success was still a long way in the future, but I was an optimist. That was why, when I sold an advertising rhyme for a pound, I considered myself launched upon the high road to fame and fortune.

Searchlights on the Ceiling

Ask anyone who cowered under aerial bombardment in World War II, particularly the Cockney who survived the winter of 1940–41, and the V-1 and V-2 onslaughts in 1944–45, what he thinks about Zeppelins and he will probably tell you they were cigar-shaped objects that made a few abortive flights over London in 1915–18 in order to unload a few small-caliber bombs. He would, of course, be right.

In his interesting book, *The Zeppelin Fighters*, Arch White-house, who made a definitive study of Zeppelins, tells us that, in the three-year period under review, German Zeppelins made 208 raids on Great Britain, dropping a total of just under 6,000 bombs, killing 528 people and wounding a further 1,156. Comparing these figures with Britain's civilian casualties of the Second World War he adds, very sensibly, ". . . the people killed were just as dead as their descendants who perished in the rubble of London during the Great Blitz." I concur, having been on the receiving end.

The house occupied a corner site between Fort Road and Reverdy Road, in Bermondsey, S.E. It was probably early Victorian and was built of that yellow-greenish brick so popular during the period of the South London population explosion, when, for the first time in the long history of the capital, materials could be hauled to a site by rail from anywhere in the country.

It was blitzed in 1940, and when I went back, in 1945, rosebay willow herb was sprouting on a pile of rubble and about the boles of three stunted trees my brother told me he had planted in 1909. The house looked much smaller than I remembered. It was difficult to believe that five of us, plus a deaconess lodger, had lived there through the final glimmer of what people now call The Edwardian Afternoon. But for me the ruin had poignancy and I was sorry the Luftwaffe had singled it out for demolition, leaving next-door and next-door-but-one untouched.

There it was, a heap of brick dust, slivers of slate and splintered woodwork, crowned with the weed that thrives on chaos, but it was that other war I remembered as I poked about looking for clues.

My first conscious experience was that of witnessing the frantic terror created by Zeppelin attacks and one should not forget, in assessing their effect upon people, that this was the first time in the human story that a civilian population was bombarded from the air and that London, and all other areas attacked, was absolutely defenseless against such attacks when the reign of terror began. The author of *The Zeppelin Fighters* made another interesting observation. Reluctantly approving the terror policy submitted to him by his warlords, he tells us, the German Kaiser issued strict instructions that raiders were to "avoid bombing Buckingham Palace, Westminster Abbey and museums." He made no reference to hospitals and orphanages, but perhaps this is not surprising. As Mr. Chips said at the time, *Genus hoc erat pugnae quo se Germani exercuerant*—this was the kind of war in which the Germans busied themselves. They seem to have enjoyed it immensely over the last two millenniums.

The earliest Zeppelin raids that I recall were those of the winter of 1917. By then residents in southeast London had perfected the kind of drill they were to practice on a much larger scale twenty-three years later. There were modest antiaircraft defenses, many of them mobile. There was a small nightfighter force. And there were shelters of a kind for those who wanted them. Most people did not want them, but sat tight and hoped, and my father was among that majority.

Warning alerts were still extraordinarily primitive. At first policemen cycled the streets blowing whistles, calling attention to a placard slung round their necks and worn as medieval malefactors wore legends describing their crimes. Later on, red lights were affixed to lamp standards and maroons were fired, a novelty that almost caused my father's arrest when my brother Bill, who played the bass drum in the Scouts, brought the entire residential section out in the streets by beating his drum in our reverberating cellar.

To a child of five an air raid was a compelling but not necessarily a frightening experience, and I recall one raid very vividly. I was lying in bed waiting for my brother to come upstairs and watching the reflection of searchlights on the ceiling. Outside I could hear two girls talking to two young men and their flirting voices were carefree and punctuated by laughter. Then one of them shrieked, "The red light's up!" and a moment later the street outside was full of tumult as pedestrians began to run for shelter.

For me, however, air-raid drill began smoothly, as always. I was wrapped in an eiderdown and carried downstairs into the kitchen, but this time there was a difference. En route there was a frenzied beating on the front door and my father, opening it, admitted a young woman who fell over the threshold, vomited and then fainted. I watched my father douse her with water and I can still see the pallor of her face that I now associate with deathbeds, a yellowish pallor framed in a mop of dripping hair. When she recovered we all assembled before the fire and I was given a scribbling pad and pencil to occupy my attention. I drew, as I recall, airplanes, tanks and armored cars. It seemed to me that these were the everyday appurtenances of life, just as khaki was the color worn by nearly all the young men I saw in the streets.

There were many other raids of this kind and occasional facets of them are stark and clear. Sometimes my mother, her nerves at breaking point, would burst into tears when anyone spoke to her, and sometimes I would watch a daylight raid (it must have been by Fokkers rather than Zeppelins) and witness the mad rush past our windows toward the shelters. Perhaps my very first introduction to the law of self-preservation was to see a muffled coster pause, dart over the crossroads outside and bawl at his wife, lumbered with three small children, "Come on, Liza, or I'll go wivaht yer!" Chivalry is at a premium during bombardments.

We heard many horror stories of devastating strikes. An aerial torpedo, the first ever fired over London, had demolished a row of houses in Albany Road, off the Old Kent Road. A scent factory, being used as a shelter, had been the scene of a direct hit. But there was one moment of triumph before we vacated the area and moved out of range in the spring of 1918. Wrapped in the inevitable eiderdown I was held up to the landing window and told to look at an orange rag floating down the night sky. It was one of the last of the Zeppelins, shot down by our expanding defense force that now included young men flying what we should now consider mobile banana crates from a Home Counties base.

It is difficult, at this distance, to decide who demonstrated more courage—the numbed German Zeppelin crews, flying on their forlorn missions and often not knowing whether they were bombing Cromer or Croydon; or the leather-helmeted youngsters plunging about the sky in open cockpits, hoping that probing searchlight beams would cone on a Zeppelin before their fuel was used up.

And as well as one moment of uncomprehending triumph there was a moment of blind, unreasoning fear, of a degree of terror that I do not recall having experienced before or since. It was during a daylight raid by Fokkers or Gothas, and I had just been released from the local kindergarten when a flight of aircraft passed overhead, far too high to identify as theirs or ours, although this did not prevent a young pessimist standing close by from shouting, "Germans! I can see the black crosses!" I did not wait for corroboration. Growing up, born as it were in the teeth of a gale of propaganda in which black crosses signified evil as surely as the swastika, I fled, amazed at arriving home without having been overtaken and impaled on one of those Prussian spiked helmets that were, at that stage in the war, coveted trophies by enterprising front-line infantrymen.

Wavering beams on the ceiling, exposing cracks in the plaster and the leering wolf in the Red Riding Hood fire screen; the rumble of "our" antiaircraft gun, said to chase Zeppelins all over London; a chalky-faced stranger vomiting in the hall; boots crashing on the pavement and a flaming rag in the sky. Perhaps a fitting introduction into the world awaiting us all in the winter of 1917–18, and somehow its images have remained sharp and clear when most of those of another war are blurred or mellowed. Yet one is tempted to ask, after more than half a century of this continuing idiocy, what military advantage was ever gained by plastering civilians with high explosive, and whether words like Guernica, Coventry, Warsaw, Rotterdam and Dresden are not indictments written by our generation into a document that contains our collective death warrant. For there is, to a Londoner in his sixth decade, a tenuous link between his earliest memories and the present revolt of the young. It is tempting to dismiss a student riot seen on television as a display of adolescent exhibitionism and mass hysteria, but one should, I feel, look for the mainspring of the demonstrations. In my own youth we grumbled, but few dared to rebel. The nuclear stockpile wasn't there; but the dole queue was, and its threat was more immediate. So if the present generation can do anything to improve, even marginally, our social and political system, so that their children's first recollections are more tranquil than mine, then I for one will forgo middle-aged cynicism, take up their slogans and even (suitably disguised) carry one of their bellyaching banners across Grosvenor Square.

Cromwellian Don Quixote

My father was the most colorful, complex and contradictory character I have ever met and you don't have to take my word for it. He baffled, bewildered and exasperated every human being who crossed his path, and this is true, not only of his family and his associates in the world of business, chapel and public affairs, but also of chance acquaintances he met on holiday, or on the bowling green, or in buses, funiculars and passport offices all over the world. This is not because he enjoyed making an impact, and throwing his personality at strangers as though it was a large custard pie, but because, deep in his heart, he had a rooted conviction that everybody needed him to solve their personal problems and shape their judgments. To me at least he reduced the professional extroverts—the Danny Kayes, the Bob Hopes, the Lloyd Georges—to the stature of inoffensive woodsprites.

He was born in Bermondsey in 1873, the elder son of a rumbustious tanner who fathered eight children, six of them girls. My grandfather, whom I never met, was an excessively companionable man and his fondness for ale and whisky chasers certainly placed a severe strain upon the household budget, but I suspect that my father, who did nothing by halves, tended to exaggerate the effects his father's intemperance had upon the family life. It is here, perhaps, that one must look for my father's insatiable appetite for uproar.

If my father is to be believed, the small house in Bermondsey, housing man, wife and eight children, was a likely backdrop for a temperance magic-lantern sequence, and throughout my childhood I took this on trust—that is, until I discussed the subject with ageing aunts. That their life was an alternation between a sufficiency and grinding poverty I have no doubt, but my own view is that pre-trade-union exploitation of labor had more to do with their shortages than had my grandfather's thirst. In an unguarded moment my father once told me that, operating as a pieceworker. Grandfather sometimes earned more than six pounds a week. In the eighteen-seventies this was getting on for affluence, even with a large family to support, but there were times when, for one reason or another, work was hard to get and every penny counted, so that as a boy my father was happy to carry a man's hot dinner for a penny a day and by so doing earn his own midday snack. This, indeed, was one of my father's proudest boasts— that he had supported himself from the age when he could run at high speed with a loaded pudding basin.

Thrown feet first into the teeming Thames-side streets, my father was a seasoned adult at thirteen. He was shortish, broadshouldered, well muscled, extremely active, highly independent and cheerfully aggressive; in the circumstances he had to be all of these things, but I never heard him complain of his lot. He took pride in the fact that Almighty God had so much confidence in him. In the meantime he helped Providence along by learning how to use his fists and how to swim. This last accomplishment was acquired, of all places, in the Surrey-Commercial canal.

He told me that he left school at eleven; but this is something else I am inclined to doubt, for all his life he wrote a stylish hand, could tot up a column of figures faster than the early adding machines and possessed a vast if disorganized store of general knowledge. He probably took his first job with a Tower Bridge tea importer when he was about thirteen and a half, and for a time was bent on graduating to the status of "sampler," a kind of taster who selected the various grades of tea imported by clippers from Ceylon and Madras. His brother actually achieved this and made a fortune in the trade; but, although even at that time my father had acquired a taste for tea (to offset his passionate hatred of stronger forms of liquid refreshment), he was tempted by the better if less regular money offered by the leather trade, and soon became what was then known as a flesher. Still later, disgusted by the irregularity of this work and having by then a family to support, he became a clerk for a meat wholesaler. He remained in the meat trade, as clerk, salesman and cattle buyer, until the moment of his great gamble in the winter of 1923.

At the age of sixteen he had succeeded in dominating his father and taking his place, like a young Napoleon, as self-appointed head of the family. His father began to give him a wide berth but managed to elude enrollment in my father's Band of Hope and continued to patronize the local taverns until he died in the first year of World War I. Years before that, when he was about twenty-one, my father had made what he subsequently referred to as The Choice.

It was made, according to him, at a street corner on a Sunday evening. The pubs were open all day every day of the week in those days (my father was to do a great deal to correct this sorry state of affairs), and The Choice was presented by two streams of people passing his home, one on its way to the local Congregational Chapel, the other, Grandfather among them, to the local tavern on the other side of the road. The conversion has about it a Victorian air of authenticity and is possibly a little too authentic, but it may be true in substance. "There they were," my father would say, thrusting out his chin and jingling his small change, "one lot on their way to worship Almighty God" ("God" was never majestic enough for my father and he habitually threw in the adjective) "and there were the others, all set on making a night of it, so I said to myself, William James Delderfield, which lot are yours? and joined the church that same night!" This was how he acquired the pennant to attach to his crusader's lance, but in a very short time the windmills multiplied until they filled my father's vision. That is to say, Daemon Drink was only the original target, a kind of range finder that he used to give him a firm seat in his saddle and a tight grip on his lance. Having run his first tilt and been greatly enlivened by it, he suddenly became aware of a whole row of windmills awaiting his personal attention, and before he was of age he was hotly engaged with three of the largest of them, The Tories, The Militarists and their age-old ally, The Brewers. I apologize for using capitals but so my father always thought and spoke of them.

I cannot imagine that any crusader ever went into battle with more zest. Banners streaming, mouth wide open in a Cromwellian battle roar, Father set to work on the task of ridding the British Empire of the menace of this godless triple alliance. If necessary he was prepared to achieve it singlehanded. Echoes of that battle have come down to me in the form of news clippings and word-of-mouth anecdotes and, judged on these sources alone, the foemen did not merit his steel. To use another Cromwellian simile, "God made them as stubble to his sword," and Horatio, not content to keep the bridge, drove the enemy all the way to Tuscany and beyond. Neither the Brewers, the Tories nor the Militarists ever wholly recovered from my father's onslaught, first mounted around 1892. They have never been the same since my father took issue with them.

At twenty-one he was the first Radical member to be elected to the Bermondsey Borough Council, a Thames-side Lloyd George with enough fire in his belly to scorch every citadel he attacked. He organized monster processions in South Park, he bombarded the press with frankly libelous attacks on his opponents, and he used the Town Hall as a forum from which to spray opponents with his unique blend of searing, semijocular invective. "The day is not far distant, I trust," says one news clipping, "when we shall burn the slums and hang the owners!" When one rubicund, honorable and gallant opponent, stung by an attack upon his profession, protested—"I am a soldier, my father was a soldier, my grandfather was a soldier"—my father leaped to his feet and demanded, "What regiment, sir? The Boozars?" As he grew older and more experienced he adjusted his sights and widened his field. He attacked, as well as Brewers, Tories and Militarists, the House of Lords, landlords en masse, magnates in all spheres of business, the Bank of England, the Navy League, bishops, prostitutes, public schools, the medical profession and, in slightly subdued tones, the throne itself. He lumped the whole lot together, as a Satanic alliance, a vast, insidious conspiracy specifically aimed at depriving the British electorate of the fruits of their costly struggle for the franchise. Looking back upon his campaigns, one could, if one was unwary, equate him with Lenin and Trotsky, but in another sense he was less revolutionary than a left-wing Tory of the period. Bloodshed in the streets would have appalled him, upsetting the natural order of things which was Rule under the Law. In later life he never deviated one inch from the party line of his youth and had even less patience with the Labour Party, then emerging as a militant political force, than with the Establishment. The fact that the Liberal Party ultimately disintegrated dismayed him not at all. Why should it, when he was still alive and vocal? But all that was far in the future. In the meantime there was the meatiest bone ever thrown to a fighting radical, the Boer War.

My father viewed the Boer War as a monstrously unjust exercise in imperial bullying. From the outset he championed Kruger, whom in many respects he resembled. In the London of his day this was not a lighthearted decision, especially after the defeats and shames of Black Week had whipped patriotic frenzy to its highest pitch since Waterloo. Yet my father warmly embraced the cause of Lloyd George and reveled in the opposition they aroused from patriotic citizens, whom my father dismissed as brewery-subsidized flag flappers. He celebrated every setback of British arms in South Africa as a heartening victory, and when it was all over and a Boer leader (De Wet, I believe) visited London, he decided that he, of all Londoners, had a personal obligation to give the guerrilla fighter a pat on the back.

This was not easy to accomplish, for the Boers were lunched at the Savoy and my father had not been invited. Social formalities, however, never bothered him. He gained entry to the hotel by announcing that he was a Fleet Street editor, flourishing his credentials (almost certainly a letter written by himself to himself on L.C.C. notepaper) under the nose of the doorman. He got to De Wet all right and he did pat his back, bellowing, "Well played, sir! Well played!" as though the Boer had just returned from the Oval. This was not a unique performance. Between the years 1894 and 1923, when he quitted the London scene, he contrived to come face to face with any celebrity who caught his fancy and almost always resorted to bluff and subterfuge to do it.

Life would have been dull for Father when the Boers capitulated had it not been for Mrs. Pankhurst, who obligingly filled the political vacuum. He at once embraced the cause of women's suffrage, and I have a photograph of him preventing a suffragist speaker being thrown into South Park pond. Certain people did receive total immersion that night but suffragists were not among the baptized. My father saw to that.

The great Liberal landslide of 1906 brought my father immense satisfaction, for it must have seemed to him that windmills were now being overturned in all directions. Enough remained standing, however, to keep him exercised, and he played a prominent part in all the social reforms and adjustments leading up to the outbreak of the Great War.

It is his attitude to this war that highlights his political traditions. For years now he had been heaping insults upon uniforms, castigating armament manufacturers, and fanatically opposing the naval race with the German Kaiser, but on August 4 he was swept away by the high tide of jingoism that engulfed the great majority of Liberals, including, of course, his beloved Lloyd George, Windmill Tilter Extraordinary. For all that, Father physically opposed the sacking of German shops in the Smithfield area where he worked and told me of one such occasion when he befriended an outraged alien who was being savaged by the mob. It was not his plight that had enlisted my father's help, but the comic nature of his protest. He had shouted, despairingly, "Go avay! I spak der Henglender ten time better than you!" This remark endeared him to my father, who at once joined the police in repelling patriotic boarders.

By 1918 he was forty-five, but even so, had the war continued another six months, he would have been in the army and the faltering German armies would have been faced with yet another major intervention. As it was, being now removed twelve miles from London Stone, he switched his dynamic energy to the local Baptist Chapel and its ancillary, the P.S.A. (Pleasant Sunday Afternoon), and also began to indulge his yearning for travel by making frequent trips to the Highlands of Scotland in order to buy cattle for his employers.

He developed a great love of Scotland and Scotsmen, among the latter Robbie Burns, who became one of his heroes, sharing a suburban Olympia with Father's two other great heroes, Abe Lincoln and Livingstone of Darkest Africa. By now, of course, Lloyd George had been dispatched to Hades for betraying Asquith in 1916. He made frequent pilgrimages to Burns's birthplace and the Scotsman's verses sounded strange on the tongue of my father, who never lost nor moderated his Cockney accent and idioms. I used to point out to my father that Robbie Burns, matchless poet that he was, had acquired the kind of reputation with women that my father would have condemned in anyone else, but in those days I had not learned that my father could plant his moral and political standards on any position dictated by personal preference. He would reply, shaking his head, "Ah, but his life was terrible, *terrible!*" implying that an eighteenth-century plowman, jostled by greedy, snobbish lairds, could be forgiven a few peccadilloes in the heather. His attitude toward women generally was equivocal. In the main he set his face against feminine practices to improve upon nature by means of lipstick, eye shadow, etc., but he never let his prejudices in this respect prevent him from enjoying the society of a pretty girl.

34

Sometimes, notwithstanding lavish makeup, he would exorcise her by declaring that she was "a nice Christian young woman!" She didn't have to be a churchgoer to qualify for this title. All she had to do was flash a smile in his direction and lend a dutiful ear to one of his anecdotes. This done she was, as it were, figuratively converted to the faith.

Busts of Gladstone, Lincoln, Livingstone and Burns cluttered the house and so did huge and oft-read biographies of this quartet, to the exclusion of all other biographies, except a book about Ulysses Grant "who won the Civil War for dear old Abe in spite of being partial to whisky."

My father's over-all approach to books was highhanded. He had read but one novel, *Robbery Under Arms*, but he brought armfuls of political and historical works into the house and sometimes borrowed others from libraries. If, in the course of his reading, he disagreed with something set down by the author, he took out a pencil and scored the word *"Bosh"* in the margin. "Bosh" was a favorite word of his, and he had a number of others, each selected and employed to express disapproval, contempt, outrage or indignation. Perhaps his favorite word of all, and one he employed fifty times a day, was *facted*, which some declared to be a shortened form of *fatheaded*, but which I always took to be a substitute for something stronger and more abusive. He had a number of phrases at his command, all fashioned to denigrate. The most popular of them were "blue-nosed thief" and "a direct descendant of Calcraft, the Hangman." The word "blue-nosed," of course, represented for Father the ultimate in abuse, for it implied that the target of the gibe was a heavy drinker and even the libidinous lagged a long way behind the drunkard in my father's eyes. Sometimes, when he wished to soften his over-all approach, he would declare that someone was a "descendant of the Impenitent Thief," a subtitle that did not carry the terrible stigma of a family tie with Calcraft, the public executioner of my father's boyhood.

One of the curious aspects of my father's lifelong assault upon institutions and individuals was that it never generated reciprocal resentment. No one seemed to take his blistering and often very effective opposition to their title, trade or political allegiance, seriously. Wherever he went, at public meeting, in Council chamber, in the street, or on the bowling green, his extravagant sallies and savage personal thrusts were received with mildness and often with masochistic pleasure. He had the enviable knack of saying precisely what he had in mind without making enemies, and I never met anyone who actively disliked him, or even resented him with any fervor.

Having regard to his publicly expressed views upon the government, it came as a surprise to me to learn, at the age of about eleven, that he was excessively patriotic, harboring a Palmerstonian contempt for all foreigners. Even the Boers fell from grace once they had surrendered. He was one of the very few people I have met who really did believe that "niggers" (or at best Caribs) began at Calais, and it was only gradually that I came to terms with this flagrant contradiction in his makeup. Its roots were concealed in the firm belief that, whilst he, as a ratepaying, enfranchised Englishman had a right and a duty to prod the Establishment, criticism by a German, an Italian or a Turk was an extremely presumptuous act on their part. I think I made this discovery the day that Charlie Chaplin announced his intention of retaining his British nationality. From that moment my father's admiration of Chaplin was unbounded, springing not from the clown's genius but from his right-headedness in rejecting American citizenship.

So Chaplin took his place in the gallery of worthies, a niche or so below those of Ewart Gladstone, David Livingstone, Abe Lincoln and Robbie Burns. Two other notables kept him company on the lower shelf. They were Mary Slessor of Calabar and James Chalmers, both missionaries for whom Father had collected pennies as a youth. Mary Slessor, no doubt, qualified as a nice Christian young woman, but his admiration for Chalmers stemmed from the fact that he had been killed and perhaps eaten by Papuans, a fate that appealed to the romantic in him.

2

As he grew old Father changed very little. His God was the same night-shirted Old Testament Thunderer, while his politics remained those of a diminished Asquith. He still insisted upon our attendance at morning service and Sunday school in the Baptist Chapel; he still refused to use public transport or buy a newspaper on a Sunday; he still expressed implacable hatred for all Tories, Freemasons, brewers, landlords, peers, bishops and Horatio Bottomley, soon to demonstrate that my father's assessment of him as a descendant of the impenitent thief was not far wide of the mark. He still jingled his loose change when he roared out his hymns in chapel, subjecting me to savage little nudges as I stood beside him and enjoining me to "Sing up!" He had always fascinated me and I still thought of him as infallible, but as the years passed I began to notice tiny chinks in his armor and the most obvious of these was his inability to judge character. I began to notice, for instance, that, for all his fearsome forthrightness he was often a tool in the hands of a hypocrite or a plausible rogue, providing he had no alcohol on his breath. If he had, he sometimes got more than he bargained for. I was once present when a bedraggled wayfarer approached him, whining that he had had nothing to eat for two days. My father thrust his nose within an inch of the beggar and bellowed, "No? But you've had a facted drayload to drink, so clear off before I give you in charge!" He had, however, a romantic's regard for picturesque rascals, and once he had prospected them with his nose he would sometimes give them a pound note or a set of heavy woolen underwear that he had just purchased for his own use. This singular lack of prescience on his part did nothing to diminish him in my eyes and he remained more or less infallible, until I became aware of a second chink, a curious lack of moral courage when confronted with absurdly trivial issues. He had always possessed enormous reserves of physical courage—he would swim a mile out to sea on a strange coast without a thought to rip tides and cramp—and on important moral issues he often displayed a terrible obstinacy, as when he insisted, against police advice, on testifying against a prominent citizen who had misbehaved in a Turkish bath. But occasionally, just occasionally, he would bow himself out of an awkward situation at the last moment and one would experience a qualm of deprivation, shock and disappointment, as though Goliath, confronted by David, had dropped his spear, opened his mouth and screamed in choirboy treble. As I say, the issues on which he faltered were so trivial that they would have passed unnoticed in a less forceful character. He once withdrew from a meeting where he was expected to propose an unpopular decision, retiring to bed and announcing that he was seriously ill. On another occasion he decided that we were going bankrupt and that every man in our employ would have to accept a trifling cut in wages. The night before this dire decision was to be made public he packed a bag and rushed off to Switzerland, leaving me to issue the diminished wage packets and relay his explanations. In fairness to him, I ought to add that the Swiss air proved beneficial for all of us. On his return a fortnight later he restored the cuts and declared that things were now on the mend, refusing to discuss the incident then or later. I soon discovered what it was that had buttressed his confidence in the balance of the pound. He had lost his passport on Mont Blanc and had a very bracing tussle with the authorities, managing to return home without a passport and browbeat all the customs officials he encountered en route.

Nothing gave him greater pleasure than a brisk sparring match with a bureaucrat. Booking a passage from Sydney to San Francisco he came face to face with an American official who had the temerity to demand the sum of five pounds for a visa. At the head of a sheepish crowd, already fumbling for their wallets, my father declared that the visa stamp was a gross imposition and refused to pay anything at all. The very notion of paying sterling for the dubious privilege of entering a country that had rejected the benefits of the Union Jack released a flood of rhetoric that would have resulted in a lesser man being seized by janitors and flung onto the pavement. In fact, something approaching this happened two days in succession but on the third day my father rose again and this time the official capitulated. Father entered America without paying the five pounds. In that respect, if in no other, he was probably unique.

He was a man who could be guaranteed to act upon impulse and some of his impulses were endearing. I remember the occasion he accompanied me to pass an oral test to enter a grammar school, a benign headmaster quizzing me, very gently, on arithmetic, history and geography. I had to be prompted on the arithmetic and when asked to describe an imaginary journey from London to Edinburgh I chose a route that would have baffled a trained bloodhound. When it came to history, however, I was on safer ground, naming the Tudors all in one breath. My father was enormously impressed with this. All the way home he kept murmuring, "Henry-seven—Henry-eight—Edward-six—Bloody Queen Mary-and-Elizabeth," using my promptly spoken answer as a spur to the pedals of his push cycle. Instead of going home, however, he passed our avenue and conducted me on a historical tour of Chislehurst Caves as a reward for my erudition. It was, I think, the first time he ever acknowledged me as a son and possibly an embryo student of Abraham Lincoln.

We shared another encounter with a schoolmaster when a somewhat pompous and unkempt man summoned him to complain of my behavior at the school. My father, a fastidiously tidy soul, took a strong dislike to the man and after announcing that the man was paid to supervise me, and had clearly failed in his duties, he turned on his heel and walked out. Then, almost within hearing of the astonished man, he growled. "Got a dirty neck! Get him to use a bar of Sunlight soap before he fetches me up here again!" He uttered no word of reproach concerning my own shortcomings but continued to brood about the schoolmaster's neck for the remainder of my brief stay at the school.

My father's work at Smithfield necessitated his rising at four A.M. to catch the first train to London Bridge. He usually arrived home at about one P.M., retiring to bed until five o'clock and thus taking his rest in two four-hour sessions. He had always been an early riser (when he was seventy-five I used to hear him chopping wood at six A.M.) and had never, to my knowledge, voiced a complaint regarding this eccentric time schedule. One November morning, however, he got out of bed, sniffed the fog, and announced that he was going to leave Smithfield and invest all his savings in a weekly newspaper. My mother, having then lived with him for twenty-five years, knew far better than to challenge this stupendous decision at the time, for once in bed, with the sheets drawn over his nose, my father was incommunicado and could not be induced to utter so much as a grunt. She would, I think, have hesitated to rouse him if the house had been on fire. Later, however, when he was shaving, he told her that he had been considering a change in his life for some little time and had contracted to go into partnership with a neighbor who was anxious to purchase a combined general shop, printing works and weekly newspaper in the West Country. The November fog had finally decided the issue. He admitted as much. Besides, he had always wanted to be an editor and was unlikely to get another chance. He put the house up for sale that very day, and within a month we were all whisked off to the West, where my father settled himself in the editor's swivel armchair as if he had been measured for it. It was the week of his fiftieth birthday.

His editorial experience was limited to writing letters of violent protest (or doughty championship) to *The British Weekly* and *The Star* but this did not daunt him. There was, he felt, a T. P. O'Connor hiding in every Radical breast and all that prevented its emergence was opportunity. The latter having presented itself he welcomed it and from that moment thought of himself as not merely a competent journalist but a provincial press baron, the equal and perhaps the superior in perspicacity of Lord Northcliffe. Locally he came near to proving it; for, just as he had never cared two straws what he said in public, now he did not give a damn what appeared under his name in print.

The impact he made upon the community has passed into local folklore. It was as though someone had been secretly undermining our small seacoast town for years and had summoned my father to press the plunger. He obliged in a matter of days, the first skirmish with reaction taking place in the office when a cautious well-wisher told him that he could only hope to succeed in a small community if he was a low churchman, a Freemason and a Conservative. My father's reply to this well-meant advice was the local equivalent of Luther nailing his thesis to the church door. He said, rubbing his fleshy nose (a habit of his when challenged), that he had been a Free Churchman all his life, that he detested secret societies, and that he would like to see every paid-up member of the Conservative Party driven into exile. His partner, himself a Conservative, was justifiably alarmed, but my father would make no retraction. Indeed, within a month he made his views public, for it so happened that there was an election pending in the constituency and my father was drawn into it from the outset. In response to his partner's pleas, he kept the tone of his editorials neutral for four issues, but early in the fifth week he happened to pass close by a lorry from which a haughty Tory agent was successfully intimidating a group of would-be hecklers standing on the edge of the crowd. Replying to a halfhearted gibe from someone in this group the speaker said, loftily, "Come forward, my friends! Say what you have to say like men! Don't hide behind those park railings like monkeys in a cage!" The hecklers remained safely out of range but my father accepted the challenge on their behalf. Grasping the tailboard of the lorry and glaring up at the speaker he roared, "Let them stay where they are, sir! One more monkey on that truck and it will be mistaken for a traveling menagerie!" Thus was the Rubicon crossed, and local Radicals took heart. From then on the weekly paper was heavily biased in favor of the Liberal candidate, and once again my father was launched upon a sea of controversy.

As time went on he became moderately drunk with power. At the slightest excuse, and often without one, he would seize his pen, dip it in bile or treacle, according to whether he was attacking or championing, and compose editorials that were often sufficiently libelous to attract solicitors' letters, all of which my father ignored on the publish-and-be-damned theory. He was only once actually prosecuted, but what might have happened had he not tired of the sport and taken to the game of bowls is still my recurring nightmare. In the meantime, before I could take over as editor, he had six pages of newsprint to fill every week without the services of a reporter. He solved the problem without difficulty, snipping news stories from the county newspapers, changing the headline and introductory paragraphs, and sending the rehash down to the keyboard operator. They called him the scissors-and-pastepot editor, and he did not quarrel with the title. Nobody, he declared, could copyright news, and his method saved the firm at least five pounds a week. The printing foreman helped him out with long accounts of sporting events and any local secretary who cared to send in a report of his club's activities could be sure of full coverage. The day after I left Shorthand College, when I was seventeen plus, he told me, quite casually, that I must now earn my keep and accept responsibility for filling the columns of the paper. It was rather like a skylarking longshoreman vacating the bridge of an Atlantic liner and handing over to the cabin boy.

From then on I did not see very much of him. He spent nearly all his time traveling around the world on money my mother, my brother and I earned for him, or on the local bowling greens, where his voice could be heard half a mile away upbraiding a partner for the erratic course of a wood. Sometimes, just as we were going to press, he would appear with the tournament scores in his hand and insist upon them being wedged into the form at the expense of Women's Institute notes or the report of a local fire or burglary. He also contributed, from time to time, to a column called "Odds and Ends," wherein he castigated someone he disliked, or larded someone who had caught his fleeting fancy. A good many people caught his fancy and often, by the time they reappeared to reclaim his friendship, he had forgotten everything about them, even their names and nationalities. He would appear in my office with a middle-aged couple in tow, diffident people usually and always a little winded by the vagueness of his greeting. "This is Mr. and Mrs. Er-Er," he would say, without a blush, "I met them in Thingummy. Show 'em the town, will you, son?" And then he would return to his bowls, leaving me with a sheaf of unread proofs and a glass blower and his wife from Staffordshire whom he had met on an Alpine peak or in a train on the way to Bognor.

From time to time, however, I would catch a kingfisher glimpse of the old William James Delderfield, the barnstormer of the "We Want Eight And We Won't Wait" days, when he cycled around the town at six A.M. on a winter's morning defacing Tory posters. Or when, in a sudden reaccess of evangelical zeal, he led a team of wandering Welsh miners in "The Battle Hymn of the Republic" at The Brotherhood, a movement he had founded to replace his Pleasant Sunday Afternoons. People grew accustomed to his unpredictability, his tremendous but short-lived bursts of enthusiasm, his savage repartee and his harmless displays of downright humbug. Somehow he offended no one, or not for long. Even the excessively pious churchwarden, who, on deciding to purchase a house my father had for sale admitted that he had "prayed for divine guidance in the matter," was no more than mildly put out when my father assured him that Almighty God was an uncommonly good judge of real estate. He continued to dun hard-working little tradesmen for small debts and remit far larger sums owed him by plausible rascals. He continued to campaign for the Liberals and to berate Lloyd George for his 1916 treachery. He still spoke of Almighty God as a junior partner in all his enterprises. He was still beguiled by the smiles and blushes of nice, Christian young women.

He had always been deficient in family loyalty, and I think this was largely because he was incapable of finding merit in a product that was not universally acclaimed, like Bovril or Kruschen Salts. Throughout my youth he had looked upon my literary and dramatic endeavors with a jaundiced eye, begrudging the time I spent at my typewriter when I might have been campaigning for Temperance, for the Liberals, or perhaps mastering the game of bowls. When *Worm's Eye View* had run half its course, however, and the local pork butcher had assured him that it was well worth seeing, he paid the theater a visit and was impressed far more by the difficulty he had in obtaining a seat than by any merit he found in the comedy. He was ripe for conversion, however, for he went again and again, and was soon a kind of season-ticket holder at the Whitehall, where his presence was welcomed by the management. Not without reason. Whenever a matinee audience was slow to respond to a line of dialogue he would bark with savage laughter, heave himself round in his seat and stare balefully into the stalls as though to shame everyone into vocal appreciation. I sometimes had an uneasy suspicion that he would forget where he was, nudge people and shout "Sing Up!" Toward the end of the run he became a magnificent publicity agent. He would accost filling-station attendants and waitresses all over Britain and say, accusingly, "Have you seen that play, *Worm's Eye View?*" and if they replied in the negative he would scowl, shake his head and say, passionately, "Ah you *should*—you *should!*" and let it go at that.

At seventy he began to mellow a little and relax some of the rigid moral postures he had maintained throughout the early and middle part of his life. He took a liking to cider, declaring it to be nonalcoholic, and he bought first one and then six Sunday newspapers. He even softened in his approach to Winston Churchill after the latter's famous Battle of Britain speech, although he could never quite forgive him for having brandy on his breath back in 1911, when they were both attacking the House of Lords.

He died in his eighty-third year and was restless to the end. His illness was brief, and he could not understand what all the fuss was about and why he was prevented by a horde of busybodies from keeping a bagatelle appointment with some of his cronies at the Y.M.C.A. Forty-eight hours before he died he suddenly asked me for a cigarette, and because I did not smoke Gold Flake I was surprised. He had never smoked any cigarette but

Gold Flake and therefore regarded every other brand as unmarketable trash. The cigarette, however, was not for him but for his doctor and I recognized it as a gesture of reconciliation. He had included the medical profession in his sweeping condemnation of secret societies, and for some reason it made me think of an incident of nearly forty years before, when he had engaged in a skirmish with the Department of Health in a small seaside resort where I had contracted scarlet fever. Scarlet fever was something to be reckoned with in those days and was one of the few things my father feared, for it had killed his eldest son. I was about to be whisked off to an isolation hospital when my father insisted that my mother should be allowed to accompany me. The authorities flatly refused, saying that it was without precedent. My father then declared that he was a London County Councillor (which he was not) and that unless they yielded to him he would inform Fleet Street that their town was a hotbed of germs, where infectious diseases were allowed to rage unchecked owing to inadequate municipal supervision. The authorities at once capitulated. My mother accompanied me to the isolation hospital.

The day after the cigarette incident he was much weaker and did not recognize anybody, but when I visited him a very surprising thing happened. He called me by my name and threw his arms around me, holding me in a bearlike grip for more than a minute. It was the first paternal embrace he had ever offered me and one of the very few demonstrations of affection he had ever made. A few hours later he was dead and it was the first time I had ever seen him in repose, for even on the few occasions I had visited him whilst he was in bed, with the sheets drawn over his nose, he was not asleep but marshaling his forces to erupt against those who denied him his rest. There he lay, bereft of indignation, without a slogan on his lips or a cause on hand to galvanize him into protest. It seemed very odd and unreal. The Brewers, the Conservatives, the Bishops and the Militarists could relax. The secret societies poisoning British society could hold their secret sessions unchallenged, and it occurred to me that if there was any substance in Father's expectation of an Old Testament heaven he was already enjoying the society of Robbie Burns, David Livingstone, Ewart Gladstone and Abraham Lincoln. He might even chance upon that nice Christian young woman Mary Slessor of Calabar, or James Chalmers, to inquire of the latter what it felt like to be eaten by Papuans. It seemed to me a pleasing thought, but then I wondered if it really was, for what pleasure would he find in a society where there was no controversy, no necessity to campaign for temperance, no threat whatever to the dearly bought franchise of the British workingman? He would, I thought, feel more comfortable elsewhere, in some political purgatory, perhaps, where he could campaign against the privileges of the Saved.

I thought of his faults and there were many, of his savage intolerance, his instability, his astounding ability to believe anything he wanted to believe no matter how hardly his judgments bore upon others, but they seemed no more than diamond-bright facets of a vivid and extraordinary personality. Without them he would have seemed naked and pitiful. Then I thought of all the boredom he had dispelled and the helter-skelter cut-and-thrust he had brought to the lives of everybody his own life touched, and also how many gales of laughter would have been lost to the world if he had learned the art of self-discipline. I could not come to terms with his stillness. I tried to lay hold of a single incident that projected him as the person he was and it was not easy. They descended on me in a shower, so that in the end I had to select one that occurred as long ago as 1930, when I was eighteen and he was fifty-seven and in the prime of his eccentricity.

He had ordered me, at an hour's notice, to accompany him to London, ostensibly for the purpose of delivering a car but actually, as I was about to discover, to steal a holiday. He was always stealing holidays, but usually he slipped away alone, leaving a mantleshelf note like an eloping bride. It was years since I had accompanied him anywhere, and I had forgotten how accomplished he was in the art of enjoying himself. We visited the Carl Rosa Opera, Lord's Cricket Ground to see Bradman play, Henley Regatta, and the A.A. Championships at Stamford Bridge, but all this did no more than whet his appetite. After the A.A. games he marched me to a long-distance bus depot and bought tickets for the Lake District, where we stayed for more than a week, climbing Helvellyn, rowing on Windermere, and generally living it up. It was during our return journey, when the bus stopped for half an hour at Coventry, that the incident occurred. My father had never lost his Cockney taste for stewed eels, and an innocent remark of mine that I had never tasted them demanded immediate action. Somehow it shamed him to have a son, eighteen years of age, who had never eaten stewed eels. It was something that had to be put right without a moment's delay.

He said we would lunch on stewed eels, and when I pointed out that we were far north of London and had, moreover, but thirty minutes to eat a snack and rejoin the bus, he brushed my protests aside as though they had been lame excuses for the brewers, or a feeble justification of the Boer War. "This joker will know where we can find someone who sells a good stewed eel!" he declared and to my astonishment and embarrassment he accosted a postman who was passing, demanding the information of him with the emphasis of a policeman seeking the whereabouts of a fugitive wife-slayer. The postman, who happened to be afflicted with a bad squint, looked intimidated and mumbled something servile but then, halfheartedly, he led the way along a main street, across the square displaying Godiva's statue and down several side streets, stopping in front of a small and rather seedy photographer's shop. "There, sir!" he said, with an air of modest achievement, "there's your studio!"

My father's unpredictable sense of humor remained dormant; indeed, I had seldom seen him more outraged and disappointed. He swung round on our guide, caught him by the lapel of his jacket and roared, "You descendant of the impenitent thief! I ask you to show me where I can get a square meal and you drag

47

me all this way to have my facted photograph taken!" The postman said nothing. What, indeed, could he say? So we abandoned
him, retracing our steps across Coventry to the bus station and
entering London on empty stomachs.

It was all there, the brashness, the intolerance, the necessity to
attack at all costs, the insistence upon gratifying the whim of the
movement. It was rude, unjust, inexcusable, but it was Father and
neither I nor Almighty God could do anything about it.

A Cacophony of Aunts

My father had six extrovert sisters, and throughout my childhood they were always within hail. They would appear and disappear on our threshold like a bevy of music-hall artistes, collectively representing and projecting the entire range of human emotions and experience, from high tragedy to low comedy, from the goose-flesh macabre to the rib-splitting routine of flailing strings of sausages. There was nothing that could happen to anyone that escaped their collective flair for seizing hold of a facet of life, kneading it as a housewife kneads dough, and hurling it in the face of the first passer-by. They were a self-elected Greek Chorus who diverted the stream of history from the world outside over our doorstep, through the living room and into the abandoned nursery that bordered our garden fence. They were, as occasion demanded, raucous, abusive, generous, tolerant, shocking, stunning, confiding, scolding and scandalous; they were argumentative, comforting, broad-minded, narrow-minded, condemnatory, encouraging and conspiratorial. Temperamentally they were extraordinarily alike, but physically they had little in common. The visit of any one of them was an event, welcomed by me and tolerated by my parents, but doubtless dreaded by our immediate neighbors, for the party walls of Edwardian terrace houses are thin and I feel sure that repercussions of their visits were registered by steel engravings hanging on the walls of Numbers 20 and 24 of the Avenue.

The senior among them was Aunt Emma, whose appearances were rare. She was a small, rather deliberate woman, with a large family and a husband who never accompanied her. As the eldest of the brood, she had, to some extent, burned herself out in the exercise of family referee before I was born and was now making her way, by slow and faltering steps, toward a blessed anonymity, rather as a tired pilgrim stumbles the last few miles to the banks of the Jordan. I respected her without ever getting to know her. She was a gladiator who had survived countless battles in the arena but was now too old, and perhaps too bemused by the clamor of conflict, to fight again. Even so she was still mildly interested in what went on out there and would, on occasion, buckle on the armor of younger sisters and give them ringside lessons in tactics.

One sister away from Emma was Harriet, the barnstormer of the tribe, who came sailing into the house like a three-decker docking in a southwesterly gale. Harriet was the acknowledged comic turn of the family and, as with all Cockneys, her humor was mainly concerned with puncturing balloons of self-esteem. Cheerful contempt for every individual and for every institution remotely associated with authority poured from her like broadsides the moment you opened the front door. She never wasted a word on greeting and, quick as she was to make an attempt to embrace you, she never succeeded in clinching. Invariably her opening salvo blasted you back into the kitchen at the far end of the passage. There was nothing unique about her visits to us. Every house she entered was a stage upon which she had been engaged to appear as the star turn, and there was no room there for anyone else, not even a walk-on performer. She always made her entry with an armful of props that she at once discarded in order that she could gesture more freely. She never required the services of a feed and was extremely impatient with interruptions, even polite queries aimed at clarifying a point she was making. Anecdotes concerning dishonest milkmen, errant husbands, pompous officials, highhanded ticket collectors, dandies, dupes and demimondaines, poured from her nonstop until the house rocked with sound and the world outside, Aunt Harriet's world that is, was revealed as a Bedlam of knaves, fools, snobs, clowns and routed jacks-in-office. Nothing escaped the mangle of her ebullience. The most trivial incident was grabbed by the scruff of its neck, turned inside out, held up for laughs, and then flung aside to fall among her litter of personal belongings. There was no lull in her hurricane of talk and when she had gathered up her umbrella, shopping bag, handbag and newspaper and backed out shouting her goodbyes, it was as though we were within seconds of the Last Trump. Anything less would have been an anticlimax.

I looked forward to the visits of Aunt Harriet, but I was always glad when my parents began to edge her on to the front porch. She undermined one's faith in the entire structure of democracy and lit a fuse beside every pillar that interposed its solidity between me and the ceiling of chaos.

Younger than Emma, but senior to Harriet, was Aunt Maud, whom I list third instead of second because she was Harriet's recoil and shock absorber. She was designed for shock absorption, fourteen stone of bone, muscle, bosom and buttock, and throughout my childhood she needed every pound of it for she was the superintendent of a large Municipal Baths, situated in a thickly populated borough south of the river. In some ways I reckoned Aunt Maud the most estimable of the brood, a widow who had been left virtually penniless and had battled her way to a responsible position by sheer force of character. She had a broad, pale face and shining, boot-button eyes that darted here and there at a speed strangely at variance with her bulk and ponderous tread. She had a wry, sardonic humor that disdained Harriet's frank appeal to the gallery but was just as devastating —indeed, more so, for its shafts were loosed from a platform of stability and seeming neutrality. She always dressed in black, and perhaps it was this, together with the amount of ballast she carried, that made her seem so formidable when reporting upon recent affrays at the Municipal Baths. To me she was inseparable from those baths. I saw her as a kind of League of Nations task force, charged with keeping the peace at all costs, even if it meant drowning her quarrelsome patrons in batches. There were, it would seem, almost hourly disputes at the baths and my aunt would blanket her antagonists as the "Tartars," and her more docile customers as the "Women." I liked to picture the appearance of my Aunt Maud on the scene of a lopsided dispute between the Women and the Tartars, and witness the instantaneous routing of the latter to the accompaniment of timid cheers by the former. I was always hoping that she would invite me to witness such an engagement, for the Tartars promised to be the nearest I would ever come to seeing the *tricoteuses* who sat beneath the guillotine, but she never did. The only time I saw her in action was when she superintended the vast public wash that followed the bursting of the Thames's banks, in January, 1927. On that day she was superb and would have made two of any of her sisters and this is not a light comparison. Any one of them was the equivalent of two guardsmen and six professional comediennes.

After Harriet came Ada, another generously built woman, with black, arched brows and a witty Covent Garden husband to whom, inexplicably, she had surrendered the initiative. This was something her five sisters could never understand, for the gift of noisy badinage was a family birthright and to yield it up, even to a husband, was like signing away hereditary acres. Ada took part in family free-for-alls but she was a one-gun battery, firing from extreme range. To every shot Ada fired Maud fired two and Harriet fired eight, but when Ada's hit their mark they rocked the opposition. Ada always appeared in green, so that I think she thought of herself as a potential peacemaker, but it was a role I never saw her enact. Looking back I am inclined to think I was wrong and that her true purpose on the edge of the family circle was to keep Harriet, Maud and the others from flagging in their full-throated exchange of *bons mots,* anecdotes, chaff, recriminations and threats. On occasions like these I always tried to position myself between Aunt Maud and Aunt Ada. Here you could enjoy all the fun of a stampede without getting trampled to death or, at best, having a custard pie rammed in your face. You had to take these kinds of precautions when the sisters were gathered under one roof for innocent bystanders were bowled over like skittles and were then subpoenaed by both sides to witness the truth.

After Ada came the family lightweights, Nell and Lou, separated from the others by a large age gap and far more nimble than their sisters. I use the word lightweight advisedly, because that is what they seemed until the atmosphere warmed up, but either one of them could more than hold her own in the way a practiced duelist, armed with a light rapier, can match antagonists armed with bludgeons. Nell was the wittiest and most forthright, but Lou had a secret weapon in her exceptionally high-pitched laugh that could divert attention and cause even Harriet to flounder for words and muff a repartee. Nell had a very gentle side to her character, and both she and Aunt Lou were generous and kindhearted, but either one of them, tempted into the fray, could be relied upon to give an excellent account of herself.

One may ask what did they quarrel about and the answer is very simple. They never quarreled at all, but merely contended for each other's attention and the attention of anyone who happened to be standing around offering them tea and buns, or inquiring after their families. I never saw an outside party challenge any one of them, much less the whole bunch. It would, indeed, have been an act of extreme folly to attempt such a thing, for six boiler factories working at full blast could never have produced the cacophony that resulted from the gathering together of any three of my aunts. When all six were assembled at a Christmas party, a wedding, or a funeral, it was as though the house was beleaguered by a vast and extremely belligerent football crowd, armed with whistles, harsh wooden rattles and bulb motor-horns. Whenever more than two of them showed up, my mother would retire to the kitchen and busy herself with sandwiches, but whilst sympathizing with her withdrawal I still think she was foolish to deny herself an entertainment of such verve and variety, for one was not likely to witness its equal anywhere this side of the Styx. It was far better than any circus or film, for what ringmaster or director would be such an idiot as to present six star performers in a single act, each of them hell-bent on topping the others' performances and cornering the attention of the audience?

"They got in through the bathroom window—lean as fiddle-strings they must've been . . ." Harriet would scream, halfway through a story of the latest attempt upon her chattels by burglars, but we never learned whether the raid had been successful or had ended in arrest and trial, because Aunt Maud, poking her finger at Harriet, boomed with remorseless insistence, "Those Tartars have been at it again! *At it*, you hear me? *At it*, and those poor Women . . ." to which Harriet would screech, "Shut up, Maud, I'm talking! I'm telling you how they got in, aren't I, Ada?" and Ada would look her straight in the eye and shout, "Hold your tongue, Harriet, and listen to my Harry, can't you?" whereupon Nell announced at the top of her voice that Harry's story wasn't worth listening to because it had blue whiskers on it, and this would touch off Aunt Lou's laughter so that no single word from anyone present could be heard until she had subsided.

As they drew together, still furiously competing for an audience, not even the bare bones of an anecdote could be rescued from the babel, but here and there a word or a phrase would emerge from the scrum like the sailing cork of a champagne bottle and describe a wide arc across the room. "My Harry! . . . My Frank! . . . My Ruby! . . . My God! The Tartars! . . . the burglars! . . . the mayor! . . . the chimney sweep! . . . How about it then? . . . You do and I'll crown you, Willie! . . . He didn't though? . . . I'm telling you straight! . . . Back up and unload! . . . Mind the baby and we'll see! . . . Oh come *off* it, Herbert, you're up the pole! . . . Never mind then, I'll see to *him* person-ally! . . . No, look here! . . . Pardon me! . . . I said, 'You're a liar, sir!' That's what *I* said! . . . Not two of 'em mind you but *six!* . . ." And I would steal away to seek out cousins, of whom there were sometimes half a dozen in and around the house, hoping to learn the substance of Uncle Harry's latest market story or whether, in fact, Aunt Harriet's burglars had been caught, or how many of the Tartars had been flung into the Municipal Baths by Aunt Maud, summoned to the rescue of the Women.

Only Aunt Nell survives to this day, and she, a heroine of the London blitz, is the only member of the family who lived to finish a story. It is awesome to sit and hear her describe the descent of land mines on Catford, or recount, uninterrupted, a shelter story from the days when she and several hundred Southside Londoners, some of them almost identical to my departed aunts, gathered in siren suits and competed for the honor of distracting an audience's attention from the crumps outside. This was indeed their finest hour, and it would have been my aunts' too, had the blitz occurred when they were young and spry. Sometimes, listening to Aunt Nell, I fancy I can hear her five sisters plaintively speaking up for themselves and demanding to be heard from the edge of beyond—"My Harry . . . My Ruby . . . My Frank . . . My God! . . . He *didn't?* He *never?* She *wouldn't?* She *did!* . . ."

Bulldozers in Arcady

Why do we equate suburbs with dullness? With boredom and personal defeat? How did the adjective *suburban* acquire the status of a calculated insult? After all, three quarters of us in the Western world live in suburbs of one sort or another, and many of them are pleasant, even fragrant places. Some are built with taste, and all are capable of exhibiting tremendous vitality. The people inhabiting them are almost always decent, hard-working folk, concerned with minding their own business, improving their standards of living, paying their taxes and, what is so often overlooked, maintaining their ancestral links with sodbreakers in tiny, lovingly tended gardens. Why else would they pour into the open on Saturday afternoons and Sunday mornings, with sleeves rolled up and tools in hand, to trim the privet, tie back the loganberry trailers and contribute to that pleasantly muted song of the suburbs, the intermittent whirr of lawn mower, the *snip-snip* of shears and the steady chink of spade?

One of the few contemporary Englishmen who finds the suburbs rewarding is John Betjeman, and no one will ever do a better job of crystallizing their elusive charm in verse. Being of John's generation I find it easy to share his enthusiasm, for the songs he sings are already nostalgic, telling as they do of corners of England that may soon be banished as finally as the meadows of eighteenth-century Staffordshire and South Lancashire. Already the writing is on the wall. Gaunt and featureless blocks of flats and offices are replacing rows of terraces and tiny, zealously maintained green patches in the outskirts of our cities. The corner shop, if it has not already gone, will soon become a super-market, with closed-circuit television keeping watch on potential thieves. The parks and recreation grounds, where lovers still embrace one another on municipal seats and children sail yachts in municipal ponds, will probably be reclassified by artful bureaucrats seeking more land to build more universities. And in those universities young men and women will be trained in sciences that will make the English suburb as archaic as the village green. Soon, I suspect, bulldozers will advance into Arcady, and when England is either a scorched desert or a clinical hell of tarmac, chromium, plastic and computerized thought, a few elderly survivors will dream of suburbs, as a few of the very old now dream of village communities in the era before the planners decided that our untidy lives needed drastic reorganization.

Before anyone is amazed that I should confuse the suburb with Arcady let me explain.

In the spring of 1918, when the people living inside the old perimeter of London were beginning to falter on account of air raids, those who could moved farther out, seeking dwellings in areas they assumed were less vulnerable. In fact, once there, they were no less likely to be killed by a stray bomb or a flying splinter of antiaircraft shrapnel. The poor, bemused devils in the Zeppelins and aircraft of that period were not often in search of a specific target and, even when they were, their chances of finding and hitting one was seven million to one. It seemed logical, however, to assume that one would be safer in, say, Hounslow, than in Hammersmith, in Croydon than in Camberwell, and one of my numerous uncles had fled twelve miles south at the height of the raids and bought a terrace house in Ashburton Avenue, off Shirley Road, in the parish of Addiscombe. It was he who persuaded my father to follow and catch an early train into the city each morning, so we moved out to the very same avenue.

To a child of six the translation from Bermondsey to the then rural district of South Croydon was as final as the movement of a succeeding generation of evacuees from Stepney to Somerset. The only difference was that I did not travel with a label round my neck giving my name, school and destination.

Perhaps no area in outer London has changed more dramatically than Croydon has changed over the last half century. Today its southern boundary is a wilderness of housing estates and shopping centers, but in the spring of 1918, when the British Army was battling to plug the gaps torn in its line by Ludendorff's final offensive, Addiscombe was as pastoral and peaceful as is most of the West Country peninsula today. Ashburton Avenue was only five minutes' walk from the ruins of the old military academy set up by the East India Company before the Indian Mutiny compelled the Crown to take over that part of the Empire. The quiet residential roads were named after Mutiny personalities—Generals Havelock, Outram, Nicholson and Campbell, all of whom had been educated at the academy. The houses in this area were a good class of property, detached residences set back from the road, and often four-storied. Farther out, toward the straggling villages of Wickham, Shirley, Addington, Down, Cudham and Westerham, where the farm land of Kent merged into that of Surrey, the countryman was unchallenged. Thatched cottages leaned on one another, interspersed with ancient pubs and shops that smelled of bran, candles and lamp oil, and on every side stretched hundreds of acres of plowed fields, studded with tufted copses. In the pastureland fat cattle grazed and chaffinches flirted in thickets, and beyond was the green twilight of the Archbishop's Woods, with its huge deserted mansion fronting a lake.

It was Wonderland to me. My experience of unspoiled country was limited to an occasional weekend in Kent. I had never seen an English spring move across field and coppice, scattering a carpet of yellow buttercups and scarlet campion, and the only wild birds I had ever seen were house sparrows and starlings. To explore there, to cross Farmer Still's meadows, to stand under his giant oaks that were growing when Edgehill was fought, to bird's-nest in hazel thicket, and pick my first bluebells under flowering chestnuts, was the most enriching experience of my life. In those days nobody I knew owned a car, and the long war had done much to discourage holidays, so that I was seeing these things for the first time and at a period in development when impressions were strong and lasting.

But, although my imagination was deeply stirred by the rural aspects of the shift, the social implications had an even stronger effect. It was here, at that time, that I came to sense and ultimately to understand, the subtle undercurrents of the English class system, something that had not impinged upon me in Bermondsey, where we all seemed to belong to one rowdy family. The suburb had a scent and the suburb had a song, but it also had a *tone* and that owed nothing to bullfinches, hawthorn, honeysuckle, whirring lawn mower and the chink of spade. To those who settled there from more congested areas, it had, however, a curious sense of security, of having arrived, of having progressed to another, loftier plane, and it is very difficult to convey this sense of social uplift to someone who has not experienced it. It had to do with the jaunty way the commuters (the word was unknown then) set out for Woodside Station on the old South-Eastern and Chatham Line, and with the presence of so many private schools that were called, for a reason I have never been able to discover, "colleges." It was to be found in the galaxy of private music teachers, the competitiveness of local rose growers, in the curtains in the bow windows and the fact that everyone had not only a back but a front garden. Suburbs like Addiscombe were not merely suburbs. They were also frontiers.

One could stand by the pregnant red pillar box at the junction of Ashburton Avenue and Shirley Road with a definite sense of having penetrated to the farthest limits of the Big City. To the north and west lay the stale, labyrinthine streets of the largest city in the world. To the south and east was the Garden of England that had not changed much since Wat Tyler's men staged their protest march against the mandarins of Richard II. It always seemed to me that London Wall was in the wrong place. It should have cut clear across Shirley Road to mark the difference between town and country.

Here, among the borderers, there was a strong sense of community, and this is not to say that the menfolk forgathered in local pubs, or the womenfolk called on neighbors to borrow cups of sugar. Camaraderie, in the true sense of the word, did not exist, but we Avenue dwellers were all conscious of having a great deal in common and an obligation to conform. Do not imagine for one instant that this obligation was in any way irksome. On the contrary, we reveled in it and went out of our way to emphasize the subtle distinctions between the ranks of the carefully graded society in which we found ourselves. No one, apart from the deliverers of coal and the emptiers of dustbins, ever appeared on the pavements collarless, and even the tradesmen who called on us for orders knew their place and used the prefix "sir" or "madam." There was very little gossiping over the garden fences and virtually no casual dropping-in, of the kind one sees in contemporary TV soap operas like *Coronation Street*. This curious sense of exclusiveness was even more apparent among the children. One was strictly enjoined "not to play" with the village children, who were collectively termed "Street Arabs." Gentle pressure was exerted to seek one's companions among "nice boys," in an income group approximating one's own, and even the games were heavily prescribed. One never saw, for instance, the children of the suburb playing at marbles, and all the time I lived in the Avenue I never came across a hop-scotch pitch chalked on the pavement. If one needed room to expand one went along to the Rec—Recreation Ground—and this was a kind of suburban Royal Enclosure set aside for us. The village children were seldom seen there, and if they appeared they were never invited to join our games. Cricket, rounders, tennis and an occasional Punch and Judy show were available behind the tall brick pillars of the Rec, but highcockolorum, a boisterous game played in school playgrounds, was left outside. Taken all round we were fearful snobs.

One would have thought that such an atmosphere was mentally crippling but somehow it wasn't. I have never since lived in a community that was as safe and ordered, and neither will I again. Nor anyone else for that matter. One knew and accepted one's place to the last decimal point. Children attending the local "colleges" did not mix with those attending elementary schools. One raised one's cap to adult neighbors, washed carefully behind the ears, and learned to speak civilly but rather distantly to shop assistants. At the same time, one took no liberties whatever with the children who lived in the big detached houses and had nannies and the use of the family Humber and telephone. The gulf between them and us was as wide as that between us and the children who picked wild flowers and offered them for sale at a penny a bunch, who stood watching the stream of traffic returning from the Derby and shouted, "Chuck aht yer moldy coppers!" My brother once picked up one of those moldy coppers. My mother insisted that he throw it back.

I often wonder, looking back, what a foreigner would have made of it all. I never met one, or even glimpsed one in the Avenue, but they must have appeared there from time to time, to return home as baffled by the English class system as they are today. No one along our terrace could have been earning, at that time, more than seven pounds a week, and I am certain most of them earned much less. But this in no way prevented them from patronizing, as only the people of the suburbs can, those who lived a hundred yards closer to the heart of London on approximately the same income.

There was no written code of behavior. No one ever prescribed in as many words what was done and what was frowned upon, what could be worn on weekdays and on Sundays, what slang was permissible and what words were not accepted as slang by decent people, when to pull down the blinds for a funeral and when to lift aside the lace curtains for a wedding. Among those who dwelt there were Anglicans high and low. Free Churchmen of every known sect, and a minority torn by Bradlaugh's "honest doubt." They were not given to gossip, but somehow, as though circulated by code notes on a hundred parlor pianos, all that transpired along the length of the Avenue became common knowledge between two successive sunsets. Trevor Sinclair, of Number Nine, had won a scholarship to Charterhouse. The "new" people at Number Nineteen were engaging a maid. Audrey Follett's wedding had been put forward at Number Forty-six, the result, no doubt, of not getting her indoors by ten, and in these circumstances how could anyone risk taking a chance in the Avenue? One slip and it was snakes-and-ladders right back to base, and who, in their senses, would face that hazard after the effort it had required to get there?

I have been back several times in the last few decades, and on every occasion the place seems to have sloughed off a little more of its identity. I may be wrong, but I have a feeling that the spurious but highly prized gentility of our suburb was destroyed by an assortment of factors. By the onslaught of the Luftwaffe, by the creation of the Welfare State, by the ball-and-chain tug of our economic malaise, by the loss of the Empire and also by the forest of TV masts that now weave a crazy pattern along the rooftops of the crescents and closes. A majority, perhaps, will view this demise as a significant social advance, but I am not convinced of this. The egalitarianism that has replaced it is as featureless as a Government White Paper and for the incurable romantic the suburb had a flavor that has disappeared as surely as flavor disappears from the prepacked meal. Whenever I wander up Shirley Road today and poke about among the new roads between the frontier pillar box and the Rec, I seem to be remembering a time as distant as Agincourt, but the song of the suburb, although considerably muted, is still to be heard. A whirr of lawn mower at Number Twenty-three. The slow castanet of hedge clippers at Seventy-three. And the scent of the suburb lingers too for those who inhaled it fifty years ago. Clipped privet and full-blown cabbage rose and melting tar in the sun on the few occasions the sun seems to shine there nowadays. For that is another secret the children of the Avenue knew so well but seem, somehow, to have forgotten. The ordered procession of the seasons that rotated, in a thousand chests of drawers. Cricket shirts and cotton frocks from Easter to September. Mufflers, hairy gloves and galoshes from early October to March.

A Multiplicity of Mozarts

Between the death of Queen Victoria and the installation, in almost every house in the land, of a reliable wireless set, a strange and terrifying malaise stalked the closes, the crescents, the roads and avenues of Suburbia. It was not a physical sickness but a kind of hysteria that took the form of chronic self-hypnosis, and in some ways it was not unlike that other, better-known neurosis, diagnosed as *folie de grandeur*, but more insidious and much more rampant. Its most singular characteristic was its selectivity. Ignoring all other members of suburban households it struck savagely at the mothers of growing children and then, having so to speak gained a hold at one end of a thoroughfare, it spread with the rapidity of bubonic plague. It was very hard to treat, for there was no medical name for it, so that I am obliged to invent one and call it Mozartitis, remembering that it was Mozart who, all unknowingly, introduced it into the Western world.

We are all familiar with the picture showing the infant Mozart seated at the pianoforte in the middle of the night, surrounded by an astounded and strangely tolerant family. There he sits in his long white nightshirt, and there they stand with raised candelabra, witnesses to his precocity. When I was about Mozart's age at the time of this nocturnal frolic this very picture, in lurid sepia, hung in many suburban parlors, but its presence near the upright piano had a specific purpose. It was there as a reminder to every child in that house that he or she, given parental encouragement and years of disciplined application, might one night assemble a thunderstruck family around the piano to bear witness to another demonstration of genius on the Bechstein, the Niedermayer or the Chappell. In that picture was the substance of the myth that began as a simple yearning in maternal breasts to bring forth genius and ended in an obsessive megalomania that banished logic, reason and the evidence of a victim's senses—particularly her sense of hearing. In passing the visitation sentenced a generation of children to a form of penance not far removed from the treadmill long since banished from our jails.

There is a curious parallel between the efforts of early-twentieth-century children to learn to play the piano and the disasters that overwhelmed the British canal companies of an earlier generation. Both were overhauled, and made to look ridiculous, by the march of science. The canals were put out of business by the railways before their courses were half completed. The piano practice of my generation was rendered vain by the invention of the crystal set, the portable Gramophone and the talking picture. All that we later victims of circumstance and maternal Mozart-fixations had to show for our lost hours of childhood was a thin smattering of "theory" and the ability to stumble through half "The Hunting Song" or "The Merry Peasant Returning from Work." The rest of the knowledge we acquired while our bottoms were glued to music stools had slipped between the edges of yellowing keys, to be carted away when upright pianos were being sold at public auction for fifteen shillings less commission.

My mother's insistence that I could, if I concentrated, become a musical prodigy, was particularly fierce, amounting almost to a mania. She had tried and failed to perform this miracle of faith on my elder brothers, but she discovered, or thought she discovered, what she was pleased to call "a nice touch" in the blundering fingers of her youngest. So that it was I who had to bear the accumulated weight of her frustrated ambition.

At the age of seven I was handed over to a Miss Dixon, a sweet, uncomplaining little spinster, who was only one in an army of suburban music teachers supplementing their incomes (and in some cases actually supporting themselves) by instructing the children of the avenues to "play nicely." God knows they did their best with us, dividing periods equally into "theory" and "practice." Each of us covered sheets and sheets of manuscript with crotchers and quavers, and each of us fairly wore out pianos with an endless repetition of scales and exercises. From time to time some of us took examinations and qualified for certificates at the Guildhall School of Music. But for all the good it did anyone we might as well have been making mudpies in our back gardens.

I never encountered one of my fellow pupils in later life who could play a recognizable national anthem on a piano, or even one who wanted to, and it frightens me to conjecture where all those hours and hours of practice went, or what they ever accomplished in terms of positive achievement. One would imagine that *something* would have stuck, a phrase or two of one of the "pieces," a tiny residual of the technicalities we imbibed, but it didn't. It all hived off during the vo-deo-do era and was either forgotten altogether or shriveled to a vague familiarity with words like *fortissimo*, the difference between sharps and flats, or the ability to play "Chopsticks."

To return to Miss Dixon.

She taught me a series of tittupy little tunes based on a "Down on the Farm" theme, and these are all I have to show for the hours I spent on her particular stool. I do not mean that I can still play them, but I can still hum or whistle "In a Quiet Wood," "Now All is Sleeping," "Cuckoo" and "The March of the Farmer's Men." My mother, dear, earnest soul, was almost hysterical at my progress, and I went on to more difficult pieces—"L'Orage," "The Hunting Song," and, of course, the obligatory "Merry Peasant Returning from Work."

I practiced these for half an hour by the front-room clock each evening, and perhaps the one consolation that was mine during those periods reposed in the certainty that, had I been released to play on the allotments or the building sites, I would have played alone. All my contemporaries, male and female, were at their pianos playing identical "pieces," except for a local genius called Taylor who had progressed as far as "An Autumn Ride."

If you chanced to pass along the avenue on a summer evening

in, say, 1921, you could, in effect, have anticipated the radio and television eras. Identical snatches of melody issued from every open window. They were all at it, one eye on the music held in its frame by a pair of brass triggers, the other on the mantelshelf clock. The only possible variant in sound would be in the Freeman house at the end of the block, where little Eric had begun five minutes after the rest of us and was therefore still at his scales.

When I moved to the West I had another teacher, one who advertised himself as a Professor. He always arrived late pleading bicycle trouble but exhaling something more convivial than the whiff of bicycle oil. The Professor did not last long in our teetotal house and I was shuttled on to a delightful old gentleman who was organist at the local parish church and possessed another vice, but one that my parents were prepared to overlook. He was a chain-smoker and had developed the most terrible cough I have ever heard, not excluding the coughs of consumptive heroes and heroines in the early talkies. When it seized him, usually in the middle of "L'Orage" or "Merry Peasant," he would shoot out his hands, smash them down upon the keys and go through a most fascinating writhing routine, generally throwing himself around in a paroxysm that made me fear for his life. Notwithstanding these alarming interruptions the time spent with him passed pleasantly enough, for at least half of it was spent dodging his frantic swipes in pursuit of the oxygen that eluded him. The other half was devoted to excerpts from Gilbert and Sullivan operas that I found far less tedious than "L'Orage." I paid a high price for this alleviation in my torment, however, for my mother, a devotee of Gilbert and Sullivan, was confirmed in her opinion that she had produced a pianist with the Mozart touch and thereafter redoubled her efforts to bring me up to virtuoso standard. Unluckily for her my tutor died, as I had always been convinced that he would, during a particularly spectacular bout of coughing, and when I was sent away to school I had a fourth tutor, a shortsighted man called Watson, whose duty it was, poor devil, to cater for all the boys at the school whose mothers had Mozart obsessions concerning their sons.

Watson was a pleasant fellow but he had a little more asperity than his three predecessors and was inclined to rap knuckles when fingers blundered. I still might have learned something from him had not his tutelage coincided with the arrival of the jazz age, when the tune "Valencia" was sweeping the country and the piano was beginning to run a poor third to the saxophone and the ukelele. If one could vamp "Valencia," what sense was there in practicing quaint and dated "pieces" like "L'Orage" and "Autumn Ride"? And who the hell would sit still and listen to them anyway? So I spent all my practice time in the school linen room playing sheet music of the period, and Watson, who had more pupils than he could cope with anyway, wrote a letter to my mother informing her that she had grossly overestimated my chances of playing at the Albert Hall.

Even then all might not have been lost if the tobacco barons had not elbowed their way into the picture by issuing coupons with every packet of twenty, to be hoarded against the acquisition of a Decca Gramophone. Once this became generally known, the upright piano was doomed. It had held its own, to some extent, against the ukelele, the saxophone and even the crystal set, but it collapsed under the combined assault of the Decca Portable and a four-tube set that could be enjoyed without benefit of earphones.

By the late twenties the evening serenade of the suburbs was becoming muted. There were breaks in its continuity as one passed along beside the privet hedges and sometimes one could walk all the way from Number Four to Number Twenty-two without hearing a single note of "L'Orage," "The Hunting Song," or even "The Merry Peasant Returning from Work." Instead one heard the steady whine of the Decca playing the Negro spirituals of Paul Robeson, the "harmonized" jazz of Layton and Johnstone, or the uncertain throb of the four-and-sixpenny ukelele (with free tutorial booklet) vamping an accompaniment to "Old Nebraska" or "Springtime in the Rockies." It was a marked drop in social tone, a plunging descent from the plateau of gentility to pavements where children had once hopped around barrel organs. A few mothers resisted it with the desperate courage of the lower-middle-class matron who sees her way of life threatened by hooliganism. My mother was not among this minority. My jazzed-up rendering of "Valencia," the sole yield of a term's music fees, reconciled her to defeat. Resolutely she slammed the lid of the upright piano and placed my dog-eared "pieces" in a music stool that later became a coal scoop, a downgrading that was symbolic of a general recovery of suburbia from its musical malaise.

I never played our piano again, and in time it was taken away to make room for a bamboo table supporting a four-tube wireless set with an amplifier as compelling as a liner's foghorn. In later life my mother would never speak of my early promise, of my "nice touch," my Guildhall certificate, or the occasion when "L'Orage" won me first prize in a local concert party tent. Yet this I know. To the day she died she was convinced that my third tutor's cough had deprived the world of a Mozart-Rubinstein, and the disappointment weighed so heavily upon her that she could never take pleasure in a radio program. For the same reason, I suppose, her eyes smoldered whenever she heard the throb of a ukelele or the whine of a portable Gramophone. It would be easy to call her a bad loser, but I fancy I can put my finger in the cornerstone of her implacability. It is one thing to see one's fondest hopes overturned by death. It is quite another to lose out to catgut, plywood and the free gift vouchers from "Ardath" and "Kensitas."

The Sad Truth About the Twenties

Among literary conventions none is more piquant than that of bracketing years into decades and giving them a special title— the "Hungry Forties," the "Naughty Nineties," the "Edwardian Afternoon" and, of course, our old friend dominated by the Bright Young Things and called the "Charleston Era." This last has, to some extent, already become a cult among stage, film and television producers.

The bracketing, of course, is arbitrary and thus a fiction. History is not as tidy as that. Decades have a habit of merging into one another, pockmarked by wars, held back or overlapped by sensational political events and current fashions, so that they soon begin to fray around the edges and no one can be precise as to where one era ended and the next began. Those who make the distinction are like frontier surveyors deprived of their apparatus, too often reduced to expediency and guesswork.

Who, for instance, can classify the fifties? Or who, for that matter, can recall anything very special about the forties after V–E Day? The thirties, as a period of foreboding, has a certain distinction, but it was mostly a period of waiting for the end of the world so that one recalls them as a time of fretful, uneasy slumber. Something like this has happened to the pre-First World War period, styled the "Edwardian Afternoon" or the "Long Garden Party." Memories of that era are fragmentary now. The youth of everyone born in the last two decades of Victoria's

reign went under the guillotine in August, 1914, and for most of
the survivors memories of the next four years are a drab pattern
of gray and black. Then, quite suddenly, the war ended and the
aged young were so astonished to find themselves alive that it was
1920 before they had time to look around and take notice. Perhaps
this explains why the subsequent decade has taken on such bright
plumage and why, of all decades with titles of their own, it
really does appear to have as much separateness as the era of
wigs and knee breeches, the Age of Elegance that succeeded
Waterloo, and the time when the crinoline was in vogue and
stovepipe-hatted domestic tyrants wore side whiskers and were
so deeply obsessed with moral principles.

There is no doubt about it. Despite all evidence to the contrary (and the evidence is impressive), the twenties *did* project
a special gaiety and have, on this account, made a considerable
impact upon the imagination of novelists and even serious historians. They are, to an extent, a freak, an odd man out, an
extrovert in a great family of introverts. They have a different
set of values, a different sound and a different tempo from any
previous or subsequent decade. Their speech idioms are now as
archaic as Chaucer's so that they seem to speak a different language than all the other decades. Every generation has its own
slang, but the slang of the twenties was not the prerogative of a
small, esoteric group, like the R.A.F. slang of the early forties,
or the beat jargon of the sixties. It was universal. It was the conversational currency of everyone who lived between 1920 and
1930, for who on earth, not having been young in those days,
would address an intimate as "Old Bean"? And who could continue to believe in the absolute innocence of the term "making
whoopee"?

The alleged characteristics of this decade have, in fact, given
it a variety of titles. Subsequent generations think of it as the
Jazz Age, the Black Bottom Age, the Age of the Cocktail Party
and the vo-deo-do era, but what astonishes those who lived
through it is the uniformity of latter-day beliefs concerning its
stridency and its tremendous vitality, as though no one had ever

been gay before and has never been gay since. Its outward trappings are rigidly period, so much so that we who were young in those days are sometimes half persuaded that we are looking at an accurate reflection of ourselves when we watch a mock-up of the period on our TV screens. It is only in the quiet moments that follow the switch-off that we can test the evidence of our eyes and ears against that of our regrets. And then, alas, comes the sobering reappraisal.

To those whose childhood and early youth were dulled and blighted by that unmitigated scoundrel Adolf Hitler, it must appear that their parents, when young, were either permanently drunk, mentally afflicted, or subject to recurring attacks of St. Vitus's Dance. Why else should the men wear tilted straw hats and striped blazers winter and summer? Why should they leap and gyrate from one Black Bottom to another, as they thrummed madly at their plywood ukeleles, uttering the while all manner of incomprehensible hoots and yowls to advertise their irrepressibly high spirits? And what, may one ask, persuaded the miniskirted maidens of that era to adopt such impossibly arch poses when wooed and pursued, with palms pressed under their chins, with sleek, shingled heads thrown over their shoulders at acute and demonstrably uncomfortable angles? I mean, what happened in addition to the party? Who paid for it? Who kept the dance floors swept? And outside, beyond the range of saxophone and uke, who governed and who starved? Above all, when did these prancing, shrieking couples sleep or perform their natural functions? Not in the brief intervals of changing records, for then they were anchored by earphones to their coy crystal sets listening to yet more jazz fed them by the Savoy Orpheans. It poses the same questions as those posed by the great Viennese Waltztime, when it is obvious that every adult male in the Hapsburg Empire served in the Hussars and every adult woman was either a countess or a serving wench in a beer garden.

Dear Heaven, if it had *really* been like that! What memories we in our fifties and sixties would have to fortify us against old age! And how bitterly we would resent current preoccupation with space travel and recurrent financial crises!

2

Let us get one or two things clear from the outset.

To begin with, Victorian prudery and the Victorian father figure did not disappear in the barrage smoke of the Somme or sink beneath the slime at Passchendaele. They were hardy animals both and emerged from the holocaust with a few minor bruises. So that there never was a great spontaneous surge toward the new freedoms by the prototypes of today's teen agers. The shackles, where they were discarded, were shed link by link and not by the chain mile. There was, for instance, no universal sloughing-off of religious observance. Families in the suburbs continued to believe in the Old Testament Almighty. Most of them continued to attend morning service, and their children thronged the Sunday schools to hear about Jonah and the Whale and what happened to the sinners in Sodom and Gomorrah. There was no weekend as we know it today. If you worked in a shop you were stuck behind the counter until late evening on Saturdays: if you plied a pen in an office you stayed there until one P.M. sharp on Saturday afternoon. Annual holidays were by no means obligatory. Some didn't take any, others took a week or a fortnight in August, and those who took a fortnight were not paid for the extra week. The discipline at most places of work was the discipline of the barracks. The discipline of the home was almost indistinguishable from that of the preceding age and I can prove it. Along my particular avenue a majority of parents kept a cane tucked behind a living-room steel engraving, its curved handle protruding like a gun from a holster. There was nothing to be gained by surreptitiously making away with that cane. A replacement could be bought for twopence at any ironmonger's where they hung outside in sinister clusters, along with the pots and pans.

But there were other, harsher sanctions, for children and adults. God was watching, and God had X-ray eyes and phenomenal hearing, so that if, in a moment of devilment or stress, you used the kind of language commonly heard in current TV plays you took good care to mutter. If it did slip out and was not over-heard on earth it went down in The Book From Which There Was No Rubbing Out, a book, one imagined, not unlike the enormous jet-black Bible that still reposed on a bamboo table in the front parlor. As for four-letter words, they were confined exclusively to brothels, the worst kind of pubs and lavatory walls, where they were sometimes scrawled by the damned and de-mented. The New Wave playwrights wouldn't have lasted three minutes in the twenties. Any one of them would have started a revolution, and their social extinction would have been im-mediate.

We knew about divorce but rarely mentioned it, except as one might mention a royal wedding, or a new speed record. Divorce was something that happened almost exclusively to the celebrated. I had nine aunts and uncles and most of them had a sizable family but I was twenty before the word *divorce* was bandied around inside the family and I was very shocked to hear it, even though a relative of mine was the innocent party. Apart from him I had never met a divorced person and never expected to.

Sex we learned about via schoolboy jokes. Nobody ever dis-cussed it at home or in the kind of newspaper that found its way through the suburban letter boxes. At rare intervals it was rumored that a neighbor's unmarried daughter was expecting a baby, and the whisper would set tongues wagging for a month, so that whenever the family's name was mentioned people walked on conversational tiptoe. The woman concerned, of course, was written off, like a sack of sugar ruined by damp. And even if the couple married, as they usually did, the circumstances of their marriage were not forgotten. Years later charitable neighbors would refer to their eldest child as "the one who came across the fields."

So much for the new freedoms. Now take a closer look at other aspects of the social scene beyond the roof garden of the

Savoy and the dance floor of Mrs. Kate Meyrick's 43 Club.

Crime for instance. It might be imagined that all those blazer-clad Romeos and bead-swinging flappers would show at least as much tolerance to the petty criminal as he receives from Bench, Press and public today. Nothing of the kind. The theft of a ten-shilling postal order was regarded with such abhorrence that a guilty party was obliged to move house as soon as he had completed the sentence he almost invariably received. Had he remained among those aware of his crime, neither he nor his family could have hoped to emerge from the cloud of odium that settled over his roof. Few would have told him the time, and no children would have been allowed to mix with his children. He was therefore advised to make for Australia, providing Australia would have him. A thief of any kind was an outcast, whether he stole a thousand pounds from a safe or a pencil box from a classmate's desk. There was only one exception to this rule and that concerned the then popular cat-burglar, who risked his neck in the practice of his profession and thus qualified for a little grudging respect. As for the hardened sinners, they went straight to prison for long terms and prison, in those days, meant punishment. There was no sloppy talk about it being a place where the emphasis was on rehabilitation. The word had not then come into fashion, and prison was a place designed for no other purpose than to dispense retribution. It was a fortress behind whose walls existed the silence rule, bread and water for the uncooperative, the cat-o'-nine-tails for the aggressive and mailbag-making or stonebreaking for all. Prisons, in 1920, had changed very little from mid-Victorian days. The only apparatus Charlie Peace would have missed was the crank and the treadmill.

It might surprise some people to learn that, notwithstanding the general atmosphere of jollity, the twenties provided some juicy murders. Their impact upon the public imagination was far greater than are today's murders. A really gruesome crime, like a trunk murder, kept Fleet Street happy for weeks and was a popular talking point over the garden fence in all the suburbs. Parents who would have blanched at the mention of birth control discussed the disposal of dismembered corpses with equanimity, often within earshot of their children. Statisticians claim that the rate of murder was about the same as today's but I cannot believe it, for in those days a murder, any murder, was given the full treatment by the press. If they were as common as they are today few items of general news could have found their way into the newspapers.

As to unmentionable crimes, of the kind attributed to the late Mr. Wilde, I suppose they too were reported, but they were not discussed over the garden fence, and it would have been courting serious trouble in the home to seek information concerning them. Ten million men had just finished slaughtering one another with gas, shell, bomb and bayonet on the Western Front, but the crime of Oscar, together with the back-street abortion, was regarded as far more reprehensible than anything that had happened in the trenches. If anyone had told us then that, within thirty years, archbishops and ministers of the Crown would be discussing such topics before audiences of millions the prophet would have been certified as a lunatic, and a dirty-minded lunatic at that. All in all is it surprising that we, in our mid-fifties, are astonished by stage and screen mock-ups of the twenties scene?

There have been great changes, however, in less dramatic areas of the social scene, and perhaps the three that strike the middle-aged as particularly significant are those concerning the Poor (then referred to by intellectuals as the "Submerged Tenth"), in the field of hired labor, and in that of education at all levels.

In 1920, the Victorian poor were still with us. Very much with us, for we met them, and avoided them if we could, in the streets of every city and every sizable market town. Forty-five years ago one could not visit a big city without seeing ragged and often barefoot children with pale, smudged faces and the inevitable running nose but their presence on the pavements did not startle us. They were the Poor, a little less reprehensible than the thief, the divorcée and the street woman, but still outside the Pale, to be patronized with the odd copper at most times of the year and possibly the odd piece of silver on Christmas Eve. I used to see some of them pass to and from a local orphanage in gray-serge crocodiles, and I pitied them from behind a screen of lace curtains. Not only because they were orphans but because, to my prejudiced mind, an orphanage was a dreadful place to have to live. For all that, the Poor did not disturb our consciences unduly. They were as much a part of life as winter sleet and summer flies. God moved in a mysterious way. He made the rich, the poor, and us, and for the most part we all stayed in line. The demands the Poor made upon us were by no means as irksome as those made, year in and year out, by our professional schoolmasters.

The Victorian ogre lingered on in the classrooms. Long after his contemporaries had been eased out of their seats in the War Office, the Admiralty, and other government departments, he was still deputizing for Jehovah in our schools with his chalk-dusted gown, his canes, and his cliché-ridden sarcasms that he sometimes used as an alternative means of maintaining his ascendancy over captive audiences. He stayed there throughout the decade, whacking, snarling, hissing and jeering, perhaps the last unstormed redoubt of Victorian self-righteousness, a man who had watched the departure of the pot-bellied hunting parson, the cavalry general, the Beadle, and the municipal water-sprinkler. And take it from me, he was not often a figure of fun. Until we were sixteen, he was a bore, a bully and a pedant in whose presence one cowered, lied and yawned.

I do not claim, of course, that all schoolmasters of the twenties were bores, bullies or pedants but many of them were and a few would have found the guardhouses of Dachau and Belsen very congenial places to work. Today, with one or two revolting exceptions that are publicized in the press from time to time, one takes for granted an avuncular relationship between pupil and teacher. In the nineteen-twenties it was rare. One either hated one's teachers or one ridiculed them. One went to school as one goes to war, to kill or be killed, to triumph or to be vanquished and humiliated and, notwithstanding the Charleston, the men in possession had the better of it for the habit of discipline was strong in the child of the twenties.

3

All those blazer-clad Sheiks thrumming their ukeleles; all those squealing flappers showing their garters . . . !

When, after a tenure of office that was probably the most successful in the history of statesmanship, Winston Churchill was banished from office in 1945, his baffled supporters at once opened an inquest. It went on for years; but, like all political inquests, it was a sterile undertaking. The truth was there all the time, staring every Conservative in the ballot box. Attlee's victory was not a victory for doctrinaire socialism but a massive counterattack, instinctively mounted and instinctively pushed home by the armies of the underprivileged. They weren't even voting at an election. They were simply getting a bit of their own back and they had a field day. Pressure had been building from below for twenty-five years.

Disregarding the minor postwar boom, the twenties was a period of great hardship for a great number of people. I do not mean solely for those who drew the dole, but for about seven people out of ten. The average wage was not much more than it had been in 1913, but the cost of living was a great deal higher. If, in 1925, a single man earned thirty-five shillings a week he held on to his job at all costs, even at the cost of his self-respect. It was that or nothing for most of the time. If a married man, with several mouths to feed, earned four pounds a week he was almost as much the property of his employer as the machine he operated. Daily women were glad to scrub the floor for ninepence an hour. Jobless men called every day at the back door and asked to cut your lawn for a shilling. And out in the street, shuffling along with their harmonicas and clarinets and accordions, were some of the men who had stormed pillboxes in Pilckem Wood and left a limb in casualty-clearing stations behind Béthune. These men did not Charleston. The mutilated among them (and there were often two in a four-man band) drew disability pensions but they still had to beg.

Unemployment climbing to three million, commercial servitude for the lucky ones, a kind of tyranny for the majority of schoolboys, and plenty of cant for everyone on Sundays. In God's name what did we have to be gay *about?* And where did a following generation find the ingredients of the nonstop revel? Is everything they say and write of the twenties a mirage or a historical lie, like that one of Merrie England, where Elizabeth's seamen died of starvation in the streets and felons were disemboweled in public? Oddly enough it is not; somehow, notwithstanding so much cant and so much cruelty, the twenties really do evoke the kind of nostalgia that reposes in their sheet music, slang, dances and cocktails. There really was something special about them and to those of us who lived through them they have a sparkle that is lacking in every other decade of this century. And sometimes it seems to me that this has very little to do with the Charleston, the Black Bottom, the vaunted new freedoms, the silent-film epic, or the dance music. Nothing to do with straw hats, striped blazers, Oxford bags, miniskirts, vo-deo-do, crystal sets, Tin Lizzies and bull-nosed Morris Cowleys. Every decade has the equivalent of all these things, but the twenties had something unique.

I think it was hope. Hope abounding. Hope for permanence and hope of progression. Hope of peace in our time and our grandchildren's time. Hope and a high expectancy that every day things would get better and better in every way. And as well as hope there was faith. Faith in the League of Nations and in the Kellogg Pact. Faith in the miraculous powers of radium, in the doctrines of Doctor Marie Stopes, and the permanence of the British Empire. There was even enough faith left over for leaders like Stanley Baldwin and Ramsay MacDonald. Every discomfort and deprivation was seen to be temporary, the result of wartime stresses and postwar adjustments. One day, we felt, the lion really would lie down with the lamb—indeed, was confidently expected to do so round about midsummer, 1932. So that when Pandora opened the chest of troubles in the autumn of 1929, half the shutters in Western Europe went up and the jobless marched on London, it was still possible to hear the voice of Hope calling from the bottom of the box. The certainty that she was there enabled us to endure the poisonous stings of all the winged troubles Pandora had loosed upon us. At least, we all thought it was Hope in that chase but it wasn't. When we took a closer look it was Hitler.

A Baptist Bonus

I never mentioned the Baptist Bonus to anyone, and there is a logical reason for this. My association with the Baptists lasted five and a half years, from the time I was six, until I was rising twelve, but it was not until I was in my middle fifties that I was even aware of that Bonus, how it was bestowed and how it accumulated. It is an odd, quirkish story but it has a place in these confessions.

The Avenue, in those days, had two aspects. Its weekday, workaday aspect, and its Sabbath aspect. The changeover occurred, for me at all events, at first light on Sunday, and again twelve hours later when Sunday, according to Greenwich, still had an hour or so to run. The only thing in the Avenue that was not involved in this weekly metamorphosis was its architecture.

Long before dawn on Monday mornings the Avenue assumed its familiar pattern of sights, sounds and smells. Fathers hurrying to catch the first Workman's Train could be heard striding along the pavements. The postman rat-tatted. Milk cans rattled. The smell of frying bacon could be sniffed in back bedrooms. Soon every Rip Van Winkle in the crescent was astir, rubbing his eyes and wondering, distractedly, where he had been and what he had done since Saturday night. The steel rims of tradesmen's one-horse vans grated on tarmac. Children erupted from almost every house in the long curve, blazers flying loose, perhaps a smudge of marmalade on chins and, where garter elastic was beginning to lose its snap, a concertina-ed stocking. Turbaned housewives appeared on windowsills, backs to the street, as they put a guardsman's polish on their glass, and here and there, according to the time of the year, a husband on holiday (or on the dole) set to work on privet that never despaired of breaking the bonds of the neat, looped chains slung between the brick pillars of entrance paths.

No such domestic scenes disturbed the heavy silences of the Sabbath and that libelous eighteenth-century traveler, who once declared that the English were a race without benefit of religion, should have spent at least one Sunday with his back propped against our red pillar box. Had he done so he would have sung a very different tune.

The scene was not so much muted as sterilized. Everyone who appeared on the pavement wore a Sunday suit, a gleaming collar and highly polished boots. No one ran, skipped or raised his voice. The tails of the dogs drooped and the chirp of the birds was faltering and intermittent, as though they feared, by introducing a single note of gaiety into the crescent, that they would forfeit Monday's cake crumbs. The silence, both before and after the brief exodus to church or chapel, was that of a well-run prison before the introduction of "association," and this was fitting, for in a way we were all doing time, sentences that would expire when the footsteps of the last neighbor, homeward bound to brisket of beef after evensong, had ceased to clatter on the flagstones.

There were well over a hundred houses in the Avenue and almost as many families, so that we could muster, perhaps, two hundred and fifty children under fourteen. It may be hard to believe in this day and age (as far removed, ritualistically, from the time of which I write as is the era of the Tudors) that of this total at least two hundred attended one or more church services and one Sunday school session every seventh day, and I do not include the few Jews and Roman Catholics who lived among us. Their approach to Sunday was at variance with ours, and on this account we half thought of them as damned well in advance. The Jews had paid their tribute the day before, whereas the Roman Catholics made their obeisance before we had rubbed the sleep from our eyes, and thereafter were licensed to treat Sunday as a holiday weekday. This boon was not for us. Anglican, Wesleyan

Methodist, United Methodist, Primitive Methodist, Congregationalist, Baptist, Presbyterian and Plymouth Brother, we all went through the motions with a sullen resignation that made the approach of Monday, school notwithstanding, a dawn to be faced with the utmost fortitude. If I sound prejudiced in this it is because I was even more unfortunate than most. My family was spiritually divided down the middle and the strain of arranging Sunday's domestic program put a keen edge on everybody's temper.

Just as my mother, a high Tory, canceled out my father's Radical vote at every Parliamentary election between 1918 and 1953, so she sought, throughout all her days, to offset the possibility that my father was worshiping a bogus God. She would have dearly loved to have been received into the Church of England, but somehow—I never discovered why—she never was. She therefore made the best of a bad job by walking two miles to worship among the Congregationalists. My father was much less dogmatic. The freest of Free Churchmen in all England, he would attend any Nonconformist service that promised to be convivial and declamatory, and the moment he settled in the suburb he poked around and finally opted for the local Baptists, like a winetaster opting for a particular vintage. He had no basic objection to my mother's preference, but considered it a violation of the marriage vows if she attended morning service and was not on hand to prepare the Sunday roast.

I have it in mind that my mother preferred the evening service but she hated cooking and although, almost invariably, she gave in and did her duty by the rest of us, she did it with scant grace and wore a heavy frown through Sunday morning and well into the afternoon. She was also inclined to become testy during the inevitable scramble to find clean underclothes. This was the first, range-finding skirmish in the Sunday guerrilla war and inevitably enlarged itself into a shouting match, with my father hopping about waving his soap-encrusted cutthroat razor and declaring that once again we would be late and make a spectacle of ourselves.

Now this, in itself, was uncharacteristic of him. Ordinarily—

on weekdays that is to say—he did not give a damn about drawing attention to himself; indeed, he often went far out of his way to make certain that he did, but on Sundays he was never the same man. It was impossible to see him as the rip-roaring extrovert he was from Monday to Saturday. A heavy and hopeless gloom engulfed him, and it was as well to keep out of his way. He was not much giving to cuffing, but every cuff I collected throughout my childhood and boyhood was administered by a hand momentarily detached from *John o' London's Weekly*, *The Methodist Recorder* or some other Sunday reading.

I suppose a number of factors contributed to his mood. One was the necessity imposed by protocol of doing without Sunday newspapers. As a political animal he devoured newsprint and no one ever succeeded in persuading him that Sunday papers were written and printed on a Saturday. Another factor was the obligation to walk everywhere as a silent protest against the employment of public transport servants on the Sabbath, thus depriving them of a chance to worship. A third was his three-inch Sunday collar. A fourth, and possibly a key factor, was the obligation to keep his voice down. All these handicaps combined to play such havoc with his nerves that sometimes, on a Sabbath evening, I could identify him with Abraham on the point of sacrificing Isaac to Jehovah.

I often think our weekly departure for chapel must have scandalized neighbors who adhered to a more rigid timetable. The Baptist chapel was only fifteen minutes' walk away, but we never, but once, arrived there on time. My father would always leave the house ahead of us, with strict instructions to follow in a matter of seconds, and these instructions were usually reinforced by threatening gestures all the way down to the pillar box, where he turned the corner at a slow trot. Trot and gestures were in themselves violations of Sunday protocol, but he probably saw them as the lesser of two evils.

My brother would leave next, taking care to keep Father in sight but not to catch him up. On weekdays he always wore his school cap at a rakish angle, but on Sunday my father saw to it that it rested squarely on his head, the peak level with his fringe. It gave him an unfamiliar and rather suspect look, as though, notwithstanding an outwardly pious aspect, he was the kind of boy who kept a catapult to fire at cats when nobody was looking. I would set off at the tail of the procession, to lose sight of both of them until I saw them waving and prancing on the steps of the little church, while the strains of "From Greenland's Icy Mountains" proclaimed that, yet again, the service had begun without us. The one occasion when we were early was the day we arrived exactly one hour before the opening hymn, my father having forgotten to put the clock back at the end of official summer time. It was the only time I ever heard him laugh on Sunday.

Sometimes, even now, I try to rationalize my disinclination to attend those services but it is not an easy thing to do. The root causes were so subtle and so various. One was the secret fear of being caught out by God, in a silent revolt against Him and all His works. Another was an instinctive distaste for the chapel itself, with its green, distempered walls tricked out in gold lines and the maddening complexity of its focal point, a stenciled text that ran clear across the wall behind the pulpit. The text announced "Hallowed Be Thy Name" but the signwriter had attempted to execute it in Gothic script so that the individual letters were difficult to isolate and spell out. Any attempt to do so blurred the vision and induced a kind of biliousness. Then again, there was the preacher himself, who wore a fixed, catlike smile, even when he was quoting Isaiah. But more daunting than any of these factors was the approach of the moment when "The Dear Children's Hymn" would be announced, and I was required to rise and warble through seven verses of "All Things Bright and Beautiful" or "Courage, Brother, Do Not Stumble," not solo exactly, for there were other penitents ranged behind me, but aware of the fact that one day, during an epidemic, for instance, I might be the only child present. It was a moment not to be contemplated.

I was always greatly relieved when this ordeal was safely past and I could put my hot penny into the offertory plate, compose my thoughts, and slide into my sermon coma until the benediction. After that there was only one hurdle to be dodged; the preacher's handshake at the exit.

We went to Sunday school in the afternoon as a matter of course, and among the regulars was a cousin of mine, a lucky dog with an agnostic father, who was spared the ordeal of a morning service and was therefore good recruiting material for the Devil. So reckless was he, in fact, that he regularly spent his collection money on chewing gum at a machine near Woodside Station. No one was more surprised than me to learn, some forty years later, that he not only had survived to become an executive in an oil-distributing company, but had reached retirement age without catching leprosy or being destroyed in an earthquake.

Sunday school followed a set pattern, an improving address by the superintendent, a hymn, a prayer, and then dispersal to classes, where we mulled over a Bible story in the hope of extracting the moral, much as a kernel is drawn from a nutshell.

All in all, it will be seen, I derived no spiritual benefit whatsoever from my long association with the Baptists, unless one counts a weekly reinforcement of belief in the power of Jehovah to punish beyond the grave. Yet a very important by-product did emerge and was to have a vital bearing on the course my life took long after I had moved over to the Congregationalists and, ultimately, to the Anglicans.

I like to think of it as a Divine Afterthought. I like to believe that God really does work in a mysterious way, and gives full value for money so long as you are prepared to give Him extended credit. After all, I had done my part. I had spent six years trying to decipher the Gothic lettering of that gilded text.

It came about in this way.

As a family we were necessarily involved in the social life of the church and this included an occasional weeknight concert that at first promised to be almost as dull as a service. Amateur conjurers conjured, amateur baritones bellowed "The Cornish Floral Dance," amateur contraltos lifted clasped hands and rolled their eyes, and there were recitations. I contributed one of these myself, a poem about a club-footed slum child with a drunken mother, who was translated to glory by instant conversion. I could hardly have chosen a more responsive audience. The very certainty proclaimed in the theme was in harmony with all the threats and promises leveled at us from the pulpit at the conclusion of "The Dear Children's Hymn." The poem was called "Tommy's Prayer," and the final verse, all I recall, ran:

> In the morning when his mother
> Came to wake her crippled boy
> She discovered that his features
> Wore a look of shining joy.
> Then she shook him (somewhat roughly)
> But the cripple's face was cold.
> He had gone to join the angels
> In the streets of shining gold.

My ego was so inflated by the thunderous applause I received that I unwisely gave an encore at a friend's Christmas party. It broke it up very effectively, with everyone sniffing as they groped for their gloves and galoshes.

The ability to hold an audience, however, is not the bonus to which I refer. This was something more subtle and, as I say, I did not acknowledge it for nearly half a century. It had to do with a man I never met, a professional elocutionist who, by some happy miracle, was booked in at the Baptist church concert on two or three occasions when I attended. His name was John Torceni and I am making a guess at the spelling.

He was not, as the name might imply, a foreigner but a thickset Englishman, and my father, who had often heard him perform, was very enthusiastic regarding his talents. All the way to the concert he kept repeating, "He's great! Wait until you hear him recite! He's great! Marvelous! Terrific!" but my father said this sort of thing about all kinds of people, including our preacher, so it is not surprising that I reserved judgment.

I don't know what Torceni was paid to appear, as star turn, on that makeshift stage. The Baptists were not well endowed, and it could not have been more than a couple of guineas, plus his supper and a return railway ticket from an inner suburb. Neither was he, in the outward sense, the least impressive, being short, plump and nearly bald, with a volatile, rubicund face, an *actor's* face, that had absorbed too much makeup over the years. Or is this the benefit of romantic hindsight? Might he not have been another amateur, who worked as a clerk or warehouseman or shopwalker by day and earned extra money giving recitals in the evening? I never knew the least detail concerning his background. I never spoke to him then or later, and he remains, for me, a name and a kindly face. That, and a beautifully pitched voice with the power to focus my attention as few people have done before or since. I remember he came downstage modestly, taking short steps and looking uncomfortable in evening dress and old-style dickey that was a bad fit.

He began, I recall, with the episode of David Copperfield and the waiter, and when the polite applause had spent itself he acted the story of two children who ran away to Gretna Green to get married, were intercepted and hauled back at the first stage. Then he recited a poem about a trio of soldiers in the American Civil War, and having warmed up on these items he gave us a haphazard selection from the works of Kingsley, Tennyson, Conrad and Goldsmith. I have never rediscovered most of the passages he selected and cannot swear to the authors. They remain for me the lost opium shop of De Quincey that assumed actuality for no other reason than to trap and enslave me. For by then, after he had held the stage for upwards of forty-five minutes, I was drunk. Hopelessly and gloriously drunk on great draughts of words, so that it seemed incomprehensible to me that I should have ever hankered after the professions of heroes in *The Boys' Own Paper* serials—a Mountie, an explorer, a pirate or the like. I knew then that whatever I did would have to do with

87

words and phrases, with the great rolling sentences that came tripping off John Torceni's tongue, conjuring up scenes and situations and characters capable of painting the bilious-green walls of the chapel the colors of the rainbow. I knew then that in some manner I would have to spin English words on a thread and that no other occupation made would make the least appeal to me. Meantime I could have sat there without food or drink until the same time tomorrow, without so much as rearranging my buttocks on the uncushioned pew where, for so many Sundays, I had awaited the announcement of "The Dear Children's Hymn."

I say I knew this, and I did, for I never afterward wasted thought on any other career. What I did not know was that the decision was not my own, that it had been made for me by the rubicund little man in a dress suit that looked too large for him and would have sat more comfortably upon the shoulders of Copperfield's waiter. And this was to remain hidden from me for a very long time, until chance dropped it on the floor of a television studio, when I was older than Torceni was when I first heard him recite. It was then that I understood with great clarity the role John Torceni had played in my life and how much I would have enjoyed meeting him and recalling our mutual flirtation with the Baptists.

They were giving me the usual half-courteous, half-cynical treatment on a late night program. Why had I become a writer? How had it all begun? At what age did I make the decision and so on. And because these stock questions cannot be answered in the way audiences expect, I suppose I answered flippantly or absentmindedly. I said, "It was because of an elocutionist called John Torceni . . ." and as I said this I understood that it had validity, that it really was so, that it was Torceni and no other who had decided on my behalf how I was to spend my days. In other words, the wrappings had fallen away from the Baptist's Bonus and as I peered at what was beneath them I wondered if John Torceni was still alive and decided, sadly, that this was improbable.

He was dead and had been for many years, but he touched me again for all that. About a week later a letter reached me, forwarded by the BBC. It was hardly more than a note written on lined paper and giving a North London address and said, without preamble, "I heard the broadcast and your admission of how you became a writer. My John would have been very pleased. As you can imagine, he loved writers, all kinds of writers." It was signed, "Mrs. Torceni."

A Love Affair

The silent screen can have had no more devoted lover than me. Not only did my passionate involvement with her endure for almost a decade; the afterglow of the adoration she inspired continues to warm a heart that has never been wholly won by the talkies or by television, despite the fact that I have made use of both, the one as wife and the other as harlot.

My love for the silent screen died a long time ago but left behind a fragrance of the kind one seeks and sometimes finds in youthful infatuations. I speak, of course, of a love that is satisfied by the shy interlocking of fingers and of a devotion when gifts of flowers and verses are adequately rewarded by a smile. It is true that, within weeks of her heartbreaking demise in 1929, I married her successor and jogged along with her happily enough for two further decades, but I never made much of television. Having no power to bestow but only to beguile, and that fleetingly, the telly is not even a satisfactory whore. All she demands of a man is a brisk address and an annual license fee.

It was very different with my first love, who would settle for nothing short of enslavement, plus the greater part of my pocket-money over a period of nearly ten years, and who received both tribute and devotion by right. It is sad to reflect that this captivating hussy is now a period joke like the bustle, leg-of-mutton sleeves, or the studio photographer's watch-the-birdie techniques. Sad and also strange, for there was a time when my generation went to the pictures as their grandparents went to church; soberly, earnestly, reverently, and in certain hope of spiritual uplift.

I can recall the moment it all began, a Saturday afternoon in High Street, Croydon, where queues stood four deep outside the Scala, featuring Charlie Chaplin and Jackie Coogan in *The Kid*. It was the queue that attracted my father. He was not a theater-going man; indeed, he thought of actors as buffoons, and of actresses as only a notch above the streetwalker, yet he stopped and made inquiries. His commercial instinct, like that of most Puritans, was very strong. He was curious to discover what kind of display could attract so lucrative a patronage.

We went in, as to a tomb, and sat down to watch the screen. The darkness pressed down on me, and I had to fight a moment of panic that stemmed from the dreadful thought that my father and I would lose touch with one another; but then the magic began its work. In ten minutes it would not have mattered to me if my father had gone home. I was hooked, or, put another way, converted. Moody, Sankey, Saint Paul, John Wesley and Billy Graham in concert could not have done a better job on me. From then on I was immune to the temptations of the live theater, the pantomime, Punch and Judy, roller skating and marbles. To take a small liberty with Mr. Jorrocks, every moment spent out of range of the silent screen was a moment wasted.

My next visit, a surreptitious one, was unaccompanied. I stole off to see Matheson Lang in *Dick Turpin*, and the eighteenth century lived for me as never before. Followed *Lorna Doone*, *Orphans of the Storm* and many other epics, chief among them breathtaking sagas enacted for me by the athletic Douglas Fairbanks in first features like *The Black Pirate* and *Robin Hood*. For at that stage, in the first grip of the delirium, I looked for nothing but physical adventure of the kind one sought in the pages of *Chums*, *The Boys' Own Paper*, *Sexton Blake* and *The Magnet*.

There were heroines, of course, but very little was expected of them in this kind of film. All they had to do was to stand around, wring their hands in ecstasy or dismay, flutter their eyelids like newly awakened sleeping beauties, and fling wide their arms as

Doug Fairbanks or Tom Mix came leaping or galloping over the battlements or the horizon, depending upon the venue of the picture. Now and again they had a short scene with the Mustached Heavy (there was always a Mustached Heavy) but with him their contribution was even more limited. All they had to do in his vile presence was to shrink, throw a forearm across their eyes and remain so postured until the Heavy was shot, pierced, decapitated or otherwise done to death. It was some time before female roles were expanded by the new type of hero tailored for Valentino.

At the age of eleven I had an astounding piece of luck. My family moved, and the move multiplied my choice of cathedrals by four, this being the number of cinemas plying in the town to which I was taken. As the cinemas were all within a hundred yards of one another, and as each advertised a biweekly change of program, eight films were available in each period of seven days. It may seem incredible that a town of some eleven thousand inhabitants supported four privately owned cinemas, but it was so. I was not the only addict.

Now cutthroat competition on this scale operated to the great advantage of the customer. Not only were the films new, but the programs got longer and longer, so that they often included two feature films, a Hal Roach comedy, a Pathé Gazette documentary and the news. If you were sufficiently hard-faced, as I certainly was, it was possible to pay your sixpence entrance money at six P.M. and stay inside until you were flushed from your seat at eleven P.M. You were thus entertained at the modest rate of just over a penny an hour. Nobody received better value for money in the old bioscope or music-hall eras. A sixpenny seat meant, of course, that you occupied a hard bench almost within touching distance of the brass rail enclosing the orchestra pit and here the screen was enormous. Gloria Swanson's eyes looked like Siberian lakes and the jowls of Wallace Beery were off-white cliffs sprouting wide areas of blackthorn. It also meant that half an hour's devotions gave you a numb posterior and a semipermanent crick in your neck, but these were trivial penalties to pay for such company and for instantaneous transportation to battlefield, medieval Paris, the backwoods of Daniel Boone, and the plains and clapboard towns of the Far West.

It was here, with my chin poised at an angle of forty-five degrees, that I served my term in the Foreign Legion, prospected the Yukon, rode into battle in plate armor, and clung with Harold Lloyd to the face of a skyscraper. It was here, a year or so later, that the sight of Valentino running a scale of kisses up and down the bare arm of a breast-heaving Vilma Banky encouraged thoughts that made me vaguely aware of the nature of the small bumps under the tunics of the girls in Form IIIa.

The magic of those evenings and matinees! And all for sixpence, obtained by any means short of theft. Birthday and Christmas presents were sold, unpopular relatives flattered, errands run, and pride pocketed, in order to keep up with the fantastic demands upon my purse. No tycoon, fighting like a madman to stave off bankruptcy, showed more ingenuity than I if Tom Mix was at the Public Hall and Emil Jannings at the King's on two successive nights. But my problems were not merely financial. There was homework and there was music practice, and somehow, by some miracle of telescoping time, both had to be fitted in between discovering how Pearl White extricated herself from the path of an oncoming express and what happened to Betty Blythe after she made her spectacular re-entry into the fire of immortality in Rider Haggard's *She*.

It was Betty Blythe who was almost my undoing. A poster, depicting her stark naked (but discreetly shrouded in leaping tongues of flame) was on exhibition outside the cinema and my mother, who had never come to terms with postwar freedoms, was alerted by my expressed preference for Betty over the rival claims of Lon Chaney just across the road. She did not know, of course, that I had already sat through two showings of *The Hunchback of Notre Dame*, and I did not tell her, having borrowed the admission money from our daily help. She came to realize, however, that I was in the grip of an obsession that bid fair to ruin my eyesight, warp my spinal column, keep me comfortably at the bottom of the class and limit my musical progress to trivial pieces at the pianoforte. So she issued her edict. One cinema show per week, preferably on a Saturday.

Poor woman. She did not understand the nature of the narcotic. A morphine addict cannot get by on one fix a week, and from that moment began a nonstop game of catch-as-catch-can, played between myself, my parents and the attendants at the four local cinemas. These latter knew me well, of course. By this time I was as familiar to them as their own torches, and it was their torches I watched, learning how to divide my angled gaze between Ramon Navarro and the probing spotlight in proportions of about two to one. Sometimes I lost out, was pinioned, led away like a bemused midget and handed over to justice in the foyer, but more often I would slip between the backrests of the front benches and make my way on all fours to a side exit and thence home, declaring that I had never left it except to visit the lavatory. In the end the campaign went to me, for my parents were busy people and their combat time was limited. I missed an important feature or two, but I could bear this, for I was now qualified to exercise a limited critical faculty.

For a year or so I continued to prefer adventure films, but the arrival of the vamp moderated my enthusiasm for sinking galleons and embattled ramparts. I became, at fourteen, a more sophisticated filmgoer, pondering the length of the close-up kisses, and the rival charms of Anna May Wong and Laura La Plante. In the unsullied infancy of my obsession I had been impatient with every inch of footage devoted to heroines, but *The Sheik* and *The Gaucho* changed all that. Now I was avid for conquests achieved without benefit of broadsides and the clash of rapier, and looked forward to the day when my own masculine approach would set eyelids fluttering and when a sloe-eyed Gypsy brunette would lure me from the path of duty, promising myself that she wouldn't be overworked on my account.

In the meantime, however, I was content to settle for a balanced diet, and all that really happened was that I came to terms with clinch-footage, giving my entire attention to the film and depriving myself of those odd moments of relaxation when I could lower my chin and get the crick out of my neck, or shift my weight from one aching buttock to the other on the sixpenny seat I occupied.

They were, in fact, days of balanced diet in the cinema, of high adventure with judicious undertones of romance. We never thought of it as vulgar sex, of course, for the screen goddesses wooed by Valentino and Navarro were impossibly remote from us and were in any case the recipients of fabulous annual incomes putting them in the Queen of Sheba bracket. In addition, according to the film magazines, it would have been impossible, even had we owned a gold mine, to catch them between marriages, for in those days it took a week to cross the Atlantic and you were still the wrong side of the continent.

In the mid-twenties the spectacle film came into its own. Epics like *Ben Hur*, *The Isle of Lost Ships*, *The Great White Silence*, *Moon of Israel*, *The Thundering Herd* and *The Covered Wagon* clamored for our sixpences and received them in a shower. I saw them all, most of them twice, and within the compass of the greater love affair I was snared in a succession of more personal entanglements. I burned incense at the shrine of Clara Bow, round-faced, cherubic, befringed "It" girl. I went off my food on Alice Faye's account, having seen her three times running in *Scaramouche*, but there were some idols who were never replaced after the earthquake of the talkies, among them Tom Mix's horse, Rin-Tin-Tin, the wonder dog, and Felix, the cartoon cat. To these pioneers I have remained faithful to this day.

There had been whispers of the talkies for some time, but it was a phenomenon that few believed they would live to see. We slotted the rumor into the category of other cataclysmic possibilities, a landing on the moon, the conquest of the Upper Amazon and Judgment Day, so that most of us were caught off balance when Al Jolson launched the revolution toward the end of the decade. Within weeks the silent screen was no more than a poignant memory, the girl next door with whom, when very young, we had exchanged pledges and bottles of scent distilled from rose petals.

I am not pretending, of course, that I did not enter upon this new affaire with considerable zest, but something of the fragrance and mystery of the screen departed on the echoes of *Sonny Boy*. The cinema pianist disappeared overnight, and so did all those cryptic, framed subtitles, like *"Oh no! You cannot mean that, Sir Henry!"* and *"Varlet! I am here to call you to account!"* Or the more tender ones, like *"Meanwhile, in the Old Vicarage . . ."* or *"I came back, you see, I came back!"* But, as though to compensate for these losses, the impact of scenes was far more immediate. In a talking picture one could involve oneself that much more deeply in duels and embraces, and there was, of course, the flood tide of melodies that emerged from features like Paul Whiteman's revues that one could always take home to bed when the lights went up and the show was over.

I cannot recall any other scientific development that captured the public imagination so quickly or so permanently. All the old classics were remade and reissued so that to me it was rather like beginning a second marriage with a more sophisticated bride. At the same time the relationship demanded far more of the senses. It had been one thing to see puppetlike figures crumple in the dust of Main Street, Hicksville, epitaphed by the subtitle *"There's only one kinda law around Big Bull Creek, Bonzo!"* but quite another to hear the crackle of gunfire and the screams of the dying. It was the same with the crowd scenes in the new epics. To the stirring strains of *William Tell* I had watched fleets of galleons heel over and sink without a qualm. Now I was caught up in the fury of the wind and the crash of green seas pounding the superstructure. I actually heard the thud of masonry as castle walls disintegrated and the protesting squeal of the door in the haunted house, and this, after the long, tranquil honeymoon with the silent screen, demanded a good deal of adjustment on my part.

I did adapt, however, just in time for the spate of gangster films, when the tires of touring cars screamed round the streets of Cicero, and the stutter of the Thompson machine gun was as essential to the story as had been the ripple of Handel's "Water Music" in silent-picture river scenes.

With the approach of the propaganda-type war film, however, the process of disenchantment began. Involved in a real war, fed up, far from home, and wearing the ill-fitting motley of the frequently posted, I could not help but take a slightly jaundiced view of high-toned sentiments expressed, week after week, by screen heroes who were obviously making a good living pointing my way to their stars. They did the telling, and I did the doing, and I suspected that, once the screen Nazis were vanquished, they peeled off their smart uniforms and went home to eat real ham and eggs while I made do on N.A.A.F.I. tea and pilchards. It was an unworthy thought but it moderated my enjoyment and tarnished the screen magic. Those who died in these films died clean, tidy deaths, and those who didn't closed the bedroom doors on their blondes and this, I imagine, is why it began to dawn upon me, after nearly twenty years' unquestioning acceptance, that the cinema was hokum.

The crest of disillusionment was topped when I was required to watch the shooting of one of my own scripts and witness a mackintoshed quartet sit in a static jeep at Shepperton and drive through a heavy rainstorm. The rain was supplied by technicians using jets of warm water pumped through a network of punctured pipes. To a pilgrim who had trekked all the way from *The Kid* and *The Covered Wagon* it was an obscene spectacle. I thought of all the wonderful moments I had spent watching Moses and his Israelites emerge unscathed from the sea in which Pharaoh's hosts perished and decided, then and there, that film making was not for me. The scars left on my heart by Gloria Swanson, Bebe Daniels, Betty Blythe, Clara Bow, Alice Faye and Mary Pickford were too raw. There was no profit in exposing them to the atmosphere of reality. Moreover I did not approve of invisible heavenly choirs, whose contribution to every film climax stunned the senses and vibrated the structure of the cinema. Instead I yearned, doggedly and hopelessly, to recapture an hour spent with my first love, when we had idled hand in hand through the Manor woods in the innocent high noon of the era, with the pit pianist addressing herself to "Hearts and Flowers," and the glycerine tears tracing their slow course down the imposing glacier of Esther Ralston's cheek.

The Far Side of the Railway Poster

Almost every family in the Avenue spent an August fortnight at
the seaside. Residence in our part of the suburb conferred that
privilege upon you, and you lost caste if you did not take advantage of it. The "high-income people"—that is to say, those
earning in excess of four hundred a year—went to ostentatious
places like Cornwall and the Norfolk Broads, and took very
good care you heard about it and scrutinized their Brownie snaps
on their return home. But the more modest among us settled
for resorts in Kent and Sussex advertised by posters displayed
the length of the old South-Eastern and Chatham Railway—
Brighton, Worthing, Littlehampton, Folkestone, Broadstairs and
the like.

The posters were a colorful feature of every halt on the Char-
ing Cross–Addiscombe Line, and it never occurred to me, during
the long, leafless winters, that the resorts they advertised were
slightly oversold. To me the posters had veracity. Here, it
seemed, the sun never ceased to shine and the piers probed almost
as far as France. Sometimes, but not often in those watch-your-
step days, a coy bathing beauty, wearing a decorous one-piece
costume was featured, but the emphasis was usually on the family and the miles of golden sands awaiting the kiddies.

Whenever the annual holiday approached I was sick with excitement, and I never recall returning home disappointed, although like every other child along the crescent I hated turning

my back on the sea and letting myself be reclaimed by those labyrinthine streets and housing estates that, even then, were advancing south and southeast at the rate of over a mile a year.

It can be imagined, then, how I reacted to my father's bland announcement, in the late autumn of 1923, that we were to sell up almost at once and actually *live* beside the sea. I don't think I should have been more astounded if he had let fall the news that, from Christmas onward, our address would be Buckingham Palace, S.W.1.

My mind raced at once to all those railway posters, and I made a rapid mental rundown on possibilities. Bognor or Broadstairs? Littlehampton or Hove? Not that it mattered, for every poster on the line advertised a marine Elysium. As things turned out, however, we were not going to any of these places, or to any resort that I had heard of up to that time. We were removing, Father announced, with an almost indecent lack of emotion, to a town situated at the mouth of the River Exe in Devonshire, and when I looked even more thunderstruck he asked for my school atlas and pointed it out to me.

There it was, in insignificant print—Exmouth, the London side of the Exe estuary, some twelve miles south of Devon's county town, Exeter. Measuring the distance with my eye I judged we should be about a week getting there.

My impressions of Devonshire at that time were necessarily conventional. I had heard about the cream and the cider. I knew that everyone down in that part of the world was a farmer and walked about in a felt, crush-on hat and a smock, with a long straw in his mouth. I assumed that the sun shone there indefinitely, just as it did at Bognor, and that inland, no matter in which direction one traveled, one was certain to cross trackless moors studded with granite boulders, or vast forests of oak and beech, of the kind seen in the second act of the Christmas pantomime. I communicated these reflections to my father, and he did nothing to modify them. In his way he too was an incurable romantic. Why else, at fifty, should he throw up his job at Smithfield meat market and invest every penny he possessed in a weekly newspaper, a printing office and a stationery shop?

We set out on Christmas Eve, stowing ourselves into the crowded eleven A.M. from Waterloo. We could just as easily have gone before or after the Christmas rush, but my father was not a planner in that sense and simply left as soon as the last trunk had been roped. It seemed, as I had anticipated, an interminable journey, and it was nearly dark when we caught the branch-line train at Exeter and ran south alongside the wide estuary to the sea. Not dark enough, however, to resolve doubts concerning the authenticity of those posters.

To begin with, sleet was slashing the carriage windows and who ever heard of sleet within smelling distance of the sea? For another thing the tide was out, exposing miles of gleaming mud flats dotted with unsavory-looking flotsam and I had an uneasy suspicion that, even in daylight, the miles of golden sands were a fiction as far as this stretch of coast was concerned.

It was too late to explore when we detrained and hauled our luggage the hundred yards or so to the impressive, three-story building that housed printing works, shop and living accommodation, but what little I saw of our new home before being packed off to bed promised bonuses one would not necessarily associate with permanent lodgings at the seaside and this in itself was reassuring. There was a flat roof reached by a short flight of stairs that ended in a movable trolley shifted with one's shoulders. There was a cavernous loft over the printing works, with a trap door through which a spread of machinery, not unlike that in the famous picture depicting Caxton seeking the patronage of Edward IV, could be glimpsed. The authentic smell of Fleet Street rose from the cogs and belts and flywheels, prompting the most extravagant dreams in a mind forsworn to the service of printer's ink. There was a cellar stocked with thousands of shop-soiled mourning cards and a stockroom where, had my mother not been on hand, I could have helped myself to a sackful of Christmas presents to compensate me for those already mislaid in the migration. I went to bed reserving judgment, lulled to sleep by the strains of the British Legion band playing "Once in Royal David's City" in the War memorial enclosure across the road.

2

I had the waterfront to myself that first, unforgettable morning, and I wonder now if the Exmouth foreshore would have made the same impression on me had it not been Christmas morning, when everybody else was cooing over their Christmas gifts. The tide was ebbing now, ripping down the river at what seemed to me a prodigious rate and pointing the line of marker buoys out to sea where the channel ran between the sea wall and half-exposed sandbanks; then on under red cliffs to the open sea.

It was utterly unlike any seaside I had visited or heard about, and it did not occur to me to make allowances for the fact that it was midwinter and all the seasonal trappings were packed away in the Council's storerooms. The sea front curved east from the toy dock for more than a mile, dunes on the left, beach on the right, and the river here looked as wide and impressive as Mark Twain's Mississippi. There was a lifeboat house and a look-out mound, a captured tank and guns, town trophies of World War I, and a string of forlorn, wooden shelters, half filled with blown sand. In a way it was a parody of the railway posters, a ghost resort that had once, perhaps, been teeming with city holidaymakers before it was engulfed in some natural disaster, like the destruction of Pompeii. It gave me a queer sensation of being an only survivor.

In the dock, forlornly at anchor, were three Continental coasters, some of the very last of the vessels dependent on sail, and I stared at them unbelievingly. They were extraordinarily like the pictures illustrating the *Hispaniola* in my copy of *Treasure Island*, and I yearned to board one and satisfy myself that it had a sparred gallery, an arms rack and a tarpaulin-shrouded stern chaser aft. I paddled around here a long time and then went along between the timber yard and the single rail track that led back to the town. On the way I had another surprise. Abandoned on a waste patch of ground was a genuine "Royal Mail," not unlike the Deadwood Coach, and I could not imagine what it could be doing there bereft of its driver and horses. It was still in good shape and looked as though it had been held up and sacked by Sioux the day before yesterday. Then, down by the tideline, I saw the bag.

It was a heavy, Hessian bag, carefully sealed with cord and weighing, possibly, five pounds. It seemed to me a prodigious stroke of luck that I should find a treasure cache the first day I set foot on the beach and I went to work on the fastenings, first with my fingers, then with my penknife. When I had removed the cord I took a careful look around before lifting it and carrying it under the sea wall. I knew all about treasure trove and was not inclined to share my good fortune with His Majesty's Receivers of Wrecks. Carefully I upended it on a weed-covered slab of rock. Out rolled a dead cat in an early stage of decomposition.

3

It was a community that grew on you, yielding its confidences grudgingly, as though, for a season or so, you were on probation. It had nothing whatever in common with the suburb. Back there, notwithstanding the tightly prescribed social code you were obliged to observe, you never really lost the sense of belonging to a vast, anonymous city. Here, in a town of eleven thousand inhabitants, who lived mainly by taking in one another's washing, you might have set foot in a new country and adopted a fresh nationality. You were no longer an Englishman or a Britisher but an Exmothian. Your loyalties belonged right here, enclosed by the English Channel on the south and the pine and bracken country to the north. And as if this was not enough to ensure your provincialism you were boxed in by two other frontiers, the tidal estuary in the west, the brick kiln in the east that marked, with its pointing stack, the urban district boundary between you and your nearest neighbor, the legendary town of

Budleigh Salterton, subject of so many music-hall jokes and allegedly populated by retired admirals, lieutenant colonels, ex-Indian Civil Servants and their army of helots.

Architecturally the town was not typical of a West Country community. Its core had been built by Regency speculators, cashing in on the new cult of sea worship set in train by Prinny when he took his rakish court to Brighton, but expansion followed the railway boom and almost all the dwelling houses and public buildings had been built in the last two decades of the nineteenth century. A few years later, in the Edwardian decade, a better class of property grew up in the open section of the town where it nudged Budleigh Salterton. We too had our aristocracy, although one had the impression that the majority of the folk who lived in what we called "The Valley" had made their pile in trade, laid no serious claim to being gentry, and would have been blackballed en masse by the real gentry in Budleigh.

Down near the river a large housing estate had been built on a partially reclaimed marsh. It was known by the slightly derisory name of "The Colony" and consisted of a dozen streets of narrow, red-brick houses, far less permanent-looking than the terrace houses of the Avenue. The tradesmen, who were the activists of the town, occupied a group of more solid-looking shops and houses in and around the town center, whereas the roads leading to the sea front were given over to landladies who made two thirds of a living out of the short summer season.

It did not take an observer long to decide that Exmouth had been a laggard in the race among British coastal towns to transform themselves from fishing village or watering place into resort. There was, even now, a halfheartedness about its drive to attract visitors, as though it had never made up its mind whether or not it wanted and needed them. In the season any number of token gestures were made. An orchestra was installed in the windswept bandstand to play popular sheet music and excerpts from Gilbert and Sullivan operas. Strings of fairy lights were slung precariously between the ornamental lamp standards. A few forlorn donkeys plied between widely spaced refreshment huts. Jerseyed longshoremen offered trips in the bay on the few summer days when the water looked calm enough to attract customers. Back in the public gardens a marquee was erected to house a seasonal concert party that returned year after year and became, as it were, honorary residents, for its clientele was largely Exmothian. It is among local quirks such as this, I think, that one must look for the real ethos of the town and of all towns like Exmouth. Outwardly they exist for holidaymakers, but actually the reverse is true, or was true then. It always seemed to me that only natives, the householders and ratepayers that is, exerted any influence upon it as a community and every one of these, including the landladies and those of the seasonal workers who did not migrate in winter, regarded the summer visitor in the way a settled and self-satisfied family might regard an unsuccessful cousin, home from the colonies and faced with a long leave on an inadequate salary. He was tolerated, fed, and given houseroom but sent out to amuse himself the moment weather permitted. In the meantime he had to take good care not to get under anyone's feet.

This became more clear to me when the spring advanced and the force of the southwesterlies, that seemed to rattle the windows nonstop from October until March, moderated to some degree, so that residents could peel off their jackets and attend to the annual ritual of erecting their beach huts, where they spent almost their entire leisure time from early May until the last week of September.

There was absolutely no nonsense about this annual chore, and it was carried out with the attention to detail that would be demonstrated by a good regiment digging in against an enemy attack. Sand was leveled, spirit levels were used, and hut sections carefully bolted together, after which the shack was lovingly painted. Then, from the coast-guard station toward a point near the dead end of the esplanade, the shanties curved in an unbroken rank, effectively cutting off all view of the sea, so that you could walk the length of the promenade without ever knowing you were at the seaside if you ignored the occasional glimpse of blue and gold between huts and where steps led down to the beach.

The Exmothians regarded these huts as summer palaces and gave each one of them a jaunty or a cozy name. One of the delights of the early part of the season was to learn these names by heart as you walked east, taking furtive peeks at the ruffled surface of the Channel. Some of the names had an ironic ring— "Farenuff," "Dunworkin," "Dunroamin," but others proclaimed the owner's indisputable right to his patch of which "Yrusb" is a fair example. Others still had a deceivingly mild title, like "The Hermitage," "Downalong" and "Restawhile," but all, one way or another, underlined the fact that the beach, every gritty grain of it, belonged to those who had weathered out the winter here and the use of any part of it by strangers was, like a soldier's leave, a privilege and not a right.

It was the same with the annual carnival. Some of the progressives once staged a carnival in high summer, thinking it might be an attraction to visitors, but it was a disappointing failure. The visitors got in the way and would not enter into the spirit of the occasion, so that soon the Carnival Committee reverted to a customary date in October, when the strangers had all gone home and we could make fools of ourselves in private.

Exmouth, at the time of which I write, was a boom town for joiners. Set an Anglo-Saxon down anywhere in the world and he will at once busy himself founding clubs and societies. In the early nineteen-twenties Exmouth was the most organized community in my experience.

There was hardly a human activity that lacked its quorum of devotees, its headquarters, its President, Vice-Presidents, Chairman, Hon. Secretary and Hon. Treasurer. There was a golf club, a cricket club, a rugby football club, and an association football club; an archery club, two bowls clubs, a miniature rifle club, a cycling club and a lawn-tennis-and-croquet club. There were bridge clubs, a multiplicity of women's clubs, a temperance club, an amateur photography club and a wireless club, and this in the days of crystal sets! There was intense political activity during and between elections, with a strong Conservative Association and a Liberal following that ran them dangerously close at the ballot boxes. Whoever you met was sure to be on the committee of one or more of these organizations and after a time you learned to identify residents by their spare-time pursuits. You could walk down the main street any day, winter or summer, and be certain of seeing window bills advertising gatherings of cage-bird fanciers, sea anglers, yachtsmen, philatelists or water-colorists, and almost every conversation you overheard concerned these things and little else unless a local election was in progress.

Exmothians took their local politics seriously enough, but the Town Clerk (paid at that time around six pounds a week) exercised the real power of executive and stood no nonsense from any of us, least of all the elected representatives. The town was very strong on amateur dramatics, notwithstanding the fact that we had four cinemas featuring Hollywood professionals but the pseudo gentlefolk living in The Valley, who did not take much active interest in town affairs generally, had monopolized this sector and it was a closed shop to the rest of us, unless you were content to stand around holding a spear, or make your sole appearance at rise of curtain dusting props or answering the telephone while the audience settled down.

The Operatic Society was more democratic but the Old Guard usually shared the leading roles among themselves, relegating all but the most talented newcomers to the chorus. All in all, it will be seen, there was a tremendous amount going on, particularly out of season, when once the town had stopped catering for visitors and could reassume its natural rhythm of sale of work, annual meeting, sporting tournament, whist drive and half-crown hop at the Church Hall (one-and-six at the Church Institute).

Occasionally there was a gala event, the visit of a warship, a conference banquet, a British Legion or Women's Institute rally, or a ten-shilling supper dance where everyone was obligated to shake the mothballs from their dress clothes and young men wearing dinner jackets were politely turned away. It seems astonishing that so much activity could be generated for nine months at a stretch by a mere eleven thousand people but it was so, and far from seeming parish-pumpy and ignoble it always struck me as the reverse, as though we were all members of one gigantic family, dedicated to leading interesting, assertive lives.

This was certainly true of the younger set, one small group excepted. Almost all of us attended the same local Council and Church Schools and moved on, at about eleven, to the co-ed Secondary School, so that we grew up, a thousand strong, knowing one another's Christian names and family backgrounds. It made for unshy matings and a relaxed atmosphere at dances and Christmas parties. It also tended to encourage early and generally successful marriages, particularly if the breadwinner had a secure economic footing in the town. The only exceptions to this rule were the younger folk who lived in The Valley, the sons and daughters of wealthier folk, who had attended boarding schools and were thus at a disadvantage. They tended to hang together— at least the males did—roaring about in tiny sports cars from which the baffle plates had been removed, and usually seen with yards of scarf festooned about their necks. I often felt a little sorry for The Valley maidens. They looked very lonely when they drifted down to change their book at Boots, but few of us would have risked a snub by inviting them to dance the Charleston at the Annual Hospital Ball, the only big social event they attended.

The rest of us, as we passed from childhood to adolescence, and from adolescence to young manhood or womanhood, tended to forget the world outside, glimpsed across the estuary, or eastward beyond Keeper's Cottage, on the road to Budleigh Salterton. We knew, of course, that things happened out there from time to time. We read London newspapers and some of us had wireless sets, or watched the newsreels between silent features at the cinema, but whatever it was it did not trouble us much, nothing like as much as Biafra and Vietnam disturb small-town dwellers today. Even the antics of men like Lloyd George and Stanley Baldwin seemed irrelevant, as though they were taking place in Stamboul or the Orkneys, whereas a front-page crime like a trunk murder did not seem nearly so immediate to us as, say, a local solicitor's bolt with his clients' funds, or a milkman's conviction for adulteration.

Life in the Avenue must have prepared me for rapid assimilation into such a community for I was thinking of myself as an Exmothian, and nothing else, within a month of that Christmas Eve journey along the mud flats. I wonder if, but for the war that shook so many of us loose, I would have had much curiosity about the rest of the world. Now that I have seen and savored a few slices of it I am inclined to think I got the worst of the bargain.

The moments I recall from that period of my life have a sparkle that is not solely a legacy of youth. It comes, I feel, from a sense of belonging and participating and also, to a degree, from a sense of permanence that seems to have departed not only from Exmouth but from every center of population in the Western world. I do not know why this should be so. Viewed as a whole, young people living in this kind of community today enjoy better housing, have far more money to spend, have a longer expectation of life, better health and a much higher standard of living than they enjoyed forty years ago. But somehow they are not as happy, or if they are they take great pains to hide the fact. Their expressions, when you see them enjoying themselves, remind me a little of the fixed grins on the faces of families depicted on the railway posters that once plastered the stations of the old South-Eastern and Chatham Line. They seem, on the whole, unaware that so much is still to be found on the far side of the hoarding.

For Your Own Good

Not long ago, when I was being interviewed on the *Late Night Line-Up* program of BBC 2, the interviewer asked me if I had any exceptionally strong views on any particular subject outside the general sphere of my work as a professional writer. I told him I had—just one. It concerned the apparently ineradicable belief among the British that corporal punishment in schools is an aid to the process of education. This is something concerning which I have always held strong views, and my failure to impress them on most of my contemporaries depresses me, for in most other respects I still consider the British to be far ahead of any other race in their assessment of human rights. This, as I see it, is one of their few blind spots, and I look forward to the day when Parliament legislates against those who persist in the archaic notion that to beat children is to improve them.

One of the most glaring errors practiced by Western legislators in the second half of the nineteenth century, especially in industrialized countries like Britain, France and Germany, was that of herding infants into barracklike buildings at the age of five to begin, what was euphemistically called, their education, and subjecting them thereafter to a system of instruction based on fear. Fear of the freely applied strap, rod and ruler and, what was worse, fear of humiliation and ridicule.

Mercifully the drive to bend and shape a child's mind to the rigid precepts of unimaginative mentors has slackened very considerably in the last twenty years. Schoolmasters and schoolmistresses are no longer the pedants and bullies they were a generation ago, and compassion has crept into the schoolroom like a fugitive out of the rain. The man who consistently flogged children for their own good, and the even more common wisecracking ironist, has been all but eliminated from educational establishments, and most children are no longer urged forward under the threat of physical punishment. At the same time the basic creed of the educationist has not changed as much as it should have done, and there is still a strong tendency among them to equate textbook knowledge with intelligence and moral stature. Examinations, if possible, have become even more vital to the child's future than they were fifty years ago, and if there is a faultier measuring stick to determine the true potential of a human being I would be interested to hear about it.

Real education, of the kind in which the advanced nations stand in such terrible need today, is not often to be found in a school textbook. It really has little to do with the kind of information fed to children by various media in a majority of school periods. Books that would help a child to discover the world through his or her own eyes are plentiful, but they are not recommended with much enthusiasm. One of the saddest trends in British schools during the last decade has been the constant efforts of narrow-headed fools to banish religious training from the curriculum on the grounds that it will prejudice the pupil! What is the next move in this extraordinary campaign by progressives? A public bonfire of the Gospels?

When I attended my first school, in the winter of 1916–17, the Victorian cult of self-help had passed its apogee. Well-meaning but shortsighted sociologists had taught the preceding generation that all the problems bedeviling mankind at that period could be solved by education, and perhaps, broadly speaking, they were right. It depended upon the kind of education applied, and this, unfortunately, was not very well understood when W. E. Forster's Elementary Education Act went on the statute book in August, 1870.

At that time, of course, the great majority of children in the

West were illiterate, and their illiteracy condemned them to a life of servitude. It was seen that if the nation was to hold its place as the major industrial power of the world it would need millions of recruits for the offices and countinghouses of the giant business enterprises that were mushrooming in all centers of population, and that an ignorant work force was not equipped to compete with industrial nations elsewhere.

A very promising start was made, at least in some of the new schools. My mother attended one of the first London elementary schools, and in later years the standard of her education frequently astonished me, especially when I reminded myself that she went out to work at thirteen. She wrote a good legible hand and could perform, what were to me, prodigies of mental arithmetic. She knew, and carried to her grave, the substance of many of Shakespeare's plays, as well as the verse of poets like Gray, Wordsworth, Goldsmith and especially Tennyson, who still had ten years to reign as Poet Laureate. She acquired, before she left, a taste for Scott, Thackeray and Dickens, and she told me that Dickens was one of the standard authors at the school she attended.

My father was less fortunate. He also attended (until the age of about twelve when he too went to work) one of the first elementary schools in London, but it seems to have had a good deal in common with Dotheboys Hall. At my mother's school there were teachers of discernment, but the disciplines of my father's elementary school were more like those that prevailed in the galleys. One of the standard punishments, he recalled, imposed upon undernourished mites of the Thames-side street, was to hold a stack of writing slates above the head and earn a flogging if it fell below a certain level.

It may seem astonishing to a more enlightened generation to learn that teachers who relied upon these methods of keeping order were commonplace in British schools at that time. Chaplin writes of them in his autobiography, and any elderly man who attended these pioneer Council schools (and many of the private schools) could verify the fact. What I find remarkable is the notion you could assist a child's mental development by free use of the goad of fear that persisted into the twenties and thirties of this century.

There is a hidden streak of cruelty in the British character that is far less obvious than that frequently demonstrated by their ancestral cousins, the Germans. Ordinarily the British are kindly compassionate people, but one would never have suspected it had one attended state schools in the second decade of this century. Here, all too frequently, reigned men and women whose methods of maintaining discipline were vicious, but the really frightening thing about this lust to control a class by the threat of inflicting pain, humiliation and misery is that it dies so hard a death among the general public of today. Recently a popular TV personality asked his audience to vote on the question of whether or not they believed in thrashing children. An overwhelming majority shot up their hands with a kind of glee, and it was obvious that they considered a progressive schoolmaster, holding an opposite view, an object of ridicule. Every now and again there is a press exposé of scholastic torture that would shock the Kremlin and the Congo into prompt action, but the legal abolition of the cane in our schools is almost as far away as it was when I was a child, and this despite the fact that almost every other nation has stopped beating its children.

I attended two state schools, the first as an infant, the second as a child of nine. At the infants' department the cane was in the offing (for five-year-olds!) but I never saw it used, although I am quite sure it was.

Discipline, however, was rigidly maintained. We were compelled to sit with arms folded on the desk and chatterboxes were silenced by having sticking-plaster slammed across mouths. Slow learners were exhibited as fools. There were dunces' caps and frequent banishments "to the corner," but I do not look back on that red-brick building with horror, notwithstanding the gloomy, cavernous impression it made upon me, or the memory of the hysterical efforts of an ageing spinster to control a class of sixty children. As long as one behaved as a robot one was not punished.

This could not be said of my second elementary school, where I spent two wretched terms four years later. The six months I was there rank among the unhappiest of my life.

This place, as I have since learned from observation, and from discussion with men of my own age, was not in any way singular. On the contrary, it was typical of the kind of establishment common at the period and, as such, a disgrace to the legislators of the post-World War I period. Neither was it peculiar to London, for my wife attended a similar school before going on to Manchester High School. Down in easygoing Devonshire there still lived a headmaster whose Wackford Squeers' antics had been checked by members of the local School Board who concealed themselves in a stationery cupboard in order to witness his brutality. This fiend, I was informed, always began the school term by flogging a random group of boys and liked to pick them from among those who had plump posteriors. He announced, as he went merrily to work, "This is what you can all expect if you don't behave yourselves!"

Years later, when I was a reporter and had this same man in my sights at the Petty Sessional Court, there was an interesting sequel to his career as a headmaster, then a magistrate! A former pupil returned from Canada after a long absence and was greeted by his old mentor with great affability. Ignoring the proffered hand, the emigrant said, "All I recall about you, mate, is that you were a bloody swine and a sadistic bully. I'd drop dead before I shook your hand!"

As to my own experiences, they left me with a hatred of cruelty to children who, in these circumstances, are quite defenseless. "Mr. Short," in the *Avenue Story*, is based on a man I met there. This headmaster would have made an admirable recruit for the concentration camp guards, who in the nineteen-forties became the personification of savagery all over the world. I was to meet one or two others who reminded me of "Mr. Short" at subsequent schools, but they were mere apprentices in the art of instituting terror compared with this wretch. They still exist, although today they are far more vulnerable to public exposure.

They will continue to exist until a nation that has abolished the flogging of criminals has the courage to ask itself why, when it prohibits the beating of various men, it stubbornly refuses the same protection to its children. Or why, indeed, it does not face up to the fact that the impulse to hurt someone has nothing to do with the process of correction and never had.

Progress, slow progress, has been made in England and Wales in this field, but it looks as if the last stronghold of the scholastic sadist will probably be Scotland, where the educational symbol would sometimes seem to be the tawse. The only escape route from poverty, some Scotsmen will tell you, is via education, and therefore, if necessary, education must be beaten into wee laddies with the strap. It is an odd belief, that persists to this day among a sizable minority up there. Do they suppose that the Scots race will cease to contribute to the arts and sciences of the twentieth century the minute the tawse follows the cat-o'-nine-tails and the thumbscrew into the museum? Possibly they do. Interrogation by torture was not abandoned in Scotland until long after it had been struck from the legal code south of the Tweed, and obstinate English prisoners were sometimes sent north in order that their interrogators could take advantage of the fact. Perhaps the time will come when recalcitrant children will be sent over the Border to make the acquaintance of the tawse.

Corrective methods on one side, some very notable progress has been made in the last few years concerning methods of imparting information to children, but here again educationists, with many notable exceptions, are not much given to pioneering. It would seem to me that far too much time is still wasted in schools in what should be a mere offshoot of education, that is to say, the preparation of pupils for examinations of one kind or another. The front was even narrower in my day. Hundreds of hours were devoted to subjects likely to benefit the few rather than the many, and the broad aim of education, to produce a kindly, intelligent, useful human being, was all but overlooked. To me—

and I admit to being an eccentric in this respect—this is what schools are for, and something to this effect should be inscribed in letters of brass over every schoolmaster's desk. Personally, I look forward to the day when the humanities take precedence over economics and to the introduction into schools of a system where the premium is on the formation of character rather than examination passes, but perhaps I am wishing for the moon. I do not know what proportion of time is still spent in the average British school on subjects like geometry and algebra, but I hope that it is less than in my schooldays, when whole vistas of time were taken up with specialist information of this kind while two periods a week were devoted to history, the only science available to us of showing where we went wrong and are still going wrong as human beings compelled to live in one another's pockets.

The teaching of English had a fair showing in the timetables of forty years ago, but in six of the seven schools I attended far too much time was devoted to what was then called "parsing," and no more than one period a week to the art of learning how to enjoy the work of men like Blake, or that splendid generation of poets all but destroyed on the Western Front. I think of them particularly, for it was years after leaving school that I made the acquaintance of Wilfred Owen and Siegfried Sassoon, to say nothing of the novelist Richard Aldington, then at the height of his fame. Why? Was there nothing in their work that would have helped young men to know and understand the challenge of Hitler in 1932, or tackle more successfully the problems of the fifties and sixties? The ideal teacher, to my way of thinking, is a bit of a stick-in-the-mud, who clings, with fearful obstinacy, to standards and methods that have little to do with the demands of "A" and "O" levels, or that idiotic and now discredited Eleven Plus, a man or woman who sees his or her main task as one of joining with parents to turn out any number of decent fathers, decent husbands, good wives and good mothers, people, let us say, who would prefer to tell the truth on a thousand a year than win a place in the supertax bracket by selling dubious insurance or even more dubious packaged holidays. He or she would lay stress on such old-fashioned virtues as honesty, compassion and tolerance, and some would have a way of making English literature and English history do much of their work for them. The best of them, I should like to think, would be the counterpart of the fast-disappearing family doctor, who knew the history of all his patients from the moment he yanked them into the world to the time when they came to him as middle-aged men with problems that were not strictly medical. He or she would be more of a counselor than a teacher, but what they imparted would remain in the minds of their pupils and, with a little luck, filter into the national ethos of the future. There were such teachers, even in the days when the unpleasant rhythm of the cane was the sound most often heard from the classroom. I had the good fortune to encounter several; and today, I am happy to say, they seem to be proliferating among the younger recruits for the profession.

It is difficult for those of us whose education ended in the twenties to have much patience with the more violent section of the Student Revolt but one area of their manifesto we should applaud. They want more say in the substance and system of their courses, and I see no good reason why, at university age, they should be denied it. When I look back on all those wasted hours with Euclid and his ilk I share the latter-day students' sense of frustration. One of the few gleams of sunshine on the news fronts of recent years has been the refusal of the young to take the wisdom of their elders for granted. Another is the occasional experiment in the system of teaching children at infant level, where the relationship between pupil and teacher is fostered by the mutual respect of the latter for his or her charges as sensitive human beings plus a ready appreciation of individuality. As a taxpayer I would be happy to see millions of pounds used annually to enlarge careful experimentation in the educational field at primary level, for it is here, not in the universities, that repose the chief hopes of finding satisfactory solutions to the mounting problems of a technological age.

Sheet Music of the Twenties

One of the few warnings issued to generations of school children that is seen to have validity in adult life is that one concerning the brain's increasing reluctance to store knowledge after the age of about fifteen. Under pressure the memory will continue to operate industriously up to the thirty mark, but it tends to become snobbishly selective, discarding all that it classifies as trash.

Nothing demonstrates this more emphatically than one's inability to capture and hold on to the lilt and rhythm of a popular tune. Achieved effortlessly as a child this becomes, ultimately, hard labor and in middle age a near-impossibility. Perhaps there is a limit on one's capacity to absorb throwaway jingles. Or perhaps the popular tunes of successive generations are so alike that confusion is inevitable. The tunes I have bottled since I was in my early twenties I could count on the fingers of one hand. Before that watershed was reached I stored away several hundreds, without devoting a single conscious moment to the task. Such tunes become, to all but the musically educated, the theme music of their youth. There can hardly exist a married couple who do not possess an "Our Tune," and there can be few to whom a musical cliché of the past does not recall a colorful segment of their personal history. My tunes were the sheet music of the twenties, spun on a hundred portable Gramophones, thumped and hooted by as many semiprofessional dance bands, strummed on teach-yourself banjoleles and ukeleles. They are poor things but I cherish them as the musically elite cherish the works of the masters. All retain the power to delight and a few, so help me, can still move me to tears.

They were, I suppose, artless tunes compared with the pop music of today. They had no heavy backing, enjoyed no artificial amplification and no kind of professional presentation. They were just tunes with a life of three to six months and thereafter a rich residual of nostalgia. Their lyrics were unbelievably cliché-ridden, their basic rhythms as ingenuous as nursery jingles telling of Little Tommy Tucker and Bo-Peep. They were all extraordinarily alike in sentiment and composition, and yet they could be classified, quite simply, to fit a mood, a measure or an occasion. Almost all of them were written for one of three dances, the one-step, the foxtrot and the waltz, and they emerged from Tin Pan Alley in equal proportions at the rate of about one hit a week. They were trivial, banal, graceless, hackneyed, platitudinous and inconsequential, and yet, in some perverse way, they have a great deal to answer for among those of us who grew up between the wars. They played a more important role in shaping our lives than any other art form, including the cinema.

As a rule the basic categories subdivided into the Moon-June-Soon variety (concerned exclusively with yearning for a mate), with a locality or with both; the "comic" numbers that were musical amplifications of traditional British jokes about mothers-in-law and sausages; the early blues numbers that were just dirges; and finally the quickstep melodies that Priestley artfully described in his novel *The Good Companions*, as "tripping-around-the-corner" measures. These last were concerned with nothing specific but were sufficiently jiggy-joggy to catch on, usually by reason of a repetitive phrase of which "Round the Marble Arch" and "Something About a Soldier" are fair examples.

We liked best, of course, the Moon-June-Soon spate and could never have enough of them. A majority of these were based upon the topography of the United States, whence most of them came, reaching us little the worse for wear. Through them we absorbed a kind of incidental geography, as from the backs of cigarette cards. They established beyond all reasonable doubt that cornfields covered the state of Nebraska, that the

Carolinas and Kentucky got far more than their share of moonlight, and that lonely pines proliferated in states like Nevada and the Dakotas. In the same way we were privileged to share an exile's longing for sun-soaked cotton plantations we had never visited and the mammies who had never left them, but they led us astray in the matter of population distribution in the States. Judged on these lyrics American cities were almost unpopulated. Almost everyone over there mooned about in shacks, cabins, hick home towns, and the far-off hills.

When you come to look closely at this avalanche of tunes, you see that they subdivide into a network of themes that are first cousins to one another. Pondering them, humming them over to myself as I drive along a congested road, competing with chart-topping numbers issuing from the car radio, I find there were about eleven leading families. Almost without exception each family produced a brilliant son or daughter, who sometimes lived to a great age. Occasionally there were two or three in one group that survived the Second World War and are, so to speak, still in business alongside their great-grandfathers like "Just a Song at Twilight" and "The Cornish Floral Dance." Most of them, however, live on only in the memories of those who mourn the splendor of their departed youth.

There was the Direct Approach family, where the loved one was actually named—"Peggy O'Neill," "Ramona," "Margie," "Sally," "Juanita," "Babette," and, of course, the girl who won all the prizes, made her fortune, and is now a dowager—the incomparable "Charmaine."

Then there was the Avowal family, a trio of prodigies who swept all before them in the mid-twenties—"Always," "All Alone" and "My Inspiration Is You." The first two are still alive today. The youngest, after a brilliant career, died young.

Then came three closely intermarried groups, expressing individual philosophies on love, the Mea-Culpas, the Claim-Stakers and the Too-Lates. The Mea-Culpas, a ham-fisted lot, made a botch of things from the outset. The Claim-Stakers picked their girl and went storming in to win. The Too-Lates had their chances and threw them away, sometimes almost deliberately.

This last-named tribe was by far the most prolific but each had their admirers. The Mea-Culpas, despite lugubrious titles, were a brash, cheerful set. Their philosophy is best exemplified by their pioneer, "Why Did I Kiss That Girl?" in which the self-accuser went on to ask "Why, oh why, oh why?" He knew he was in terrible trouble, but he was still prepared to sing about it. The Claim-Stakers were a unique bunch with uncertain temperaments. The first of them, "Yes, Sir, That's My Baby," was aggressive but later on the family sobered down, often to the point of being maudlin, so that we got "Meet Me in My Dreams," the fabulously successful "Goodnight, Sweetheart," and the jubilant "Paddlin' Madeleine Home."

On the heels of these comparatively cheerful people, however, trod a sad, masochistic tribe wailing their regrets and misjudgments down the years so that sometimes it would seem to me that the world was populated by star-crossed lovers and that, to be even moderately successful in the lists of love, one had to possess shrewd judgment and have any amount of luck. "Souvenirs," "She Don't Wanna," "I Wonder Who's Kissing Her Now?" "Brokenhearted," "Mean to Me" and "Somebody Stole My Gal" were the sodbreakers in this territory, but they were followed by scores of others, all lachrymose and all, to some extent, self-accusing. There was "Little Old Church in the Valley," "I Met Her in Monterey" (I left her and flung away the key to Paradise!), "I Can't Give You Anything But Love, Baby," and even "You're In My Heart" (but never in my arms!). Their laments engulfed the entire Western world, warning cheek-by-cheek waltzers and foxtrotters that nothing but heartbreak awaited them. Nobody heeded their warnings. It was always something that would happen to somebody else, like a car accident or a burglary. We glided on, moving as one to the mournful croak of the saxophone.

As if to offset these Dismal Jimmies there arrived on the scene about then the Promise family, singing of better times in the immediate future and heralded by the trip-trippety "Red, Red Robin," the optimistic "Blue Skies," the heedless "Singing in the Rain," and the earnest "Every Step Towards Killarney's One Step Nearer

Home." And after them, sometimes side by side with them, came the Hellraisers, like "Let's All Go to Mary's House."

In the meantime, however, there had been a shift in locale. Some numbers continued to proclaim the merits of various states of the Union, but there was a creeping tide of sheet music allegedly originating in Latin countries and these tunes had gained a firm hold by 1926, when the sensational "Valencia" swept the dance halls and bandstands, to be followed by its slightly tipsy brother, "Barcelona" (I'm one of the nuts of), the gentle "In a Little Spanish Town," the brisk "Sunshine of Marseilles," and the haunting "Night in Napoli" that really belonged in the what-might-have-been school.

With the arrival of talking pictures in 1928–29 there was a revolution in theme. Numbers suddenly became more sophisticated and we had to adjust to new moods, new places, new atmospheres. The silent pictures had not had much influence upon sheet music. Cinema pianists, half hidden in the gloom of the pit, were conservative practitioners, loath to abandon the rigidly prescribed accompaniment to various forms of action. Running water on the screen demanded the obligatory Handel's "Water Music," and a parting between lovers, or a close-up of an orphan, could only be accompanied by "Hearts and Flowers." Under the terrible pressures of the talkies these traditional tinklers were washed right out of their pits and into unemployment queues and sometimes into the gutter, where a few continued to play "Hearts and Flowers" on portable pianos. As I have confessed, I was a silent-picture addict but the only two popular tunes I can recall as being directly associated with the cinema in the early twenties were "Song of the Bells" (written for the epic *Hunchback of Notre Dame* and anticipating the era of theme music) and "Felix Kept on Walking," a jingle that introduced the forgotten forerunner of Mickey Mouse and Donald Duck.

The talkies removed the inspiration of sheet music from country to city. Without our realizing what had happened, all those cabins and pines disappeared. Charles Farrell and Janet Gaynor, ukelele accompanied, sang numbers about a different kind of lover wooing against a Wall Street backdrop (quite unheard-of up to that time), in their "I'm in the Market for You." Then came a spate of revues, and we adjusted to our lovers huddled on a bench in the park instead of under the moon in the Deep South. The lyrics changed, many of them showing sparkle and originality, as in "Broadway Melody," another city-inspired song. Then came "Tiptoe Through the Tulips," "If I Had a Talking Picture of You" and the slightly more subtle "Little White Lies."

I have overlooked the purely comic effort, a direct descendant of the Edwardian music-hall song. There were plenty of these all the way through the twenties, and some of them had a tremendous vogue, notably "Yes, We Have No Bananas," "Horsey, Keep Your Tail Up," and later on, "How Do You Feel When You Marry Your Ideal?"

In the meantime, however, no changing fashion, not even the Charleston-Black Bottom tidal wave that had its own anthem called "Crazy Words, Crazy Tune," could oust the indestructible Moon family. Throughout the entire period the Moons were present at every party and every shilling hop. Among the most popular and long-lived of them were "Carolina Moon," "Kentucky Moon," "Moonlight on the River Colorado," "When the Moon Comes Over the Mountains" and, in 1929, "All by Yourself in the Moonlight," that had the distinction of introducing a popular but short-lived dance step called the Heebie-Jeebies.

The rhyming techniques, alas, did not improve. In all these songs we had the same immortal groupings, and to ring the changes on them the lyric writers must have ransacked the poets as far back as Herrick and Waller. There was the blue-you-who-new-true grouping, the again-rain-pain-refrain and the year-dear-near-fear-appear. Lonely always went along with only and heart with apart. Kiss was seldom without miss and, dare was always coupled with pair, where or despair.

Laugh at them and patronize them if you will. In their time they made the world a gayer and a happier place than it is today. And at the risk of raising the blood pressure of music lovers I am obliged to admit that they qualify as my personal Unfinished Symphony.

A Crusoe By-product

To some degree we are all subject to Robinson Crusoe hangovers. Defoe was at pains to emphasize the loneliness and desolation of his hero, but as motorways proliferate, housing estates eat up the landscape, sonic booms crack ceilings, and more and more Nosey Parkers appear on our doorsteps demanding to know our mother's maiden name and how much profit we made from the sale of a prewar lawn mower, the modern tendency is to regard Crusoe as a man who never learned to count his manifold blessings.

For my part I was never wholly convinced that Crusoe did not enjoy his isolation, particularly in retrospect, but it was not his separateness, his thrilling adventures with cannibals, or even his ingenuity that made him one of my boyhood heroes. When I thought of him it was not as the traditional figure in a homemade goatskin suit ruling a solitary domain or as the owner of a Man Friday. My admiration did not spring from his ability to make do and mend, or to seek the path of righteousness among savages and rum-swigging pirates, but from his ability, at the very outset of his isolation, to construct a raft capable of transporting goods across the lagoon from the wreck to the beach.

I cannot say why this single workaday feat of his should have impressed me so much but it did. To an extent it colored my entire boyhood and led me into endless trouble with authority for, from the age of seven until I abandoned the project eight years later, I was obsessed by a determination to construct and sail a seaworthy raft. Indeed, even at fifty-plus it remains one of my unfulfilled ambitions.

My first egregious attempt was made upon the golf-links pond at Addiscombe, in Surrey. There were six artificial ponds cut in a rectangle behind one of the larger bunkers and I imagine they had something to do with the irrigation of the course. They were deep, scummy and full of newts, and children who were not bemused by Crusoe's salvage operations were content to prowl along the margins with jam jars attached to pieces of string. I was more ambitious. I saw the largest of the ponds as a lagoon, and a railway sleeper embedded in the mud as the bare bones of a Crusoe raft. Somehow I prized it loose, armed myself with a pole, and set off toward the farther shore. I was no more than five yards from starting point when the sleeper rolled over and I daresay I would have drowned had I not retained my hold upon the heavy pole. This supported me until I could be dragged ashore and wrung out. The only cautionary dividend that resulted from this, the very first of my experiments in navigation, was a horrid fear of lockjaw, for a splinter from the pole wedged itself between forefinger and thumb. For days after the incident I identified every yawn as the forerunner of tetanus.

I attributed my miserable failure to the fact that the railway sleeper was waterlogged, and the incident taught me nothing about the niceties of balance and counterpoise. A year or so later, after a prolonged forage for materials, I built a real raft of wooden boxes nailed together with laths. With two friends to help me I carried it three miles to Ham Farm Pond in the Elmers End district, where I set sail in shirt and trousers with the utmost confidence. This time the raft floated, but although the surface of the pond was calm I might have been riding Atlantic rollers, so varied and energetic were my capers to remain aboard. From the shore it must have appeared that I was performing a Lancashire clog dance on a very small stage, and the entertainment terminated with a flourish as I rolled backward into eight feet of water.

I was so disgusted with my handiwork that I abandoned the raft there and then and having spread my shirt on a navvy's almost-extinct brazier, I went off bird's-nesting in soggy trousers, returning to find my shirt reduced to a couple of charred sleeves.

The shame of walking home through busy London streets in nothing but squelching boots and a pair of gray-flannel trousers lives with me yet. My mother, a careful soul, was extremely annoyed at the loss of a good shirt, and I was forbidden to leave the garden for the rest of the holidays. This was fair enough, but it seemed to me unjust that my mother should lay the blame upon my two friends, whose role in the adventure had been limited to helping me carry the raft to the pond and who had, in fact, expressed grave doubts concerning the seaworthiness of the craft. But mothers are like that, always at pains to find whipping boys, being unable to accept the fact that they have given birth to an idiot.

Time passed and I moved to the seaside, where materials for building a seaworthy raft and opportunities of testing it were available to anyone with enterprise. I began assembling the basic structure in our yard as soon as the winter storms subsided, but I had learned a little from experience and it seemed to me essential that I should take steps to overcome the tendency of all rafts to angle themselves in calm water. I solved the problem, so I thought, with empty petrol cans, a dozen of them fastened to the sides and ends of the structure by lengths of parcel string. It was a tiresome and noisy contrivance to convey through the town to Mudbank, a mile or so up the Exe estuary, but I managed it in the company of a dedicated and pessimistic friend called Whitworth, who was very interested in the petrol-can theory and wanted to see for himself whether or not it was sound.

In theory it was. The raft did not tip and for several minutes I was able to stand upright and even propel it along, but I had made the mistake of attaching the cans by fastenings as long as a dog-lead, so that whilst they remained buoyant my weight was sufficient to depress the platform below the water to a depth of about thirty inches.

Whitworth, watching gravely from the bank, told me it was an engaging spectacle, similar to that of witnessing Saint Peter's attempt to emulate Christ on the Sea of Galilee. I moved along, he said, without any visible means of support and no apparent link with the oblong of bobbing petrol cans. When the first of them filled through rust holes that I had not taken seriously I slowly disappeared, reappearing beside the raft when we both rose to the surface.

My faith in my ability to construct a raft ebbed with the tide at Mudbank; but, like Crusoe, I graduated thence into the boat-building business. I made a whole fleet of boats but all, for one reason or another, were even less buoyant than my rafts. No matter how painstakingly I calked them with pitch and canvas there were always enough leaks to sink or capsize the craft in a matter of seconds. Time after time I struggled ashore leaving the results of days of careful construction and mortgaged pocket money in the shallows. As it was a point of honor to venture to sea in my clothes I was obliged to exercise a good deal of ingenuity in drying myself before returning home. Once I stood for an hour in a limekiln, but usually I sat glumly before a fire of driftwood, pondering my errors and promising myself that one day I would set to sea in a craft of my own design. I never did; but, in a way, I compromised with fate, completing a deep-water voyage in a vessel I had extensively modified.

Down near the old jetty was a large red canoe made of light timber and canvas. It was called *Tornado II*, and it seemed to be derelict, like all the rafts and boats I had built or abandoned in the last few years. I made inquiries and discovered that it had been built by a young man called Ridge and that he was willing to sell it for the sum of ten shillings. I did not possess ten shillings, but Ridge settled for a down payment of one shilling, with the rest in weekly installments. He was good enough to give me some advice concerning the canoe's performance in the water. "She's inclined to capsize," he said, thoughtfully, "she needs stabilizers. With a couple of stabilizers you could get as far as the Warren and back!" I was elated with the prospect. The Warren was a sandy peninsula studded with wooden bungalows that jutted into the Exe at the point where it entered the sea, and the current running between the sandy spur and our jetty was strong. I had never been to the Warren but I had gazed across at it for years. If you could imagine it without the bungalows it looked exactly like Crusoe's island.

I went to work on the stabilizers, two broad planks attached to the central ribs of the canoe by little iron brackets, and I saw to it that I used screws instead of nails that had proved so unreliable in all my previous endeavors. They seemed to work splendidly during trials in shallow water and I chose a calm day and an ebb tide for my attempt to cross the Channel.

The weather was propitious, but other factors were not. On my way out of the back door I was waylaid by my father, who gave me a fat sheaf of bills to deliver in person. They were, as I discovered later, not ordinary bills but irate demands for the settlement of long-overdue accounts. Accounts of this nature were always presented by hand. I should have remembered this when my father said, "Wait for the money!" but I wasn't listening.

The outward voyage was an unqualified success. The stabilizers worked perfectly, and I made the quarter-mile crossing without any difficulty, using a shortened oar as a paddle.

The Warren too came up to expectations. All the bungalows had been wrecked by winter storms, and there was an authentic air of desolation on the peninsula with any amount of wreckage on the beach. I spent a pleasant three hours over there, forgetting that the tide had turned and that a great weight of water was now pressing upriver. I was not long in discovering this, for *Tornado II* was at once caught in the current and swirled slantwise across the estuary in ever-decreasing circles, responding not at all to my frantic attempts to steer with the paddle. Halfway across it slipped out of my grasp and from then on I could only remain rigid and pray. I could swim, but not that distance, and not in that kind of rip tide. The canoe circled and circled until the town was more than a mile downriver and I was approaching the scene of my earlier disaster at Mudbank. Then, with a violent bump, the canoe grounded on a mud flat and heeled over in about two feet of water. Monotonously I was catapulted into the shallows and *Tornado II* disappeared, carrying with it eighteen weeks of pocket money.

It was only after I waded ashore that I remembered my jacket was in the locker and it was the presence of that jacket that enabled me to pinpoint the spot where Tornado lay submerged. As I watched, a stream of my father's savage demands for settlement floated toward Topsham, a seemingly endless chain of sodden envelopes that would never raise a single blush on the cheek of my father's debtors. I was not much concerned about these bills but I was about the jacket, so I sat shivering in the cabin of a beached trawler to await the turn of the tide. It came at last and I was able to retrieve the coat and make some assessment of the extent of the damage. *Tornado*, I discovered, was a write-off. The locker door had burst open and only a projecting screwhead had prevented my jacket accompanying the bills upstream. The starboard stabilizer had been wrenched off by the shock of the collision and the rib to which it was attached had parted from the canvas hull. Full of water the canoe was as immovable as Crusoe's first boat, the one that was too heavy to be launched. I left it there, wrung the water from my jacket, and set about making the inevitable driftwood fire before going home.

I paid half the money for *Tornado* before Ridge relented and canceled the remainder of the debt. It was a season for debt-canceling for, not unexpectedly, few of my father's demands were met by his debtors. As time passed, the unanimity of their silence puzzled him. "Funny," he would say, musing over the books, "not one of them had the manners to write and ask for time to pay! Not *one!*" and then he made a round of calls and wrote off more than half of them because the bowling season had opened. Father never looked at his ledgers between the months of May and October.

Somewhere, high up the Exe, his letters beginning "Dear Sir, *Unless* . . ." lay on some remote bank among the flotsam of Exmoor and the jetsam of the town dock. Near them lay the last of my hopes of emulating Crusoe in his salvage operations off the coral reef.

Just Cyril

They pointed him out to me that first Sunday as the son of the Sunday-school superintendent. They said he was incorrigible, wild, unpredictable as a bronco, and that nobody had ever come close to taming him, and they were right.

His mother, a sweet, gay soul, with a delicious Devon burr, was my Sunday-school teacher and that same afternoon she asked me home to tea. "You and my Cyril will find a lot in common," she said, and she was a good judge. We found so much in common that she ultimately despaired of us both. At time of writing she still survives, a very lovable old lady of ninety-three. I consider her survival to that age a miracle.

He was one of the tallest boys in town, five feet ten inches at thirteen, with incredibly long legs that carried him along as upon stilts. He had a small head with sharp features and eyes as bright and restless as the Pied Piper's, and in a way he was a Pied Piper. Children of the more enterprising type followed him gladly, and within hours he and I were boon companions. It was the most rewarding friendship I ever made, for in Cyril's company every day was an odyssey, packed with thrills and perils.

The partnership got off to a slow but satisfying start, Cyril's mother serving an enormous Devonshire tea consisting of chudleys bursting with Devonshire cream and strawberry jam, consumed before a huge fire in his living room. Everything about the house was huge except the kitchen, supervised by a long-suffering maid called Thirza, who gave notice (on Cyril's account) about once a fortnight. The top floor housed Cyril's father's archaeological collection, hundreds of flints and fossils, but these were of no interest to Cyril. He was a boy who preferred to live in the present. He showed me his sister's Raleigh motorcycle and promised to take me pillion-riding on it. He also showed me a sliding panel leading from his father's cutting-room to a cellar, where, so he said, his father's grandfather had concealed smuggled brandy. It did not seem a very probable story, particularly as his father was a strict teetotaler and the house was mid-Victorian in design, but I believed it. By that time I had accepted Cyril's house as a base from which the most extravagant adventures might be launched so long as Cyril was around.

Our partnership was almost literally dissolved that same week, soon after he had shown me a small brass cannon, ill-advisedly cast for him by a very thoughtless uncle who worked at the Dock Foundry. Cyril told me that he was in the process of manufacturing sufficient powder to fire a shot across the bows of motor traffic passing up and down the street outside his father's premises. I accepted this as a brag until I actually saw him at work, methodically hammering match-heads and ramming the grains into the mouth of his cannon.

He seemed to know a great deal about the techniques of Elizabethan gunnery. When the base of the cannon was solid with powdered match-heads he inserted a piece of lead taken from my father's printing works and after that a tight wad of cotton wool. Then, the cannon mounted on the surface of his father's cutting counter and anchored to nails driven into the underside of the mahogany, he produced a candle end and one of Thirza's hairpins. He heated the hairpin in the candle flame until it was red-hot and then rammed it into the touchhole.

The resultant roar set our ears singing and the cutting room reeked like the gun deck of an embattled man-o'-war. At first it seemed to me that the experiment had gone awry. The recoil tore the cannon from its mountings and hurled it against the cutting-room door, but when the smoke cleared away we could follow the course of the shot across the counter, through the glass panel of shop door, across the shop counter, through the plywood backing of the window, and into a box of shirts offered in the January sale. The shot was still too hot to handle when we recovered it from the folds of linen. Cyril pronounced himself more than satisfied with the potentialities of the cannon. The shot had furrowed the counter as well as breaking the window and puncturing the shirts, but the awful trail of damage did not seem to bother him at all. He did not even refer to it and I left him hammering match heads for a second trial.

I was summoned to the house later in the week to find the kitchen a shambles and Thirza in the process of packing. It seems that Cyril had fed so much powder into the cannon that it had not responded to the red-hot hairpin, so he had held it over the gas-stove with a pair of tongs. The explosion that followed wrecked the kitchen, split the cannon and robbed Cyril of his eyebrows and eyelashes. He looked very odd without them. Contemplating his riven cannon he had the appearance of a young Mongolian monk who had just survived an ordeal by fire.

Cyril's mother was able to talk Thirza out of leaving but there was another crisis in the kitchen some months later when Cyril cut open a down cushion, emptied its contents over the bannisters into the stairwell and shouted, "Anyone ever see snow in June before?" His father was a tolerant man, but there was trouble over that and even more over a new mackintosh that was splashed with whitewash aimed at me as I was climbing through the sliding panel during a game of smugglers.

Whenever life seemed stale and profitless I used to cross the road and inquire of Cyril what was new. He never disappointed me. Within the hour something quite extraordinary had occurred and usually it had to do with something Cyril was making. One time it was a long rope ladder assembled for the purpose of reaching gulls' nests on the cliffs. We made it from clotheslines and pieces of notched planks taken from protective fencing that enclosed my father's printing machinery. It was not a conventional rope ladder formed of rectangles but a succession of knotted lengths, with struts inserted between knots so as to form a chain of diamond-shaped footholds. It did not look at all practical, and his father, seeing it, forbade him to use it, so that we had to wait until he was shut away in his top floor painting scenery for the spring missionary play before we could test it, descending from Cyril's bedroom into the backyard. Cyril, as the stronger of the team, elected himself anchor man and increased my confidence in his ladder by tying one end of it to a crossbar and wedging the bar into the window aperture before taking the strain.

With some difficulty I descended below the level of his window and was poised above the steep-sloping scullery roof when Cyril heard his father approaching and urged me to step off the ladder and take refuge on the roof. He shouted down that his father would confiscate the rope ladder if we were caught and he was going to pull it up and hide it in his bed. It was a most unreasonable proposition but when I protested he supplemented his demands by shaking the ropes so emphatically that I was obliged to jump for safety to the kitchen roof in order to avoid falling into the asphalt yard. He then withdrew the ladder and closed the window before his father came in but I was less fortunate. A few slates had been removed from the scullery roof and replaced with squares of glass and one of these smashed as I slithered down the angle of the roof, broke my fall on the gutter and dropped into the yard with a jolt that jarred every bone in my body and cracked my glasses. Then Cyril's head appeared again at the window, urging me to hide in the outside privy before his father could investigate the crash of glass. He did not warn me that his privy door was fitted with an exceptionally strong spring. I pushed it open and it swung back on me with such force that I was laid dazed and bleeding in the yard. The episode closed with my transportation to the living room, where Cyril explained away the entire incident by saying I had fallen into the yard during a gallant endeavor to retrieve a ball wedged in the gutter. During the interval, when all attention had been concentrated upon me, he had planted the evidence. The rope ladder was thus saved from confiscation and later Cyril used it to get into a cave he had never previously entered. On that occasion, however, I insisted upon being the anchor man, and it was some consolation to note the extreme difficulty he encountered disentangling his feet from those diamond-shaped knots.

Cyril was the most optimistic person I have ever met. Nothing could daunt, defeat or depress him, and I think the secret of his ebullience lay in his ability to switch his attention from one goal to another the moment he ran into a major difficulty. He once constructed an odd-looking coracle from his mother's wardrobe drawer, using strips of her box-room blinds soaked in pitch to seal the cracks. He boiled the pitch in my mother's porringer and casually returned it to me while it was still warm from the kitchen range. It was quite ruined, of course, and I at once threw it away. My mother did not connect me with its disappearance, and that was how I was around to help him carry the boat to a slipway under the pier. It floated until he was in five feet of water. Then it sank, slowly and rather gracefully, and Cyril reacted like a conscientious captain, standing in it until only his narrow head showed above water. One of the most rewarding aspects of Cyril was that he never held inquests upon his failures. On this occasion he waded ashore, stripped, dried his clothes and went home to practice assegai-throwing in his father's fossil gallery.

The really surprising thing about Cyril's family was that its members never learned how to isolate him from the apparatus of destruction. It sometimes seemed to me that his father, mother, sister and uncles were people who went out of their way to pickle rods for their own backs. There was that cannon, specifically cast for Cyril by his uncle. There was his sister's motorcycle, a permanent source of challenge in the yard. And there was that bunch of genuine African assegais that his father borrowed to lend authenticity to the Sunday-school missionary play he was producing.

We had been looking forward to the missionary play for many weeks and had sometimes watched Cyril's father at work on the scenery, a Zulu kraal surrounded by a dozen cardboard palms. Every Sunday-school scholar had a part in this epic. Some were cast as godless Zulus, some as white hunters all but extinguished under pith helmets, and the rest, including myself, as zealous missionaries financed by the Congregational Church to preach the gospel of Christ. Cyril, lucky devil, got the part of Cetewayo, the Zulu chief, appearing naked except for black bathing trunks and smeared from head to foot in charcoal. He was also given a real assegai to carry, and even at rehearsals this seemed to me an act of sheer madness on the part of his father.

And so it proved. At the dress rehearsal, when all the little Zulus were squatting outside their kraal awaiting mass conversion, Cetewayo was missing, and the rehearsal had to stop until he could be found. Everyone was told not to move as a photograph was being taken and it was during the actual flash that the schoolroom door crashed open and Cetewayo's assegai sang through the air to pass between producer and photographer and stick, quivering, in one of the tubs containing palm trees.

It was the only occasion that I saw Cyril's dedicated father lose his temper. He did more. To the onlookers it appeared that he had gone berserk. With a scream of rage he tore the assegai from the tub, leaped from the stage and pursued Cyril down two flights of stone steps and into the street. I believe he would have skewered him if he had overtaken him en route, but fortunately he did not. Some instinct warned Cyril that he was running for his life and he went hell for leather into the busiest section of the town with his father still in pursuit. It provided, they told me, a very unusual spectacle for the late shoppers of our town. One does not often witness a maddened Sunday-school superintendent chasing a Zulu chief along busy gaslit streets, with a tufted assegai in his grasp. Cyril escaped, and his father returned to the rehearsal shamefaced and wind-blown. The assegais were at once withdrawn and replaced with raspberry canes, tipped with silvered cardboard. As a punishment Cyril was banished from the cast, his father standing in as Cetewayo, a giant among his tribe. The punishment did not bother Cyril overmuch. With his entire family out of the way he did something he had been yearning to do for years. He climbed out of a top-floor window, straddled the roof as far as the end of the block where he could look down on the Methodist Chapel opposite his father's premises and tormented rival Wesleyans with a peashooter. Nobody traced the source of his hard-hitting peas, and he stayed up there unde-tected until he judged his parents would be returning home.

He was a very inventive boy. As well as the boat and the rope-ladder he constructed a powerful crossbow that could shoot iron railings through dustbins and when the nights drew in he in-vented a popular nocturnal game, played in the narrow courts and alleys that were the heart of the old town. He called the game "Dismal Swamp," because it was inspired by a book on run-away slaves that he was reading. The apparatus, like all the stage properties used by Cyril in his lifelong game of make-believe, was the genuine article. From his father's museum he had acquired a long ox-driver's whip that could produce terrifying cracks, and with this instrument he chased the rest of us up and down drang-ways and in and out ill-lit courts on a succession of joyous winter evenings. The whip, plus Cyril's habit of living all his parts, made the game an exciting one. It was important to keep out of range of that whip, and when Cyril, always the plantation boss, was close on our heels there was genuine panic, as when he cornered five of us in a cul-de-sac where the only possible refuge was the court's communal privy. We fled there, all five of us, intending to barricade the door but in our haste and the dim light we did not notice that a mountainous old crone was already enthroned. Within seconds she had five boys and a whip-cracking overseer on her lap, and she carried her complaints to the proper authority, in this case the chairman of the local housing committee. Here was proof, she argued, that the court stood in need of more than one privy.

Cyril was by no means a callous boy, but he could be thought-less, as when he tied one of his victims to a ringbolt, lit a slow-burning firecracker under him and forgot about him in the excite-ment of hiding in the churchyard and watching choirmen on their way to practice stop to pick up a bogus parcel attached to a length of string. He was always careless with his own and his parents' property, but he touched off a town scandal when he extended his depredations to municipal preserves. He and I once took refuge in a bed of dahlias when we were pursued by the head gardener whilst sporting in the locked enclosure after dark. We got off unseen but I blushed to see my editor father's leading article in that week's *Chronicle*. He prescribed the birch and Borstal for the local vandals who had flattened the town's most spectacular flower bed.

I often wondered what made Cyril the kind of boy he was, but it was not until I talked with his mother in later life that I got a clue. All his ancestors had been blue-water men and perhaps his father's initial error was to sire a throwback and put him into the tailoring trade, instead of shipping him off to Java as a cabin boy.

The climax in our friendship was reached when, after a conference between the local headmaster and our parents, we were packed off to separate boarding schools, but before we parted we shared one last adventure. It left me knee-and-knuckle-scarred for life.

Cyril had always promised to take me pillion-riding on his sister's motorbike, and on his fifteenth birthday (you could drive a motorcycle at fifteen in those days) he kept his promise. Until then I had believed his statement that he could drive was an empty boast, but I should have known better. His driving, like everything else he did, was a little erratic, but he could certainly manage the machine and told me he had gained the necessary experience by driving it up and down the drangway behind the house whenever his sister was out of the way. We got as far as Honiton, fifteen miles away, that first day and the only incident that frightened me during the journey was a prolonged speed wobble in a rutted lane. The following day, however, we were not so lucky, at least, I wasn't. Speeding up the main Exeter highway Cyril drove along a one-way traffic stretch where they were resurfacing the road. In order to avoid a head-on collision with oncoming vehicles he swerved into a section of loose flints, skidded, accelerated, came out of the skid and neatly rejoined the negotiable highway fifty yards further on.

In the process, however, he lost me without even knowing it. I was picked up by a kindly farmer's wife and given first-aid in her kitchen. I had escaped with lacerations on the hands and knees and when I emerged, swathed in bloodstained bandages, I was just in time to see Cyril shoot by in the direction of home looking left and right for his missing passenger. He found me on his third return trip and we proceeded back to town at a slightly moderated pace. When we were putting the motorcycle away I thought he might comment upon my injuries but he did not. He said, thoughtfully, "Funny that! I kept talking to you over my shoulder all the way to Exton, and it was only when I left the ground at the humpbacked bridge that it struck me you might have fallen off. I looked there first as a matter of fact."

Good old Cyril. He did become an outfitter after all, and later still a local lifeboat enthusiast, but in between God relented and gave him some five years in the Royal Navy fighting the Axis powers in the Mediterranean. It is no mystery to me that Mussolini's fleet achieved little or nothing during the war, or that the Mediterranean never became Italy's Mare Nostrum. How could it while Cyril was around and licensed to kill?

"*You are invited to . . .*"

The first of them arrived with the laggard Christmas cards and the New Year bills. Stiff, mini-envelopes, enclosing a card decorated with forget-me-nots in the top right-hand corner. And underneath, in the round childish hand of the host, "*You are invited to my party on . . . at . . . R.S.V.P.*"

Your popularity was regulated by how many you received in the slack season, between the day after Boxing Day and the date the Lent term opened in mid-January. And how many you got, of course, was directly related to whether or not you had been able to persuade your own parents to give one.

In this respect I was singularly deprived. There had been a time when my mother was a grudging but conventional hostess. On my eleventh birthday, however, our house had been filled with male friends, and the more enterprising of them had broken all the springs of the drawing-room sofa whilst using it as a trampoline. From then on, until I was eighteen and more interested in romance than acrobatics, my mother set her face against house parties. It took her seven years to forget those tortured sofa springs.

I could always reckon, however, on about seven or eight invitations, and they had a curious uniformity, as though, generations ago, British mamas had met at a national conference and drawn up a basic program for the terrace-house or semidetached-house party. One could reckon on getting an almost identical menu at each of them. Green jellies, pink blancmange, seed cake, shop pastries, bread and butter, brown or white, jam and Devonshire cream and jugs of yellow lemonade to supplement the tea demanded by eccentrics. The games were also identical. Musical Chairs, General Post, Blind Man's Buff, Pinning the Tail on the Donkey, Winking and—the *raison d'être* of the party—Postman's Knock. The source of music was the same. A brown upright piano, out of tune and with one or two dead notes, happily at extreme ends of the scale. Even the dresses worn by the girls were a uniform; green or pink satin or organdie, fluffed-out hair ribbons to match, short white socks, strap-over shoes. The only variation lay in the size of the bunchy bows worn in their hair.

Whenever you set off for one of these parties you carried a small brown-paper parcel under each arm. In one parcel were your patent-leather pumps and in the other an obligatory gift for the host, unwrapped with shrill cries of, "Oh, you *shouldn't* have!" But you always made sure that you did.

They got off to a slow start, with everybody inhibited by Sunday clothes and parental warnings to be on their best behavior, but around the crowded tea table things loosened up a little and the mildest joke or gaffe was greeted with shrieks of laughter. When you weren't laughing you wore a fixed grin that soon began to hurt a little. Crackers were pulled and paper hats donned. Soon the floor began to look like a beach after a Bank Holiday.

Then, if they were wise, the parents withdrew to other parts of the house or even left the house altogether, and the program opened with one or two decorous pastimes that did not involve kissing. Nobody played these with much enthusiasm. They were rightly regarded as a kind of overture before the curtain rose on the real performance.

About seven-thirty the party got into its stride, sometimes assisted by the steady whine of the Gramophone, but there was never enough room to dance. It always astonished me how a front parlor, even when fitted with a folding partition connecting it to the dining room, could accommodate so many boys and girls, plus its furniture and the decorations. Sometimes there were as many as thirty of us packed into one of those brightly lit rectangles, but parties thrived on overcrowding.

With the nonkissing games disposed of we usually settled

down to Winking, which was a kind of warm-up for the real thing after supper. Winking was played in a very sportsmanlike manner—that is to say, one often winked at girls one did not want to kiss but for whom one felt sympathetic because they looked so glassily hopeful. Then, an hour or so before it was time to go home, the real fun began, and the host or hostess would announce Postman's Knock. Silence descended on the circle so that it was sometimes possible to hear the soft flutter of the fire or the buzz of a trapped fly who had mistaken the rising temperature for summer and was making an exploratory journey along the sash of the steamed-up window. You would sit there hoping until someone you hoped would ask for you had been summoned. If you were lucky the summons came and you spent a breathless moment in the gaslit passage before pondering who to name when the door opened and the postman reappeared. Too often, alas, one was tempted to ask for the same girl but that didn't do and savored of the closed shop. Couples without these scruples sometimes did their damnedest to hog the game but this wasn't encouraged and an indignant clamor would soon put a stop to it.

The actual kissing was formalized. Its technique had been mastered at the cinema, and both girls and boys wanted to conform, if only to prove they were sophisticated. The boy placed one arm behind the girl's shoulders and the other round her waist. The girl poised her chin at an angle of about forty-five degrees and steadied herself by holding the back of the boy's head. She then closed her eyes. In all those games of Postman's Knock I never once remember kissing an open-eyed girl. No words were exchanged. Silence banished shyness and the embrace resolved itself into a ritual, solemn but satisfying. Lips met and party frocks crackled. Then, without a word, the embrace would dissolve and one would be left alone under the popping gaslight mantle. You had scaled the summit of the evening, and now there was nothing left but to stay there as long as possible.

The parties usually broke up about ten-thirty, with a flurry of mackintoshes and cries of "Thank you!" and "Goodbye" and

"Nice Time." For some reason you did not escort girls home from parties, as you invariably did from public dances. Everybody left separately, or was called for by an indulgent parent, and at only one party, given by a very daring girl called Edna, can I recall the dispensation of alcoholic drinks for the road. It was elderberry wine, but it seemed to make everybody drunk, and my mother was very shocked when I mentioned the fact and from then looked upon my hosts as depraved. Luckily for all of us she did not tell my father, who would almost certainly have registered a protest on paper and might even have picketed the house with his Band of Hope.

Do boys and girls entering their teens today still hold these Christmas parties, or have they been banished forever by the telly? If they are held at all, I feel sure they are far more sophisticated affairs, for I cannot imagine anybody dressing up in their best suit or party frock in response to an invitation card framed in forget-me-nots. Neither can I visualize the sturdy youngsters of today, most of whom are a foot taller than were our generation at the same age, enjoying a game of Winking and Postman's Knock, to say nothing at all of Pinning the Tail on the Donkey. Perhaps they have their own version of our post-Christmas house party, with the radio turned up to full blast and games of Consequences that would provide Mr. Kinsey with some interesting data. I wouldn't know, for I haven't attended one for nearly forty years, but the memory of those I did attend lingers like the scent of lavender in a seldom-opened drawer. Sometimes, when I pass along the older streets of the towns and suburbs where I lived as a boy, I recognize the actual numbers of red-brick houses where such parties were held and glance at front-parlor windows behind which all the boys and girls within easy walking distance erupted and embraced one another at the foot of the stairs. It all seems as far away as Wassail and as outmoded as the minstrel's lyre, and I hurry on, for I hear the clock ticking at a faster tempo than it ticked on the mantelshelves of "Chez-Nous," "The Laburnums" and Number 10, Cedar Close.

PART TWO

Bells Across the Moor

Bastion of Privilege

Was it Julian Grenfell, Sassoon, Robert Graves, or one of their front-line contemporaries who took his first, appalled look at the glutinous battlefield of Passchendaele in 1917, and exclaimed, "Great God! It's worse than School!" Whoever it was, the remark is revealing, and I wish someone would use it as a counter-broadside during one of those perennial debates aimed at abolishing public schools, establishments that left-wing politicians still regard as bastions of privilege.

As stated, I attended seven schools between 1917 and 1928, and only the last of them was "public" in the sense implied. I enjoyed my time there enormously, but this is not to say that I ever thought of myself as privileged for having worn its cap and blazer. Indeed, there were occasions when I thought the exact opposite, looking over my shoulder at feather-bedded day-school boys, much as the underprivileged of Paris looked through the locked gates of Versailles at pampered nobles. For whatever one can say for or against public schools, one is obliged to admit that a mercurial temperament and a tough hide is needed to enjoy such privileges they have on offer. It was said of mine that its pupils made excellent soldiers. Nothing worse was likely to befall them on active service.

It was not the intention of my father that I should complete my education at this type of establishment. As a fiery radical, who had been storming bastions of privilege all his life, he bracketed public schools in his mind with breweries, stately homes, episcopal palaces and the Cavalry Club, but he could never be bothered to study handouts and when it became imperative for me to leave the Exmouth co-ed school he handed me a sheaf of brochures and told me to take my choice. It was typical of him, as was his scornful dismissal of the incident that brought about an abrupt change of school.

This incident was known at the time as the "Brickworks Affair," and its inflation into a tiny local scandal illustrates the vast distances we have moved in half a century toward the establishment of a permissive society. Today the "Brickworks Affair" would not crease the forehead of the most exacting headmaster or parent, involving as it did no more than a little innocent horseplay between the sexes on the way home to tea. It was very different then, however. Any overt expression of the sex urge between adolescents was apt to be regarded as a prelude to debauchery. When it became known that a dozen of us were exchanging pledges and kisses in the disused kiln five minutes' walk from school one might have judged, from the resultant uproar, that the boys had opted to train as White Slavers and the girls were earmarked for the streets.

When it blew over, and staff and parents were satisfied that there was no likelihood of an abrupt rise in the local birthrate, my father came to the conclusion that the best way to insure his leisure against interruption throughout what remained of my adolescence, was to put distance between us. That is how, in brief, I came to qualify as a potential enemy of the militant left, likely, indeed almost certain, to man the wrong side of the barricades when the October Revolution was launched.

This long-anticipated event, it appeared, promised to coincide almost exactly with my enrollment in the junior ranks of the oppressors. The General Strike took place during my first term at West Buckland, but it proved a mild upheaval and taught the British what they should have known—i.e., that the prospects of a Continental-style revolution in England are almost as unlikely as that of teaching them how to make carnival, how to transform Sunday into a public holiday, or how to win a war and come out of it more solvent than the vanquished. There are certain spheres in which the average Briton is less likely to succeed than the

Australian aboriginal, and making a revolution is one of them. He will master the trade of hotelier long before he understands how to overthrow an elected government.

I had, of course, many preconceived ideas about life at a public school and all of them stemmed from books published in the latter half of the nineteenth century. *Tom Brown*, of course, was one, and three others were *The Bending of the Twig*, *The Hill*, and *The Fifth Form at St. Dominic's*. These were buttressed by a weekly injection from the late Frank Richards, the prolific recorder of the japes at Greyfriars and St. Jim's in *The Magnet* and *The Gem*. The stage background built by these industrious carpenters took a severe battering before it was replaced by a more solid structure. The process occupied, I suppose, the better part of a year, during which I learned, albeit slowly, that a dormitory feast seldom expanded beyond the furtive sucking of a few acid drops, that fat boys were not necessarily butts, that the smoking habit, far from being confined to bounders and weeds, was considered a manly accomplishment, and that the luxury of a study, enjoyed by Tom Brown from his first day at Rugby, could not be anticipated until one had plodded all the way from second form to sixth.

The school buildings occupied a western spur of the Exmoor plateau, six hundred feet above sea level. The nearest market town was six miles distant, the nearest railway halt two miles, the nearest village a mile and a half. All three were out of bounds.

The school had been founded by a muscular Christian, himself a pupil of the famous Doctor Arnold, but it was not to Arnold that he looked when he approved the architectural layout. I have it in mind that his inspiration went back somewhat further in history—say, to a Spartan barrack for defaulters—and he apparently overlooked the fact that Sparta enjoys a Mediterranean climate. The wind charged through the stone corridors like an army of howling Cossacks, and in my time there was not a stitch of carpet or, for that matter, a fiber of linoleum. Knotted wood, slate and granite enfolded us, and there was never room for more than three at the classroom heating-pipe alcoves. It was said by those who did not qualify for these places that to lean against them was to court constipation, but I never put the theory to the test. At fourteen I was a medium-sized boy, but West Buckland catered for farmers' sons and there were at least three hulking Jan Ridds in each class.

The full force of these disadvantages did not strike me until my second term, for I joined the school in April and we had a long, hot summer ahead of us. Soon after the commencement of the autumn term, however, I raised a splendid crop of chilblains and became resigned to dying young, possibly of exposure.

The headmaster, a very genial soul, had inherited the Spartan tradition. At sixty-plus he was still playing in the scrum of junior games and on one occasion had a game suspended for half an hour while we combed the trampled mud for his false teeth. He had a number of eccentric beliefs, and one in particular was responsible for implanting in my mind the belief that I was unlikely to survive my first winter on the moor. The bathhouse was situated in a vast covered playground on that side of an open quad furthest from the dormitories. Boys were required to make their way there in pajamas and dressing gowns. As a preventive against catching cold on the return journey the headmaster instituted a system of cold showers, supervised by a prefect. I was warned of this in advance but dismissed it as terror propaganda, fed to all new boys. It was even so, however, for on stepping out of the bath I was steered into another, where the prefect in charge baptized each boy with three large pans of ice-cold water, "To close the pores," he reiterated, quoting the headmaster.

I have dwelt on the cold, but there were times when the over-privileged were tortured by heat. It was pleasant to lie all day long on a rug in the shade of the plantation watching, without seeing, important cricket matches, in honor of which two dull periods had been canceled. One dozed, or read *Monte Cristo*, to the accompaniment of scattered applause and self-conscious cries of "Oh, well *played*, sir!" but summer idylls such as this were not to be had for nothing. Our contribution, as juniors, was enlistment in rolling gangs charged with the task of keeping the pitch

in good order for the Somerset Stragglers or Devonshire Dump-
lings. It was the kind of labor performed in the Peruvian silver
mines by the enslaved Inca.

For specified periods throughout summer terms teams of eight
conscripts dragged a horse roller up and down the level turf
between the wickets, two members of the team supporting the
shafts, where the horse should have been, the other six pushing
to maintain momentum. The overseer, a prefect or a cricket color,
pretended to push, but had more important obligations—to keep
the bondsmen at their work with a cricket stump.

One way and another there was not much time for waiting
one's turn at the heating-pipe alcoves. Everyone in authority had
been indoctrinated with the spirit of Henry before Harfleur.
Someone was always around, winter and summer, to ensure that
our sinews were stiffened and our blood summoned up by prolonged sessions of violent movement within a ten-mile radius of
the naked ridge.

West Buckland, then and now, was a famous running school.
In the autumn and Lent terms there were, in addition to biweekly rugby games, early morning P.T., Saturday penal drill for
defaulters, and a weekly Cadet Corps parade, a series of testing
cross-country events, eight in number, over the tracks and folds
of moor and pastureland. They were not the usual, easygoing
jog-trots of my day-school days but highly competitive events,
averaging three to four miles out and upwards of two miles in.
On the outward course whippers-in kept gasping and stitch-
tormented laggards closed up. On the home run it was every
man for himself, the honor of his house and Saint George, or
possibly Saint Phaidippides with a postscript from Marathon.
After one of these events your calves ached abominably and
usually to no purpose, for only the first forty into the quad
scored points.

If, on a Wednesday or a Saturday half-day you were, through
some oversight, not actually participating in a field sport, you
were under an obligation to watch a First Fifteen game against
a neighboring-town side or visiting team. Bad weather (and up

there a blustery day on the plain was a tornado) was no excuse for frowsting in a classroom with a P. G. Wodehouse. Gauleiters flushed the small fry into the open and thereafter patrolled the touchline as official cheerleaders. Every now and again, as you struggled to shorten your neck against the storm, a cricket stump would prod you in the small of the back and a senior would growl, *"Cheer, you bastard, cheer!"* It was as well to respond with the high-pitched and plaintive cry of "Come *alonggg*— school!"

Years later, when Fleet Street split its sides at the expense of the Fascist claques, lining the streets of Rome and Berlin to applaud Mussolini and Hitler, I often wondered if the commentators were men who, as boys, had been numbered among the privileged. If so, they must have forgotten those Banshee wails flung into the wind along touchlines throughout the length and breadth of England. But I never did forget those occasions, having served claque-time myself. I am still astonished when I catch a glimpse of a football-match crowd on TV and reflect that here are men—aye, and women too—who are eager to pay for the privilege of shouting encouragement to players.

The diet at West Buckland in the mid-twenties was equivalent to that served to indigent prisoners in the Debtors' Ward of the Marshalsea, a century before. It included porridge (sugarless if you were low in table seniority), murky toast, strips of meat that would have passed for the boucan eaten by eighteenth-century pirates, potatoes—warts and all—lashings of cabbage, cindered hard-bake, thin custard and scrape, the sole, official issue at six-o'clock tea unless you bought extra at the tuckshop. Tuesday was a red-letter day. We had a sausage apiece for breakfast. So was Thursday, but then it was fishcake, and on Saturdays an egg. There was no issue of jam at the final meal of the day and the tea, served in large jugs, was unsweetened. Somehow the privileged thrived on it but the regular arrival of tuck-box parcels may have accounted for the fact that, according to my reports, I grew an inch a term.

I seem to have forgotten penal drill, reserved for classroom defaulters on Saturdays. This was a kind of mobile field punishment, organized on Army lines and I was not to see its like again until, in 1941, I escorted a prisoner to an R.A.F. detention barracks. Each penal mark awarded during the week earned a defaulter fifteen minutes' drill consisting of alternate bursts of hefting an eight-pound First World War rifle and doubling round the quarter-mile circuit of the school buildings. It was an excellent substitute for more conventional training and some of our best athletes emerged from the penal squad, where the same faces appeared every Saturday afternoon.

It might be imagined from the foregoing that life at West Buckland was a purgatory, that growing boys could hardly wait to kiss their hands to the place and scramble aboard the train in search of less strenuous servitude elsewhere, but this is very far from being the case. One or two new boys drifted away after a term or two and were seen no more, but the great majority of my contemporaries can be seen swilling beer and swapping stories at the annual Old Boys' gathering at the school each Whit Monday, when a bar is set up for them in order that they may lubricate their reminiscences. On these occasions they are shown the many improvements in fabric, diet and home comforts, by a new generation of masters, but they are not impressed. It sometimes seems to me that they equate the installation of Aga cookers, a gymnasium, a fire escape and new lavatories with the dissolution of the British Empire. I can only assume that the Anglo-Saxons are a masochistic race, or perhaps the answer to the deeply rooted affection we all feel for that gaunt huddle of buildings on the Exmoor ridge can be found in *Tom Brown*, particularly in that early part of the book, where Tom reflects on the compensations of the discomfort of an all-night coach ride up to Rugby ". . . the consciousness of silent endurance, so dear to every Englishman, of standing out against something and not giving in."

My own attachment for the high, isolated plateau where I spent the better part of my adolescence is less complicated. I remember it as a series of discoveries, some of them magical, a few frightening, but all of them absorbing to someone with a predisposition to translate observation and experience into word pictures. To cite them all would fill a book but I can recall a few outstanding ones. Bluebells, covering the steeply angled slopes of a North Devon woodland and a late afternoon sun playing hide-and-seek with the course of the Bray; the pleasant sound of ball snick-snacking on willow, capped by the harsh but somehow reassuring clamor of the school bell swung by a jolly, buck-toothed boy called Shaw, killed in a Lancaster bomber in 1942; the massed pit-pat-pat of rubber shoes—"stinkers" as they were called—on the surface of Exmoor farm tracks as we ran, two hundred strong, across the folds of the moor; school entertainments, made by us for ourselves alone, including the annual Gilbert and Sullivan opera; a few microscopic triumphs, such as running second in the Senior steeplechase; and rather more egregious failures that provoked laughter, always laughter, that seemed sometimes to have taken permanent residence among all that stone, slate, knotted oak and the ineradicable smell of boiled greens; strings of improbable nicknames and faces to go with them, "Juicy," "Bummy," "Romeo," "Daffy," "Waso," "Bouncer," and "Legweak"; "Buster," "Gobber," "Tightass," "Stalliio," "Beaky," "Bo" and "Puddleduck," some of them dead within ten years, and their official names added to an earlier list on the stone cross at the head of the east drive, a majority alive, balding and paunchy with, here and there, a grandson at a greatly enlarged school that has finally rid itself of the smell of boiled greens.

These things and a sense of belonging that was more intimate than the community tug exerted by my home town, an easily detachable segment of life that can be framed in the memory, to hang there until an impersonal nurse draws a sheet over the bed and goes out, closing the door.

Church and Mrs. Stanbury

The French writer Taine, who visited Britain and had some interesting things to say about it in the middle of last century, was smitten by a kind of mental palsy when contemplating the English Sabbath in London. "Sunday in London in the rain," he wrote, "the shops are shut; the streets almost deserted; the aspect is that of an immense and a well-ordered cemetery. The few passers-by under their umbrellas, in a desert of squares and streets, have the look of uneasy spirits who have risen from their graves; it is appalling . . ." It is indeed, or rather it was, for in some (though by no means all) parts of the British Isles, the gloom has since moderated. It had not done so to an appreciable extent when I was a child.

Sunday was always a day of penance for me, reared as I was in a Nonconformist home, and although, since the end of World War II, gallant attempts have been made by the British to Continentalize their Sunday, these efforts have not really succeeded. There exists, deep in the subconscious of the English, the Scots and the Welsh, a guilty awareness that there is something desperately wrong about appearing on a sea front with an ice cream and a transistor on the Sabbath, so that the quirk of conscience moderates the enjoyment of all but the reckless.

M. Taine might have returned home supposing that a Sunday spent in the country was a less chastening experience, but he would have been wrong, then and now. I sometimes watch people getting through Sunday in the long, straggling streets of Devon villages, and they always look to me as if they are returning from a disappointing hanging. They are never sure of their direction and mostly idle around in blue-serge suits, dropping match stems over the bridge and watching them float downstream. They not only seem ill at ease but insufferably bored, so much so indeed that one is inclined to take seriously Osbert Sitwell's wry comment that Sunday murders in Victorian suburbs had their source-motive not in greed or hate but in the stifling ennui that settles over places like Balham and Catford on a Sunday. For my part, and notwithstanding all the attempts to inject Sunday with a swaggering gaiety in recent years, I am always relieved to wake up and remember it is Monday and I can return to the blessed rhythm of my life. I was relieved as a child and I am relieved today, although now, when my time is at my own disposal, this must be dismissed as prejudice.

I entertained some hope, when I exchanged home for boarding school, that my Sundays would brighten up a little, but I should have known better. Six days a week the school was a lively, tumultuous place, but on the seventh the familiar Sabbatarian shroud descended upon us, enveloping masters and boys in folds of yammering boredom. We hung about in our best suits awaiting attendance at matins at the local church, trudged home to a cold and meager lunch, hung about waiting for evensong that occupied most of the afternoon, returned to school again for tea, and finished off the insufferable day with a period of prep, half of which was devoted to composing the weekly letter home. I could never find anything to write on that sheet of ruled foolscap. My inventive powers had been anaesthetized by the ordeal of the hours that preceded the exercise.

There was, however, a single ray of light that penetrated the fog of a school Sunday, and so welcome did it prove that even now the memory of Mrs. Stanbury sidles up and gives my hand a comforting clasp whenever I am sufficiently depressed to contemplate the British Sunday.

I can only compare her to a rustic Mrs. Do-As-You-Would-Be-Done-By, in Kingsley's *Water Babies*, a consolation prize for those who had performed the obligatory offices of the Christian and undergone two successive baptisms of boredom in the pew. Boys on their way to church walked, for the most part, in glum and decorous silence, a small and forlorn reinforcement moving up to a front-line trench after an all-too-brief respite in reserve, but every now and again a boy would leap and scuffle. He was thinking of Mrs. Stanbury's little window and his chances of getting there before it was blocked by a surging mob of pie and pasty purchasers.

The services at that church were so dull (and, to me, a Nonconformist, so incomprehensible) that I sometimes wonder if they were designed as a subtle infliction of punishment for sins of omission during the week. We had one preacher who sermonized, during one entire term of thirteen Sundays in a row, on the reformed prayer book, subsequently flung out of Parliament as promptly as though it had been a Papal Bull. Some of the more daring of the seniors did make one attempt to voice their protests and did it in an original if blasphemous manner. They deliberately emphasized the response to "Lord have mercy upon us . . ." with a sustained and beseeching shriek that emerged as *"Christ!* Have *mercy* upon us!" but it did very little to relieve the monotony, and I was driven to seek other means of diversion. The most successful, I recall, was carving my name on the backrest of the pew in front by means of my teeth, and it was a somewhat desperate measure, for the taste of varnish was as bitter as gall and the name and initials required thirteen letters and three full stops. But this was no more than a palliative. There was really nothing to do but think about Mrs. Stanbury and the smell that emerged from her ovens, and to reflect that, in church at least, the rule of the survival of the fittest operated in favor of the juniors, who filed out first and were given a head start over the starving vanguard of the fifth and sixth forms.

It was exhilarating to participate in that mad stampede over the bones of the long dead. We could never break into a run until we had rounded the church tower, but then, with its solid structure interposing between us and the nearest master, we shed the last of our respect for authority and the place wherein we walked. At the first of the leaning gravestones the second-formers would break into a trot, and when pressed from behind they would accelerate to a canter and finally a gallop as the mob stormed through the lich gate to gain access to the road. From here it was only about fifty yards to the Stanbury farm-yard, a morass broken by unhewn slabs of granite. It was diffi-cult to cross this hazard at a fast run, but most of us managed it, fountains of mud spurting from the crevices as we converged on the tiny, barred window of Mrs. Stanbury's kitchen.

If you were among the first fifty you could get a glimpse of the interior, where stood Mrs. Stanbury herself and her smiling daughter. But Mrs. Stanbury was not smiling. Week after week, term after term, year after year, she was concerned for the safety of her fabric and would say, standing with freckled arms akimbo, "If you bra-a-ake my window you'll pa-ay vor'un!" Nobody ever did break it, but I like to think that her fears had substance and that long ago, years before I was born, somebody's clumsi-ness had inspired this weekly warning. For Mrs. Stanbury was that kind of person, an institution as rooted in that place as the church tower itself. I suppose, when I met her, she was no more than fifty, but she somehow gave an impression of having baked pies for boys who wore crepe armbands on account of Prince Albert's death.

She was stoutish and very solid, with gray hair and strong, tolerant features. That she was fond of boys was never in doubt, for, when every last inch round the window was occupied by juniors, reaching out like a swarm of beggars at the grille of a medieval monastery, we could overhear her genial conversation with the privileged prefects and first-eleven colors assembled round the open fire.

She had a nice sense of the proprieties and treated these great men like favorite sons, sometimes teasing them about the looks they directed at her attractive daughter, sometimes cracking a broad jest about family matters at the farm. Once she set the kitchen in a tremendous uproar by announcing that the local doctor had just left after "circumscribing the baby's dickey."

This remark, of course, passed instantaneously into school legend.

But she had joviality to spare for the underprivileged, and once she had made up her mind that her window would not be shattered by the press, she began passing out her stream of hot pasties and apple turnovers in exchange for our pennies.

For those of us who could not afford threepence there was a supply of delicious currant cakes at a penny apiece. Not even boys entirely without funds were denied her bounty. She preferred cash, of course, but she practiced a credit system and when, come half-term, her patrons could only pay with promises, she would look them indulgently in the eye and say, "Right! Us'll zee 'ee then, virst Zunday o' new term!" She kept no books, but she had very few bad debts. To pay Mrs. Stanbury's backlog on the first Sunday of term was an insurance against hunger in the future, for her memory was exceptionally good and I have heard her say, albeit regretfully, "No, boy, youm still 'way be'ind, baint 'ee?" to the future casualties of Carey Street.

Her fare was impeccable. The pastry was firm and crisp and just the right shade of brown, and inside those generous envelopes was plenty of meat, potato and onion, or the choice fruits of her adjoining orchard. One had no fear, after matins, of spoiling one's appetite for lunch or, after evensong, of spoiling one's tea. All that awaited us on those long tables back at school was a sliver or two of cold mutton or beef, a splodge of potato and a slice of beetroot, with tapioca or semolina to follow. And for tea there was nothing but scrape. It took us longer to eat Mrs. Stanbury's fare than to polish off the Sunday lunch or tea, for in Stanbury's yard we stood oblivious of the Exmoor sleet, munching with precision and husbanding crumbs in the hollow of the hand. And all the time, beyond the slim bars of the threatened window, we watched the blue and crimson flames of apple logs light up the dim interior, and cocked an ear for the banter of the prefects responding to one of Mrs. Stanbury's jests.

It was a scene made up of contrasts. Inside the kitchen it was warm and cozy, and outside, exposed to the full force of the gale, it was cheerless, or would have been but for the contented expressions on the faces of a hundred munching boys balanced on ridges of granite that divided the farmyard into a delta of sludge. There was contrast too in the general appearance of the customers. Above the knee they all had a Sunday look, neat, well-brushed jackets, spotless Eton collars, scrubbed faces and plastered-down hair, while below the knee the race across the gravestones and through the miry yard had left them spattered with the midden. Usually our faces were turned toward the window, where a little of the comfort within reached out into the open and the rise and fall of Mrs. Stanbury's burr and full-throated chuckle came to us as a benediction, the like of which we had not received in church. One and all we loved her, for her baking, her credit, and the sly gleams of humor she shed on Sunday.

She was one of us, attached by that stampede over the graves of dead Stanburys to what she referred to as "Sku-ell." For her, "Sku-ell" was a city, the capital of her world, the change house of successive generations. She knew everybody's nickname and everybody's attainments. Sometimes I think she knew everybody's potential and could have selected, with far greater accuracy than the headmaster, those among us who would be likeliest to succeed in politics or in commerce, those who would make good husbands and those who needed watching. Nobody who took part in that graveyard race and stood before her window ever forgot her. They forgot each other but not Mrs. Stanbury, the weekly dispenser of hot pies, hot pasties, and threats of legal action concerning her kitchen glass.

Every time I sink my teeth into a hot pasty or an apple turnover I think first of brown varnish and then of Mrs. Stanbury. Not surprisingly these flavors are linked, the one exorcising the other. Only a few indecipherable scratches remain on the backrest of the pew opposite my seat in that church but Mrs. Stanbury triumphed over her exertions and finally retired. There must be a connection between longevity and lifelong association with hungry, sermon-dazed boys. Perhaps the spectacle of seeing generations account for the results of a day's baking in ten minutes flat rescued her from the dangers of gluttony and kept her as vigorous into her seventies. That, and the tremendous prospect of standing in her kitchen to pounce upon and sue the very first boy to fly through her shattered window and roll at the feet of the privileged.

By Courtesy of Isaac

Charles Dickens, who began his career as a Parliamentary reporter, is said to have declared that acquiring a knowledge of shorthand was equivalent, in terms of effort, to learning six foreign languages.

I do not know what form of shorthand Dickens used. When he began to practice as a reporter, Isaac Pitman, the patron saint of private secretaries and the business men who delight in pinching their pretty posteriors, was a young man evolving his system and Pitman did a very great deal to simplify the art of recording verbatim speech. I owe him much, but not on account of the role he played in equipping me for a profession. I passed out at eighty words a minute, and subsequently increased my speed to about a hundred and twenty words a minute, but Isaac could never have decoded more than a word or two of my squiggled accounts of court proceedings, political speeches, and thunderous evangelical sermons. I took outrageous liberties with his system and evolved a shorthand of my own.

My debt to him is of an entirely different kind. He led me, unwittingly perhaps, into some very pleasant pastures in the year 1928–29, for the commercial college I attended on leaving school had but three male students and perhaps three score potentially accessible inamoratas, any one of whom was capable of distracting a susceptible seventeen-year-old from learning how to distinguish a hook *r* from a hook *l*, or a thick stroke from a thin. Could it possibly matter in that kind of company? Is it any wonder that my progress, in a room spilling over with Thisbes, Isoldes, Juliets, Helens, Lauras and Cleopatras was slow, that my attention wandered a little or that my principal, a conscientious man, had doubts concerning my fitness to sit for the qualifying examinations at the end of that first term?

There are some days that lie luxuriating in the memory like lazy surfeited guests too charming to be told they have over-stayed their welcome. The day I enrolled at Fulford's Business College is one of them, a still, golden time in mid-September, when schooldays were done and the business of earning a living was indefinitely postponed. It was then, I recall, that I yearned for a rich and indulgent relative who had never learned how to debase the currency of youth and was still willing to invest in it to the tune of, say, a couple of hundred a year, to continue until I qualified. Had such a godmother presented herself I should have been there yet, a graying, balding lotus-eater at the feet of Isaac Pitman. She did not, of course, and I had to make the best of nine fleeting months with a couple of mediocre passes in shorthand and typing at the end of them, and a grudging second-class cer-tificate in bookkeeping. I can type, and I did, as I say, master shorthand to some degree, but that bookkeeping certificate was a polite forgery on the part of an excessively kindhearted tutor.

We are not here, however, to discuss the commercial arts. That first day, I remember, I was hard-pressed to keep my at-tention focused on the elementary *p*'s, *b*'s, *chay*'s and *gay*'s, on the *st* loop and the *shun* hook. It was easier to raise my head from the exercise and repeat, soundlessly, the vowel key sentence, "P*a*-m*a*y-w*e*-*a*ll-g*o*-t*oo*!" for if I half-closed my eyes in simu-lated concentration I could see miracles that would have ban-ished all thoughts of his system from Isaac Pitman's mind had he witnessed them before he grew that Old Testament beard, and even later if, like me, he had been lately released from the monas-tic seclusion of a Spartan community on Exmoor. Most of those miracles have slipped through the net of the years leaving noth-ing but a few crystals of wonder, but a handful remain, trophies of William Wordsworth's inward eye and bliss of solitude.

There was, for instance, the sunbeam on a blond curl that had escaped from Ena's bandeau, a spectacle worth at least a dozen

FOR MY OWN AMUSEMENT

"P*a*-m*a*y-we-*a*ll-g*o*-t*oo*"s, and perhaps a brace of its traveling
companion, "Th*a*t-p*e*n-*i*s-n*o*t-m*u*ch-g*o*o*d." And besides Ena,
given to looking over her shoulder, was Muriel, who had jet-
tisoned the bandeau in favor of an Eton crop and had the coquetry to go along with it. To Muriel's left, praise God, was
Jacqueline, all fluff and freckles, and to the right Barbara, whose
interest in Mr. Pitman was clearly flagging, for every now and
again she extracted a lipstick from an enormous handbag, made
some slight adjustment to her Cupid's bow, and then glanced
through a sheaf of holiday snapshots, one of which she was kind
enough to let fall. It was, of course, a snapshot of her in a one-
piece bathing suit of the kind then worn by the Mack Sennett
girls. She never asked for it back and I have it still, the one solid
dividend of that day's silent communion with Isaac.

I asked for no more than to sit there, a shy and silent Brigham
Young getting his second wind before making up his mind who
should accompany him to Utah. The choice was not easy, nor
was it simplified by the arrival of the demure Stella, whose per-
fume and comparative maturity drove Isaac and all his works
right out of mind. For Stella, nineteen and classic-featured, was
an instructress, who bent low over the desk and smilingly deprived me of my pencil in order to illustrate the intricate subtlety
of grammalogues and the effortless grace of phrasing. Stella's
flow of instruction reached me like the murmur of an Arcadian
stream. On her softly compressed lips "P*a*-m*a*y-we-*a*ll-g*o*-t*oo*"
sounded like the laughter of nymphs bathing under Mount Pel-
eus. Her rendering of "Th*a*t-p*e*n-*i*s-n*o*t-m*u*ch-g*o*o*d" was exquis-
ite, a line sung to the accompaniment of lute and lyre, and had
I been her sole backward pupil I doubt if I should have progressed far beyond the diphthong. As it was she could devote all
too little time to me, for Fred and George clamored for her.
They too were having difficulty with their suffixes.

It was a garden where no weeds grew, where, almost every
new day, you could discover new and rarer flowers. Our orchestra was the rattle of the typewriter and the ping of the carriage
bell. Assiduously we stenciled and gamboled in about equal pro-

portions, and all the time the sun played its gentle teasing game with Ena's curl. Muriel continued to glance archly over her shoulder, Jacqueline's freckles multiplied, Barbara made methodical adjustments to her Cupid's bow, and Stella, high priestess of that enchanting establishment, continued to move among us, incanting her litany of key vowels and occasionally laying a cool hand on mine to guide a stumbling pencil that stumbled more on that account.

This state of near-trance did not endure for more than a day or so, but Isaac, bless his hirsute memory, had many other delights in store for his disciple. Toward the end of the week, Muriel, boldest of his acolytes, smiled and dropped a lid on her hazel eye in a way that seemed to me to make light of grammalogues, whereas Jacqueline, catching my admiring glance, blushed so that her freckles went in as though it was coming on to rain. Soon we were all on Christian-name terms, and I would not have thought it possible that I could make such haste to the station each morning for fear of missing the nine-twenty-five that carried me and my homework to Isaac's shrine each weekday.

The ritual of that place had none of the rigidity I had found in other temples of instruction. One could move unchallenged between desks, unclogging the clubbed keys of Barbara's Remington, feeding a stencil into the rollers of Jacqueline's Underwood, seeking an interpretation of ambiguous squiggles on Muriel's notebook and sometimes, during a lull in the stream of devotions, communing one with another on the world outside, the king's illness and convalescence at Bognor Regis, Sir Henry Seagrave's new land record of 231 m.p.h. in the *Golden Arrow*, Paul Robeson's rendering of "Ol' Man River," and the prospect of giving Isaac the slip when spring came round and seeking our own river where boats, they said, could be hired at sixpence an hour. Our increasing familiarity with Isaac's loops and hooks made written communication easy and intimate. We were among the first since the ancient Egyptians, I imagine, to exchange vows in hieroglyphics and once I even caught myself writing an ode to my mistress's eyebrows in characters that Shakespeare would have found unintelligible, although Isaac might have deciphered a couplet here and there where "delight" mingled with "excite" and "dear" with "near."

The examinations came round with all their tremulous excitement and over-modest protestations of failure. "I had to use gallons of donkey-blood" (typescript erasure fluid) "on Para Two . . ."; "I couldn't read a word I had written but I remembered the dictation, wasn't I lucky . . . ?" And Stella's softly voiced refrain that is the theme song of that place—"So feed into the typewriter that the dull side of the carbon faces the operator . . ." Squeals and groans when the results were published. A sly celebration in a threesome skiff with Muriel and Jackie. A coffee and bun in the most fashionable restaurant in town and the ostentatious deposit of a threepenny tip for the waitress.

And then it was behind me, like school and the nursery, an Alma Mater I can never pass, notwithstanding hideous traffic risks, without a fond, sidelong glance, so that I do not see Isaac Pitman as most people see him, full-bearded and serious-eyed, the embodiment of the mid-Victorian cult of earnestness and self-help, but as Puck, the faun whose mission it was to open all the windows on commerce and infuse a tender theme into the metallic rattle of the typewriter. Sleep well, Father Isaac, wherever you are. You were a poet in spite of yourself.

Under the Cloche Hat

I

West Buckland, like every school of its kind, was necessarily a monastic establishment. Ordinarily we did not so much as exchange speculative glances with an eligible female from the time we boarded the train at our nearest main station, until the moment we were dumped there thirteen weeks later, on the first day of the holidays.

A very great deal has been written concerning the enclosed aspect of public-school life, with emphasis on the sinister atmosphere segregation of this kind is likely to produce. In the interests of truth I have to state that I saw no evidence at all of homosexuality during my schooldays. Maybe I was lucky. Or maybe it was so exposed on that high, windy ridge that romantic friendships withered in the Exmoor downdraft before they could mature. There was, I recall, a little innocent ragging about associations between seniors and juniors, but I would take my oath they fell far short of the charges leveled at larger, more famous schools in the last few years, mostly, I suspect, by memoir writers and novelists with a hopeful eye on the best-seller lists. A majority of the two hundred-odd adolescents with whom I shared this period were hard at work cultivating more conventional relationships through the post with schoolgirls encountered during the holidays, and there was often a pooling of experience arising from a communal recognition of handwriting when letters in a girlish hand (sometimes in scented envelopes) were

flipped the length of the breakfast table when mail was distributed. A little blonde who was writing regularly to me would use
a large, blue envelope with heavy gold edging, and the entire
house grew interested in her, supposing her to be a person of
some consequence on this account. Her letters usually arrived
on my plate spotted with prefects' porridge.

The secretive among us would make great efforts to evade this
kind of publicity, but there were others who took pleasure in
boasting of their conquests, displaying photographs and sometimes reading their letters aloud. I sometimes wondered if this
happened at girls' boarding schools, and the unworthy thought
did something to moderate the tone of the protestations I dispatched to various quarters of the realm.

In the main, I think, we idealized women. Jokes and quips of
the cruder variety were usually reserved for masters' wives, or
the odd young woman, buxom, red-faced and broad of beam,
whom we met in the farmyards within easy walking distance of
the school. We tended to think of girls our own age as fragile,
ethereal beings, like the heroines in paintings by the Pre-Raphael-
ites, and in this sense we were a long way behind the times. As
I was to discover within a few months of leaving school, the girl
of the nineteen-twenties was anything but ethereal, but the discovery, once you adjusted to it, was a relief. They were, in fact,
a lively, vivacious, captivating, capricious breed, and the collective word for them—*flapper*—suited them very well.

The high noon of the flapper lasted for about a decade, from
the early twenties until the early thirties, after which the genus
suddenly disappeared, like the unfashionable bosom of the period.
Somehow the flapper was unable to survive the frenetic period of
the middle and late thirties, when Hitler went on the rampage
and the young became gloomily obsessed with politics.

Few under twenty gave a damn about politics until the Slump
of 1931. All through the twenties the teen-agers I met were content to live each day as a separate existence, and this despite a
shortage of jobs and a standard of wages that would bring industry to a standstill today. Rightly so, I might add, for every-

where one looked in those days one saw injustice and inequality of the kind that threw a shadow over the late Victorian and Edwardian eras. Despite this, however, there was an air of flirtatious triviality, and a zest for the passing moment, that seems to have deserted us all in an era when the young enjoy licenses that would have appalled their parents forty years ago. Whenever I hear that protest song, the one that fathered so many successors, I am tempted to add a verse beginning, "Where has all the gaiety gone . . . ?"

I remember them all so well, those cloche-hatted flappers, epitomized by the Hollywood "It" girl, Clara Bow, on whom the late-comers modeled themselves. They were the first generation in the West who could walk abroad wearing makeup without being regarded as tarts, the first to have made available to them a supply of cheap, ready-made garments that had dash, style and individuality, the first, probably, who would cheerfully date a boyfriend without thought of marriage. They were thus social pioneers, but pioneers without a specific goal or a cause, and this made any kind of association with them exciting, colorful and inconsequential. Their skirts, after 1926, were nearly as brief as the micro-mini-skirt of the late nineteen-sixties, and they had, as a rule, pretty, twinkling legs, even if their shape as a whole was odd by today's standards, losing its sex-appeal an inch above the bottom to become rather squarish and sexless as far as the shoulders.

This, of course, was due to the abdication of the pinched waist and the bosom, so dear to their mothers and grandmothers. From around 1926, until the early nineteen-thirties, there wasn't a waist or a bosom to be found outside a graveyard, where they were the prerogative of smug-looking angels perched on expensive marble tombstones. The popular dresses of the period fell in a straight line to the hips, and if your appraisal of a flapper had been limited to her middle section you might just as well have been looking at a boy.

This boyish look was emphasized by the frantic shearing of tresses that began about 1924. First the bob, considered recklessly daring by its innovators (I knew a girl who cried all night after submitting to the scissors), then the shingle, that removed nearly all the hair from the back of the head, and finally, in 1926, the Eton crop, that was not so popular as its two forerunners. Later on, a reaction to the Eton crop introduced the page-boy bob, with hair combed straight down and curled under in a roll, and a year or so after that the long bob, the last individual hair style of the genuine flapper. In all the styles the fringe was popular and sometimes the Victorian kiss-curl, added as an afterthought. Long boots, when they became popular in the mid-sixties, were reckoned kinky, but they were no more than a revival of the "Russian" boots worn by many of the flappers and wholly approved by the male. Within this over-all framework, however, there were many substyles that had their day, sometimes quite a long day. One, I recall, was the pinafore frock, usually worn with a beret. Another was the bolero. A third was the sunray skirt, with its galaxy of pleats.

The flapper had absolutely no pretensions about being devious, intelligent or ambitious, and herein, I think, lay her charm. She was content to be feminine and made the very most of her physical endowments, with no specific aim other than to attract a man physically and encourage him to make the running. Looking back, their renunciation of all other designs seems at one with the Victorian girl, but this was the only thing they had in common with their grandmothers. They knew and cared nothing about what was going on outside the world of sheet music, the fashion houses, scandal in high places and, to a degree, the internal-combustion engine. Very few of them bothered with books or newspapers, but they devoured an avalanche of twopenny magazines and usually had one protruding from the outer flap of their patent-leather handbags. They used a great deal of slang, and the words they used sound very archaic today. A film was a "flick," and a fast operator was "mustard" who "qualified for the Wandering Hand Society." Words like "topping" and "spiffing" signified their approval, but I do not recall their equivalent for "square" or "grotty." Mostly they left their sentences unfinished for want of a terminal point, their enthusiasm boosting them from one subject to another in a series of short, breathless rushes. In short, if you were looking for a soul mate among them you were wasting good mating time. They believed vaguely in God but would have shown embarrassment if you mentioned Him or His works. Parsons made them giggle. They were inclined to switch on an aggrieved expression if you tried to test their political opinions, as if politics were slightly indecent in mixed company. They were all excellent ballroom dancers but very few of them could drive or swim, although they enjoyed pillion-riding and prancing about beaches in skirted, one-piece bathing costumes. In every way they went to great lengths to proclaim their new freedoms, but there is a curious contradiction here, for they responded warmly to old-fashioned courtesies on the part of the male and were overwhelmed if you sent them flowers or a poem or a thinly disguised Valentine card. A verse or two of homemade poetry, composed in their honor, was almost certain to advance your cause, and they were alert to good manners and chivalric displays in public. For all that there were very few fools among them and the great majority knew precisely how many beans made five when it came to dispensing favors after dark. I would say that they occupied a position exactly halfway between their Victorian ancestors and the young women of today who proclaim their sex liberation almost nightly on television.

2

She was walking slowly along the esplanade on a Good Friday reconnaissance, gray beret perched at a provocative angle over her right ear. Her dark hair swept in a smooth curve down the other side of her face, the "Pola Negri" or "Vamp" style, that was in vogue about the time I quitted the Exmoor monastery and began to look about me and see what I had been missing up there. I had not had sufficient time to learn the conventional gambits so she willingly helped me out, as flappers usually did with beginners. She approached me and demanded to know the time.

We went down the slipway and along the deserted beach, exchanging tidbits of information about ourselves, and she gave me careful instructions where to be at a certain time in the vicinity of her home that same evening, adding that I was not, on any account, to show myself but was to use the cover offered by her father's macrocarpa hedge.

This throws into relief a curious technique the flapper used on these occasions. She liked to pretend to herself that she was still lumbered with a chaperon, that watchful parents were jealously concerned for her honor, as though she was contemplating elopement with a fortune-hunting scoundrel. It was pure fiction, of course. Even in the mid-twenties the new freedoms were beginning to have an impact on parents but the pretense added spice to assignations.

I met her at the appointed hour and we walked out of range of the macrocarpa, exchanging rather formal kisses modeled on the silent-film close-ups we had studied, and endearments borrowed from the same medium. Then she did a curious thing that went some way to erasing the Pre-Raphaelite image I had of young women up to that period. Solemnly, almost ritualistically, she shed one of her beaded garters, presenting it to me as a keepsake and a reminder of our first meeting and doing it so artlessly that it would have seemed preposterous to put an improper construction on the gift.

It was, as I see now, a typical flapper gesture, proclaiming not wantonness but liberation, and I accepted it clumsily, wondering anxiously where I could conceal it when I arrived home. I wish I knew what became of that green, beaded garter. It would qualify as an interesting period exhibit now that garters have followed the farthingale.

Betty, the first of them as far as I was concerned, had her

declaration of independence, symbolized by her beaded garter, but they all had something original to offer. That is to say, they did not rely exclusively on their charm, plus a few shillings' worth of cosmetics, a "Pola Negri" hair style, and an off-the-peg jumper suit or pinafore frock. They put as much imagination into the business of projecting themselves as a modern commercial concern buying time on television. They each had a gimmick.

The word was not in circulation in those days, but it must have been on the etymological drawing board, for it is by their individual gimmicks, woven into the pattern of their several personalities, that I distinguish them one from the other. What they had to sell was very marketable at that time—gaiety, infectious optimism, and any number of lighthearted embraces and stylized end-of-film kisses. Seldom much more, but we, their escorts, did not quarrel with this. It was that kind of society in the late twenties. We weren't out looking for trouble, and a deep emotional involvement meant trouble on an impossibly low budget, so that although we were well aware the flappers were leading us up the garden path we did not hold it against them when they slammed the summerhouse door.

Muriel's gimmick was a shy, downcast glance that passed for modesty among those but slightly acquainted with her, but she had something far more practical in reserve. It was her mother's hard, shiny, imitation-leather couch, a mute but extremely vigilant chaperon on the occasions you were invited into the front parlor after a dance at the Church Hall or Institute. I swear that couch was human. As long as you conducted yourself like a gentleman it stayed neutral, but at the least show of ardor it projected you straight onto the floor, the rapid movement inevitably reducing romance to farce. Muriel was, of course, well aware of this and exploited the propellent properties of that couch shamelessly. So, I think, must Sweeny Todd have regarded his barber's chair, an ultimate in secret weapons.

Gwen was more sophisticated. She could play ragtime and although she was very pretty, and fairly forthcoming under the stars, my tenderest recollections of her were not, as one might imagine, the moments we danced together or sat out in the Plantation, but the occasions when she asked you into the house, sat down and rattled off "Old Nebraska," "Valencia" and "Swanee" on her upright piano. She had a way of looking at you over her shoulder as her fingers skimmed the keys, and although her glance might be said to have contained promise, it was veiled in mockery. She was using that piano to keep you at arms' length. In my mind's eye I can never picture Gwen without her walnut piano, just as I can never see Muriel out of range of her slippery couch.

Cis and Kathy had color fixations. I cannot recall Cis ever appearing in anything but pink, or Kathy wearing anything but royal purple. Cis was one of the few flappers who did not succumb to the beret but went right on wearing a cloche hat beyond the turn of the decade. They were usually of pink straw or velour and they suited her very well, for she was a dainty little brunette, with fine brown eyes. The hat acted as a kind of arbor from which she could survey you without committing herself. Kathy always looked regal in her purple dance frocks and was more dress-conscious than most flappers. She was an expert dancer and was anxious to teach you all the latest steps, showing the greatest forbearance when you steered her into a collision or stood on her toes.

Perhaps the most authentic flapper I ever consorted with, however, was Esther, who insisted on spelling her name Esta. Esta had gone to tremendous pains to absorb the "Pola Negri–Theda Bara–Clara Bow" techniques, for she somehow succeeded in combining the nonchalance of the vamps and the allure of the famous "It" girl. The circumstances of our first meeting are typical of the way Esta went about things. She was standing on the pier, propped against one of those machines that stamp names on strips of tin. Her dark hair ("Bible-black," Dylan Thomas would have called it) was Marcel-waved, and the undulations were exposed by the extreme tilt of the almost inevitable gray beret, in her case worn so far back on her head that it was in danger of falling into the sea. It was an obvious ploy on my part to set the pointer, stamp my name, and then pretend to ignorance as to how one extracted the strip of tin from the machine. When, in her estimation, a sufficient number of seconds had elapsed and she had subjected me to a careful and expressionless scrutiny, she reached out very slowly, pulled the ejector lever and smiled. It was the smile of a tolerant mother indulging an enterprising three-year-old. It was also the beginning of a very rewarding holiday.

Esta had set her heart on a Decca Gramophone and to get it she was obliged to assemble a thousand Kensitas coupons. That first day she enlisted me in the crusade and I smoked Kensitas, much against my will, for close on a year, after which she wrote and told me she was deeply committed to a boy working in Germany and the correspondence between us must now cease. I could never decide whether this decision on her part was dictated by the fact that she was in love or by the arrival of the long-awaited Decca Gramophone.

3

I was relatively inexperienced then and still had a great deal to learn about flappers and flapper techniques, but I was an earnest pupil and I enjoyed my work. One of the first things that impressed me about their techniques was the gap between promise and performance. The flapper pulled out all the stops except the essential ones, so that one never lost the impression, even in the company of the boldest among them that, whilst they worked hard at persuading you they regarded mother's advice and the Gypsy's warning as old hat, one was left in no doubt that they had pondered and approved both. This provided them with a kind of yardstick to measure the dishonorable intentions of every man in the world and rarely failed them in an emergency. They would, for instance, never venture beyond a couple of small ports, or one glass of rough cider, and they had a way of classifying their escorts into categories, all the way down from the too ardent to the impossibly dull. For someone who had spent three years in the exclusive company of males it was a testing apprenticeship and conclusions about the way in which the feminine mind worked were hard to come by. Gradually, however, one learned by trial and error, and it was an enriching experience, particularly for someone like me, bent on earning a living by writing fiction. And because I still live within a few miles of the parks, lanes, beaches, cliff walks, sea-front shelters and front parlors where all these encounters occurred forty years ago, there has been for me a rewarding bonus. Every now and again, in a surge around a Christmas counter, in a supermarket, on a station platform, or in a crowded café, I see a face I can identify, the face of one of those adorable flappers, and a glimpse of any one of them leads me to contemplate what the newspaper and TV pundits call the Generation Gap. It occurs to me then that this too is an illusion, for the gap is so certain to close that there is no profit whatever in making a song and dance about it. For there they are, these quiet-spoken, well-dressed, carefully corseted grandmothers, buying toys or cereals or raspberry sundaes for grandchildren, or seeing grown sons and daughters aboard the London train. Sometimes we exchange greetings or a half-smile but not often, for our associations were brief and none of us were concerned with putting down roots at that time. It is best, I think, to savor the past without exhuming it, to hear behind the clatter of café china and the hiss of the departing Golden Hind, the toot of saxophone and the click of heel taps on frosty pavements, when these elegant matriarchs were bobbed and shingled and babbling happily about "topping" bands and the "spiffing" time they had had at the British Legion dance.

It is in the frame of the dance hall that I remember them best, as they were when I had hair on my head, for it was there that their spirits soared like champagne corks and promised romantic ecstasies through an eternity of youth. The one thing that puzzles me about them is the location of the moment in time when their transformation began, when they stopped being flappers and began to train as matriarchs. Perhaps it was the day the last notes of the Jazz Age were drowned in the diatribes of the

Führer and the vaporings of the Duce. Or perhaps it was the day they fell in love.

4

As I say, the cult of flappery did not long survive the Great Slump. Pola Negri and Clara Bow passed into legend. Tilted berets, cloche hats, bobs and shingles went out of fashion, to become symbols of the Charleston era. Skirts came down below the knee, to remain there, alas, for a whole generation and then soar again like the end of a long night. But here and there a lonely flapper survived, recognizable by her glances, her mixture of pertness and archness and, above all, by her techniques in beguiling men. It was my destiny to meet one in dramatic circumstances on a warm summer night in the year 1941, by which time the flapper had become almost as dated as the Victorian masher.

I was hitch-hiking back to an R.A.F. camp in the Midlands after an unauthorized weekend leave. Because I had no pass the time factor was important and traffic was disappointingly light. To increase my anxiety, some idiot in the Tewkesbury area inadvertently rang a church bell, and church bells in those days signified invasion. There I was, forty miles south of my station, without a pass and likely to qualify as a deserter when Nazis parachuted into the shire. At last a car stopped and offered me a lift to within a mile or two of my camp and I scrambled in very gratefully. It was driven by a young civilian, and his passenger was a very pretty girl whose angled beret reminded me of happier days. The young man was one of those motorists out to prove something—perhaps a belief in their own im-mortality—by driving at high speed on sidelights but it was a brilliantly moonlit night and we made good progress until we ran between a belt of trees into deep shadow. Here, before he could switch on his masked headlights, we collided head-on with a herd of cows straying on the highway.

The impact was savage. One cow was killed and another injured. The car was badly damaged and the driver and myself stumbled around in a dazed condition, wondering how to set about clearing the road. For a few moments neither of us were much concerned with the girl, but then we saw her, wandering unconcernedly around the wreckage. She was humming snatches of a currently popular musical-comedy song and seemed totally detached from the incident, as though she had been a spectator rather than a passenger in the car. "The radiator has taken a frightful beating," she announced, cheerfully. And then, "Silly cows."

Her detachment was fatal to the driver's self-control. He blurted out that the car had been borrowed from his father's garage without permission and that the wounded cow in the ditch was not alone in needing the service of a humane killer. I thought the girl would be touched, but she wasn't. All she said in reply was, "There's a lane there leading to a farm. These will be that farmer's cows. We'll roust him out and get some transport. It's getting a bit late, isn't it?"

Her self-possession hypnotized me. I went with her down the lane beyond the trees and into a brilliant patch of moonlight, where she stopped and fumbled with her handbag. "Derek's sweet but upset," she said. "Could you hold this a moment?" and I found myself angling a pencil torch and a hand mirror whilst she applied fresh lipstick. Comment and action were so typical of the flapper that I felt myself whirled back to 1928 and was not in the least surprised when she tucked her arm cozily through mine, squeezed my hand, and drew me on toward the farm buildings. I wasn't sure what was expected of me. It seemed to me hard on Derek that he should wreck his father's car and lose his girl friend to a stray airman all in one night, and a moonlit night at that, but I soon discovered she was far more concerned with her strategy than with me. She said, as we knocked on the farmhouse door, "Don't say a word about the cows. Not yet."

The farmer appeared with his pajama jacket tucked into his trousers and she flashed him a smile that would have compensated any man alive for the inconvenience of being dragged from sleep at two A.M.

"We've had a slight accident," she said, "back on the main road. Nobody hurt. Could we use your phone?"

The man said he would brew some tea and as soon as he had disappeared into the kitchen she lifted the receiver and asked for a number. It struck me as curious that she should have the number of the local policeman so pat but not nearly so odd as her greeting when the callee came on the line. She said, in a soft, dear-old-bean voice, "*Keith,* darling? Sorry to spoil your beauty sleep but I'm in a jam. I've pranged about half a mile south of the 'Haymaker.' Be a cherub and fetch me, there's a dear." She listened for a moment and then replaced the receiver. "He'll be along in twenty minutes. I'll see to the tea while you ring the policeman. Tell him to bring a butcher with a humane killer." She drifted away while I made the call. The policeman was less cooperative than Keith.

I suppose, until then, I had misjudged her, assuming that I would be the one to explain to the hospitable farmer the true nature of the accident back at the spot where Derek was contemplating suicide. When we had finished our tea, however, she said, equably, "Thank you. That was lovely. It was cows, straying all over the road. Black and white cows. They materialized out of nowhere . . ." The farmer did not wait for her to finish. He shouted "Jesus Christ!" and was gone in a flash. We heard his gumboots thumping on the surface of the lane and when the sound had died away she said, in the same equable voice, "Poor Derek. He seems *so* upset. Come along then, I shall insist Keith runs you back to camp. What a lovely night, isn't it?"

She tucked her arm through mine in the coziest manner and we went out and down the lane to the main road. Lights and figures were bobbing about and there was a continuous rumble of conversation. Keith arrived five minutes later and the girl and I jammed ourselves into his two-seater. Derek did not accompany us. He had business with the policeman and said good-bye ruefully. The girl blew him a kiss. Another typically flapper gesture.

Some Well-meant Advice
to Postal Wooers

The cozy practice of bundling, so long practiced in Wales by courting couples pressed for time and separated by distances, is no longer in vogue. It had, indeed, been long discontinued when I had need of it.

They tell of young men working in remote country districts walking miles after laying down their tools to enjoy bundling sessions into the small hours, when, presumably, the hardy fellows would start back, to be on hand for work in the morning. It says a good deal for the ardor and steadfastness of the early Victorian Welshman. If he would go to these lengths to spend a couple of hours beside a girl sewn up in a bag, it is not surprising that his descendants had the strength of mind to take over the BBC, the British banking system, and most of the lucrative posts in the T.U.C. and the Parliament at Westminster.

Today, I imagine, the practice of bundling has been rendered obsolete, even in the remotest of districts, by the availability of the secondhand car and higher wages earned by couples contemplating marriage. Very little courting, I would say, is practiced nowadays on foot. In the minds of the young, mobility takes precedence over everything, including romance. For my part, I was lucky enough to be on hand for the earliest stage of the used-car boom, but this did not solve the worst of my difficulties, the two hundred-odd miles between East Devon, where I lived and worked, and South Manchester, where my fiancée, May, had her home. In any case, several courting years had passed before I acquired a battered Austin Seven and in the interval the only means available to effect a meeting was the London, Midland and Scottish Railway.

The fare from Exeter to London Road, Manchester, was thirty shillings and sixpence in those days. I remember this particularly, because, at the time of my first trips, I was earning thirty shillings a week and had to scratch around for the odd sixpence on Friday night before I could buy the return ticket. I always traveled to Manchester overnight, leaving at ten-twenty and arriving at London Road about six A.M., the journey including a longish stop at Crewe, where I sometimes think I must have spent about a third of my life.

Occasionally, very occasionally, May would travel south to Exeter, but we eventually worked out an ingenious system of saving time and money by taking advantage of the numerous football excursions to London that started from Exeter and Manchester simultaneously and cost a mere ten and sixpence. On these occasions we would rendezvous at Euston or Paddington, according to the time of arrival of our respective trains, but London had little to recommend it as a trysting place for courting couples who were not resident in the capital. The parks were available, of course, but as we had both been traveling all night we found it something of a strain to spend an entire day walking the graveled paths and as for privacy, the Welsh bundlers were far better off than we were, even in a two-roomed Welsh cottage. At least the parents below were in favor of the match.

We enjoyed those football excursions nevertheless. We would linger over innumerable coffees in one of the three Corner Houses, visit museums and art galleries, and take advantage of a seat placed opposite a celebrated mummy or a famous painting. And always, before the day was over, we took a tube to the Tower of London, the Bloody Tower and the Byward Tower being two places where a limited amount of privacy was available, particularly in the slack part of the day. The Beefeaters, I discovered, were far more tolerant than the park-patrolling Metropolitan policemen of those days, who seemed to have received special instructions regarding provincial courting couples. The Permissive Society was a long way ahead of us and policemen always scrutinized us as if they were trying to relate our faces to photographs in the police files.

On these excursions I sometimes approached the physical hardihood of the veteran bundler, cycling the twelve miles from Exmouth to Exeter, traveling overnight to Paddington, walking about the capital all day, traveling back to Exeter by night, and cycling home again at four A.M. on Sunday morning. May, for her part, showed equal determination. She made the two journeys by night and on her return walked four miles from London Road station to her suburb in South Manchester. Courting in those days was hard on the pocket. It was harder still on the feet.

This period in our lives lasted four years, and during that time British railway stock must have taken a small, upward leap. We saw one another, on the average, about six times a year but on only eight occasions during that time were we able to enjoy each other's company for more than a few hours. This was when we went off somewhere for a holiday, to the Lakes, to North Wales where we met, or to a southeastern resort, a daring thing to do in the early thirties. Finally, we got engaged on the battlefield of Hastings, and I like to think that the shade of Harold, himself an extremely energetic traveler (he covered the distance between Stamford Bridge, in Yorkshire, and Pevensey, in Sussex, at an average speed of thirty-two miles per day) added his blessing.

When, in 1934, I acquired the Austin Seven, I mistakenly thought our distance problem was largely overcome. An early Austin Seven would do more than forty miles to the gallon, and petrol at that time could be bought for one and a penny a gallon, but the car was already elderly and it did not do to press her along. Whenever I did, one of three things happened: either the carburetor needle stuck, and I would have to loosen it and blow bubbles into the chamber until it cleared; or I would get a puncture; or, for some inexplicable reason, the horn would sound without my assistance and begin a long, high-pitched, uninterrupted note that must have infuriated hundreds of sleepy families

in the villages of Gloucestershire, Worcestershire and Derby-
shire through which I passed. I soon learned to take it leisurely
and once, on a return trip, I was fifteen hours driving from
Cheshire to the Devon coast.

It will thus be seen that we were obliged to do most of our
courting through the medium of the Post Office. In the period
under review, actually from autumn 1931 until we married in the
spring of 1936, we exchanged an estimated total of five hundred
and twenty-five letters apiece—that is to say, an average of about
three each week, not including parcels and postcards. I am sure
this is not a record. Some couples I knew wrote to one another
every day, but all the same it was no mean achievement. With
stamps at three halfpence apiece we invested a further seven
pounds in romance, a sum equivalent to fourteen football excursions.

There is a good deal to be said for postal wooing. It develops
both the handwriting and habit of marshaling one's thoughts on
paper. When you haven't seen your fiancée for months, and are
still concerned with keeping her interested, you are required to
exercise a good deal of ingenuity. As a professional yarn spinner
the correspondence was part of my long apprenticeship. In addition, it must not be imagined that an interminable exchange of
letters is a tedious occupation, even for those who are not looking
for marginal benefits. To begin with, it tends to reduce partici-
pants to a state of suspended animation, so that the very sight of
the postman is an occasion, like the appearance of funnel smoke
off the coast of a castaway's island, or the sound of distant bagpipes heard by the besieged garrison of Lucknow, or was it Arcot?
Moreover, in those days, there were three deliveries a day, even
in country districts, and no nonsense about first and second class.
The exchange of news and endearments was thus far more rapid
than it would be today. A letter posted in Manchester by seven
P.M. was virtually certain to drop through a Devon letter box by
noon the following day. This, I suspect, would be regarded as a
minor miracle in an era of landings on the moon.

There was another enlivening aspect, a kind of game to be

played one with the other. Tiffs were sometimes promoted by an ill-judged remark or omission and involuntarily prolonged, long after the heat had gone out of the exchange, the dispute being sustained by crossed letters. This, of course, added to the excitement surrounding the arrival of every new letter and sometimes the slightly counterfeit quarrel had to be terminated by a telephonic exchange.

We did not use the telephone as much as we might have done. May did not have one in the house (very few people did in the early thirties) and if we wanted direct communication it had to be done through a fixed call, booked to a call box. A telephone booth is not the most comfortable place to wait on a winter's night in Manchester, so we usually reserved this means of communication for briefing each other on the estimated times of arrival of the football excursions, information concerning a rendezvous, birthdays and the like.

It is generally accepted that one enjoys hard-earned cash more than a windfall, and this logic applies to those obliged to do their courting through the post. In other words, having each gone to so much trouble and expense to come within range of one another, postal wooers are not disposed to waste as much time in bickering as couples who live within bawling-out distance of one another. Every meeting is a great adventure, every parting a tragedy played on a low key. Marco Polo, embarking on an odyssey to Cathay, could not have been more braced and expectant than I when I lowered the misted carriage window and looked into a murky dawn, to discover that I had begun my vigil on a Crewe railway siding. Or when, rattling along at a steady thirty-two miles per hour, I passed through Matlock, saw a signpost to Cheadle or Stockport and realized that the long haul through the dark was almost over. Or, for that matter, when I passed the local railway station and noticed a poster advertising a ten-shilling excursion to watch Arsenal and West Bromwich Albion contend for the F.A. Cup. On these occasions I would tell myself that one day I would actually attend a professional football match.

In view of all this I feel qualified to give postal wooers of a later generation a few broad hints. If you are not in possession of private transport keep a close watch on British Rail announcements. By so doing, you can save yourself money, even nowadays. If one or other of you possesses a secondhand car, then in God's name, keep it serviced. Otherwise all manner of frustrations might beset you miles from nowhere in the middle of the night. If you are passing rich, and both of you possess private transport, then study the map of the British Isles very carefully and hit upon a halfway house, but if you do this be sure that it is set down in a depopulated area. Cities were not built with courting couples in mind. If, on the other hand, you are situated, as I was, in the first stage of the saga and limited, in the main, to dependence upon the postal service, then buy your stationery in bulk. If you exchange as many letters as we did over so long a period you might save enough for a down payment on the marriage bed.

PART THREE

Fleet Street in Lilliput

The Mandarins

In the early summer of 1929, with the world slump just over the horizon, I joined the staff of *The Exmouth Chronicle*, my father's weekly newspaper, as general reporter and spare-time ledger clerk. Times were hard, and my starting salary was five shillings a week, plus a withheld thirty more for board and lodging at home.

It seems, looking back, a modest sum, even for those pinch-penny days, but my father had not learned the knack of adjusting to the passage of years. To him the value of money was static and had he owned a vineyard he would have paid for labor at the rate of a penny a day, citing Holy Writ as a precedent. I was seventeen then, and he had gone out to work at twelve for about the same weekly sum as I received. His views concerning money survived another world war. Even in the early fifties it was difficult to persuade him that five pounds a week did not put a man in the supertax bracket.

At that time, Father was fifty-five and his obsession with the game of bowls coincided with a conviction that forty-three years of steady toil is as much as can be expected from a human being. He opted out, transferring the paper to me as though it had been a bicycle that required to be kept in reasonable running order, and I like to think this was a manifestation of faith in my latent ability as a journalist. Doubts regarding this, however, continue to linger in the mind. More probably he never gave a thought to the dangers and complexities of placing his destiny in the hands of a youth so utterly lacking in experience. The prospect of a libel suit had never cost him a moment's sleep. He had been walking hand-in-hand with libel and slander ever since he entered local politics at the age of twenty-one. By 1929 he and they were boon companions.

I learned by trial and error—the only way anyone can learn to be a newspaperman—and sometimes the element of error brought me within hailing distance of disaster. More often, however, it brought me into conflict with the local mandarins; for, whereas it was easy to learn the rules of evidence whilst attending sessions at the local Magistrates' Court, it was very difficult indeed to acquaint myself with the sensitive areas of the fifty-odd individuals who ranked as mandarins. They all had an Achilles' heel, and it was essential when interviewing them or reporting their speeches to know what would enlist them as patrons and what would incur their wrath. I soon learned to identify them and set about studying them in detail, a technique now discernible among stalwarts who interview national mandarins on television. In those days, however, there was little in common between Fleet Street men and small-town provincials like myself. The Fleet-Streeter could be, and often was, very cavalier with human material, basing his style on story value. The province-based reporter had to live with the people he wrote about, and I was never able to convey this sober fact to London news editors, who sometimes employed me on local stories that made national headlines.

I recall one occasion when an agency sent me to interview the son of a millionaire, whose father had just died in the Channel Islands, leaving a relatively untaxed fortune. The beneficiary, not unnaturally, refused to confirm that his father was a selfish capitalist, who had made his money in Britain and then escaped to Jersey to ensure that it did not find its way back to the Chancellor of the Exchequer, but he knew me by my Christian name and consented to give me an interview on the plans he had for building a model farm. In the morning an account of the interview, cunningly slanted to coincide with a newspaper's initial policy line, made original reading, particularly for me, the alleged source. The dead millionaire was pilloried once again and not a word concerning the model farm appeared in print.

For the next few days I waited for the mine to explode and sure enough it did, at a local charity ball, where the new millionaire was the principal guest. We met one another in a crowded dressing-room and pointing a derisory finger at me he roared, "Look at him! The Yellow Press lapdog! A scoundrel who would sell a fellow townsman for thirty pieces of silver!" It took me nearly a year, and the offices of several mutual friends, to get on speaking terms with him again, and talk him into subscribing to our local relief fund for the Gresford Colliery disaster.

Confrontations of this kind were rare, but during my apprenticeship period it was all too easy to tread on a mandarin's tail and start a chain reaction. The only certain way of avoiding trouble was to familiarize oneself with the full range of local eccentricities and foibles, to discover what made each mandarin tick and write accordingly.

In one of the best of his many short stories about English provincial life the novelist H. E. Bates describes a journalist's endeavors to examine, run down and expose the true character of a local worthy. The story is called *The Late Public Figure* and has, for me, great authenticity. The journalist's discoveries in this particular case were unflattering, and I would not like to imply that all our local mandarins had feet of clay. But the comparison is there nonetheless, for each one of them had a public face and a real face. If, like me, you sat at their feet for more than a decade, you could while many tedious hours away making guesses at the thoughts that were passing through their heads whilst the rhetoric poured from their mouths. You could do more than this. Soon you could see them as they had appeared to their school fellows forty-odd years before, how they were regarded by their families, and then make a guess at how much they were likely to tip waitresses who did not know them. The sum total of these informed guesses was rewarding, for sometimes you could assess them as fallible human beings instead of self-inflated figureheads, comic turns, or the platitudinous old bores that they sometimes seemed in public. As the years passed I mellowed toward them and when, one by one, they died, I was genuinely sorry. A Micawber, a Pickwick or a Quilp had been lost to me. Here and there, as I grew older, I made friends with survivors, for by then I had come to understand that they did what they did, not, as I had once assumed, from motives of self-aggrandizement, but from an instinctive desire to serve that lies buried in most Englishmen, particularly Englishmen rooted in the shires.

I can think of three who seem to me fairly representative of the kind of men who ran our town in those days, and I see them as standard-bearers for one or other of the sectors of town life I chronicled, day in and day out, for twelve years. There were many such sectors but those of local government, good works and the Church were three of the most important and often overlapped from my point of view.

There were, at that time, eighteen urban district Councillors, who conducted a monthly public meeting round the horseshoe table, presided over by the Chairman, our substitute for a mayor, and guided in their duties by the Town Clerk, with some assistance from the Town Surveyor and the Chief Financial Officer. The Councillors were divided into what I always thought of as progressives, who wanted the town to expand, and diehards, mostly retired residents, who opposed all changes. Collisions between these factions provided me with a monthly headline. Tremendous heat was generated round that horseshoe table from time to time, and the controversies, at this distance, look absurdly parochial. Should the railings round the Strand Enclosure be removed or strengthened? Should the tank and guns remain on the esplanade as a permanent reminder of the town's contribution to victory in 1918? Should we change over from gaslight in the streets to electric power?

The dynamic champion of change on all these occasions was the one member of the Council who proclaimed himself a working-man, a van driver by profession, and an unrepentant Socialist in days when British Socialists were suspected of being financed by the Kremlin. His name was Bert Humphries and he was a delightful character from my viewpoint, for he provoked any number of civic shouting matches, with the Chairman banging away with his gavel in a vain attempt to restore order and dignity to the chamber. Bert, however, did not have a spark of malice in his makeup and was always prepared to shake hands with all his opponents after the meeting. Chubby-faced, given to extravagant practical jokes, and inclined to corpulence even as a young man, he was Devon born and bred, and possessed a curiously offbeat West Country accent. He was the only man in town familiar with political theory and threatened us with the arrival of a Socialist millennium by 1940, at the latest 1941. Snatches of his genial rhetoric return to me: ". . . Milyons of workin' men won't be denied their rights . . ." "Here we are, back where we started out, time o' the universal franchise . . ." And sometimes, egged on by a sense of innocent fun, he would exaggerate his dialect, beat his chest and bellow, "You all know who I be! I'm 'Pudden' Humphries, born in the shadow of the gasworks!"

From the first I believed Bert to have a future in the national Socialist party and I was right. After countless melees in the Council chamber, exchanges that he always described, with his broad, schoolboy grin, as "spuddles," after innumerable victories on behalf of the locally oppressed, he gravitated to union official-dom and became a West Country organizer on behalf of the Transport and General Workers' Union. He survived all his one-time opponents and attended all their funerals, genuinely regret-ting their demise, for he esteemed them not only as fellow towns-men but as targets. He was, I suppose, an old-fashioned Socialist even then, for his ultimate loyalty was to his home town rather than Transport House. I recall some of his elaborate practical jokes, as when he organized the erection, on an open field facing a row of select, detached houses, of a huge board painted with the legend, "Site of Hi-Wun-Lung's New Chinese Laundry." It was accepted at face value by all the residents, who at once organized a petition and presented it to the estate-office officials responsible for administering the land in question.

I was once the victim of one of Bert's practical jokes. He bribed a boy to bring in a small ad, offering for sale a parrot owned by a local sea captain. The bird was alleged to be a non-stop talker, answering to the name of Polly, who turned out to be not a parrot but the sea captain's garrulous wife of the same name. The captain, whose address was given, was extremely abusive when the paper went on sale and Bert, hovering in the background, delighted in the blasphemous threats he directed toward me and the staff of the *Chronicle*.

A mandarin cast in a very different mold was Major Arnold, a small, shuffling, walrus-mustached ex-regular officer, who somehow got himself elected to both the Council and the Magisterial Bench. The Major was the most uninhibited elder among our city fathers, and some of his antics, performed with a curious innocence, set the town in an uproar. His election address was a minor classic and I wish I could quote it in full but I recall only that it began: "I was wounded at Dargai. They got me through the liver in the first rush. Vote for the old soldier who has fought and bled for his King and country . . ."

The Major was not a success in the Council Chamber. Mostly he looked as though he were asleep, and dreaming of Afghan rushes and Sikh counterattacks in the Swat Valley, but he was a never-ending source of entertainment on the bench, for he contrived to give the impression that all the business conducted there was make-believe, that cases could be shrugged off when it was time for a chota peg, or when sounds of something more entertaining drifted into the court from the street outside. I remember once, during a long and intricate motoring case, when a dozen witnesses were resolutely engaged in a lying match concerning speeds and skid marks, the skirl of bagpipes was heard and the Major, who had seemed to be sound asleep, braced himself and suddenly vacated the chairman's seat. A witness, understandably baffled by this abrupt movement, stopped in midsentence, and the eyes of everyone present followed the Major's purposeful shuffle the length of the magisterial dais to the window, where he drew aside the curtain. "Dagenham Girl Pipers!" he announced, with the slow smile of a gratified child and then, shuffling back to his seat and nodding at the witness, "Carry on, carry on!" It was only after the gale of laughter had subsided that I recalled that the Gordon Highlanders had played a prominent part in the battle for Dargai in Victoria's Jubilee year and that the Major had gone down in the first rush.

The Major often employed this sort of gambit to relieve the deadly tedium of the petty sessional court and we were always pleased to see him slumped on the bench. One day an application for an affiliation order had occupied us throughout the morning and part of the afternoon, the respondent resisting all attempts on the part of a shoal of witnesses (including two Peeping Toms and a mother-in-law elect) to saddle him with the paternity of the child. I am inclined to think the Major missed even the spicy bits concerning waving grass, the parlor couch and the alleged exchange of whispered endearments, but he opened his dormouse eyes as the respondent's solicitor announced, "That's my case, Your Worship," and sat down. The Major then blinked three times and said, aggressively. "We find defendant guilty. Any previous convictions?"

Bert and the Major qualified as light relief in the routine of filling an eight-page newspaper once a week, but there were mandarins whose long, rambling speeches, and sustained avalanche of platitudes, sometimes kept us imprisoned in hall or committee room for two hours before we could extract from the meeting a single paragraph embodying the decision. By far the most long-winded of these was the wealthy owner of a chain of stores who had retired from business to devote himself to good works. He was earnest, plump, pale and beaky, so that he looked like a benign owl when he was pecking through his notes, and he covered a very wide front indeed. Wherever you went in search of copy he was sure to be there, usually in the chair, and as he was a generous subscriber to dozens of local causes we were obliged to suffer him gladly, especially if the causes he supported brought printing orders into the office. I recall him particularly because of a certain irony that attended his funeral.

The cortege started out from his home, a large house at the top of a narrow drive that gave on to a busy and equally narrow thoroughfare. I ran a hooded Austin Seven in those days, and its engine had as many eccentricities as the mandarins. For a reason I cannot recall, all the local pressmen, with myself at the wheel, were late for the funeral, and having no opportunity to beat the cortege to the lich gate we decided to join it at the house. Turning into the drive, however, I had carburetor trouble and stalled the engine at the very moment the hearse was setting off. There was no room to pass, and low, grass-covered banks made it difficult to push the car off the road, so the press was instrumental in delaying the man who had so often made it miss its deadline.

There were perhaps a score of residents who popped up at almost every annual general meeting and hardly one among them who did not enjoy indulging in a long, prolix waffle. They were there as figureheads, however, and left the real work of the movement to the honorary secretaries, a terse, efficient breed, as impatient as we were to push on to the relevant part of the agenda. We—the secretaries and the press, that is—would sometimes commiserate with one another by eye-rollings and gestures of despair, as the figurehead rambled on and on, pottering among anecdotes that lacked a punch line, and groping for well-worn phrases to thank honorary auditors and scrutineers. It is interesting to recall that this rarely happened when the meeting was convened by women and chaired by a woman. Women's meetings were refreshingly businesslike and cut most of the corners, the chairman silencing the wafflers from the platform. I have always held that if Parliament were made up entirely of officials picked from Women's Institutes and Townswomen's Guilds, we should solve most of our social and economic problems in a single session. They have a way of sifting the relevant from the inconsequential and are not much given to self-glorification.

One prominent townsman to whom I looked for a steady supply of news did not qualify as a mandarin, inasmuch as he never concerned himself with public affairs but concentrated manfully on a business that was, in a sense, everybody's business. He was our most prominent local undertaker, whose detachment from the local junketings was impressive but spine-chilling. To look at him, to see him going softly about his work, helped to restore one's sense of proportion but it also reminded one that time was flying and that nothing mattered much, not even the disputed switch from gas street lighting to electric street lighting. Death was out there waiting for all—that is, everyone but Jabez, who had somehow wrung the secret of immortality from the gods and would be on hand to make a tidy job of the youngest and healthiest among us.

Perhaps his detachment encouraged this belief—that and his trick of measuring the most pompous of us with his expert eye. He invariably referred to his customers as "parties," as though he were conducting mass burials at one or other of our church-yards, and it was some time before I could persuade myself that his approach to his work was in no way disrespectful but tradi-tional, for he came from a long line of local undertakers. Jabez had some interesting theories about Death. He would call sooner, he claimed, if one was unfortunate enough to possess a short, thick neck but could be kept at bay a long time if one was reluc-tant to invest in life insurance. It was his experience, he declared, that parties with short, thick necks rarely reached the allotted span and usually came his way well in advance of it. Similarly, parties known to be heavily insured had a way of dropping off soon after the first big premium was paid, almost as though they had been nudged by avaricious relatives.

He would sit on my office table when he came in with his biweekly list of departures and chat cozily about his associations with the deceased, so that his profession would shed its natural gloom and assume the aspect of a learned profession, deserving a long and arduous apprenticeship. He was never surprised by death, not even when it struck haphazardly among the able-bodied. It was as though he had been privy to what was about to happen and it had, in a way, been arranged for his benefit. Yet he was a craftsman and spared nothing to do his customers credit.

He could convert the most modest funeral into an event of great dignity and sometimes mild hilarity, for he was not merely the undertaker on these occasions but a family counselor, who gave advice both before and after the event. He could also be relied upon to recall all manner of amusing stories about the dear departed. Nobody ever challenged him or his decisions. He was the local Diogenes, dispensing wisdom from an enormous vat of experience.

Jabez must have been a wealthy man by the time I met him, but his dislike of ostentation extended to his way of life and dress, especially his dress. All the years I knew him he possessed but two suits. One was informal and was worn during preliminaries; the other was his gala attire for the actual interment. Both must have been bought at least twenty years before our first encounter, for the informal suit, that had once been gray, was now dark green, and the trilby hat that went with it was a defeated ruin that had weathered countless southwesterly gales as he cycled about his business in the high season of the trade, between late January and early March. His graveside clothes were cut from more lasting material and had withstood the weather fairly well, but the nap had disappeared from his topper that had weathered a shade of black one might look for in the feathers of an elderly crow sitting out a shower. In either suit, however, you could never mistake him for anything but an undertaker, for he had a long, measured stride and held himself very erect, a gait and posture acquired during the hundreds of miles he had walked between lich gate and grave, chapel and family plot.

I grew very fond of Jabez, but this did not prevent me from transporting him, root and branch, to one of my early novels. He appears there as he appeared to me under the somewhat Dickensian name of Sleek.

I had a bad moment on this account. A few days after the appearance of the book on the bookstalls I saw him striding purposefully toward me with an unfamiliar gleam in his eye. A sore conscience made me wonder how I could possibly excuse myself for conferring upon him, without his prior consent, a different kind of immortality, that of the printed word stowed away in the British Museum, where at least one copy of every author's book must survive. I had underestimated human fallibility. Clapping me on the shoulder he smiled his thin, wintry smile and congratulated me on what he described as "a rare pen portrait of X," naming a rival and less distinguished local undertaker.

From that moment I have never been overworried about the possibility of libel. There exist, here and there, a few Englishmen prepared to accept the mantle of the scoundrel in fiction and sue. But no promise of damages will tempt an Englishman to don the motley, climb into the ring and consort with clowns.

Jabez was not immortal after all. In the fullness of time he died, just like everybody else, but to me at least his death was an affront, a welshing on the part of the gods who had promised him immunity. He was, however, a ripe old age and long past his work, so it seems superfluous to add that his neck was long and thin and that his passing did not occasion so much as a tut-tut at the head offices of the giant insurance corporations.

Lilliput Goes to Press

The working week always began with copying out the tide table and the selection of six jokes from a book of funny stories. They were trivial tasks, but they could not be overlooked. The local anglers fished by the tide table, and the local housewives looked for the jokes. Mercifully, the latter were partial to chestnuts.

Then, at eleven sharp, the petty sessions opened and the week's batch of malefactors filed into the dock. All kinds of malefactors, the stricken and the defiant, the indifferent, the brazen, the penitent and the thrice-damned. Motorists who had passed halt signs; cyclists who had ridden through the night without a light; farmers who had allowed cattle to stray on the highway; milkmen who had watered their milk; poor devils who had exposed themselves and were bewildered by the furor that followed; the odd thief or professional wayfarer who had made a bottle of methylated spirit serve the purpose of rose-colored spectacles. Sometimes the sessions were over in fifteen minutes, sometimes they dragged on into the afternoon. The evidence varied little week by week. Every accused motorist had sounded his horn twice and held his speed down to below twenty m.p.h. and most of them stuck gamely to their stories under cross-examination. The thieves and the wayfarers seldom disputed the facts, most of the former going forward to the Quarter Sessions, the latter cheerfully accepting six months or less as a means of settling their housing and subsistence problems for the winter. All in all it was the dullest job of the week.

As soon as I returned to the office to transcribe my shorthand notes I covered the old kitchen table with a clean sheet of brown paper, fixing it there with drawing pins. This was a memo that couldn't get lost and onto that sheet of brown paper went everything that would certainly happen, would probably happen, or might happen up to the paper's deadline at five-thirty P.M. on Friday evening.

Small towns are not as sleepy as they look to the outsider. The variety of fact and prospect was immense. Every week I witnessed events and made calls that many Fleet Street men would not witness or make once a month, perhaps once a year. The local undertakers appeared, quietly and deferentially, with their lists of forthcoming burials, and the information they brought me was jotted down on the table top. Every address would have to be visited, perhaps twice, for sometimes the weekend intervened between the death and the funeral. Brides-to-be and their triumphant mothers called with wedding folders (all routine questions printed in advance); and I would look hopefully at the section "*Any other information*," because it was only here that I could hope to find data that would vary the lead-in. It was a relief to switch from "*A pretty wedding was solemnised . . .*" to "*One of the best known athletes was groom at . . .*" or "*The Honiton lace veil of the bride's grandmother was worn at . . .*"

I liked a quiet afternoon on Monday. I could finish the court column, write up a wedding or two well in advance, and make a few before-the-funeral calls. If I was lucky I could also edit the W.I., Girl Guides, Sea Scouts and National Trades Union contributions. I always welcomed this material, for every week I had eight pages to fill. But it all needed editing and often cutting, and so did the notes sent in by all the other unpaid reporters describing sports events that I hadn't had time to attend.

On Tuesday anything might happen, including the monthly Council meeting, where the progressives and the diehards stormed at one another and every other paragraph in the committee reports was referred back. The mimeographed agenda the Town Clerk sent me was a godsend. Sometimes, if I was pushed for time or short of copy, I could work away with scissors and pastepot and snip whole chunks from a committee's report, consigning the movement of a single lamppost to the immortality of print. But all this was mere routine. What I looked for from Tuesday onward was the unexpected, the dramatic, the trumpet call announcing events that qualified as news as distinct from padding.

I usually heard that call before I had finished reading Monday's galley proofs. The single maroon would explode over the town, and I would drop everything and hurry toward the fire station. If the engine had already gone I pedaled in pursuit. Usually it hadn't but was awaiting its quota of spare-time firemen. Three times out of four it was only a chimney fire, but now and again I would arrive in time to assist the police save valuables from real flames. It was important that I should not stand aside on these occasions. The police helped me every day of the week, and if I could give their chances of promotion a small nudge by writing *"P.C. Newman did a magnificent job at the scene of a disastrous fire in Jubilee Road last Tuesday . . ."* it was both seemly and advisable to do it. Besides, lending a hand would loosen the tongue of the householder and whet the edge of the story. If I hadn't won his confidence he wouldn't have told me that his losses included a home-made crystal set and his father's certificate of merit for saving life in the Messina eruption in 1908.

There were fires, wrecks and accidents. Fires and accidents were bread and butter and made tolerable reading, but a wreck was a sugarplum. It meant not only a spectacular lifeboat launch, and a picture or two, but lineage for London papers and news agencies. It was frustrating to stand spelling out names to an impatient subeditor in a drafty sea-front telephone kiosk, but who cared if the story made a London front page and brought in thirty shillings?

There were inquests, any number of them, even in a town with fewer than 12,000 inhabitants. All kinds of inquests, from the aged laborer who had somehow succeeded in drowning himself in four inches of water, or hanging himself with a lavatory chain, to the distressed gentlewoman who had collapsed in her morning bath or taken an overdose of sleeping pills. They were solemn but not necessarily depressing occasions. It depended upon the age of the victim and the amount of pain involved. It was here that you were given a quick peep into the lumber rooms of minds and had a chance to measure the stresses contributing to a suicide, or hazards that awaited the unwary and absent-minded. It was the darker side of town life that balanced, with curious exactitude, its carnivals, jamborees and tournaments, its plays, operas, concerts, annual meetings and sales of work.

Wednesday was always a busy day. Almost everything that happens on a local beat is motivated by tradesmen, the social and sporting trend setters of the town, and Wednesday is their day for extracommercial activities. Reporting a sale of work was a deceivingly simple chore. It was essential to listen very carefully to the names you were given and link stallholders to the correct stalls. To fail in this respect was to invite a frigid visit from the overlooked or the misspelled as soon as the paper went on sale.

There was a bonus at every amateur stage presentation, for here you were not a reporter but a critic. You could exult, patronize and damn with faint praise. And if the entertainment was second-rate and you were ill-disposed you could even sneer —providing, of course, that the society's programs and bills had been set up in somebody else's printing works. It was a working apprenticeship in show business.

In the eleven years I was a provincial reporter I saw everything from *Uncle Vanya* and *Ghosts* to *Rookery Nook* and *Charley's Aunt*. I saw *The Mikado* five times and *The Pirates of Penzance* four. At W.I. gatherings I must have seen nearly every one-act play printed in the English language.

We had our naturalists and our highbrows, and they too demanded their share of space. I sat through one series of lectures on Ornithology and another on British Portraiture. At lantern lectures I scribbled in the dark about the dangers of venereal disease and then ran across the gaslit streets to the Institute to learn something of Mayan architecture. Sometimes, even now, I am astonished to find myself at home inside an encyclopedia. Did *you* know that Gainsborough's feathery brushwork on his foliage was considered superior to his portraiture? Or that one-eyed planters keep their field hands at work by dropping a glass eye in a tumbler on the steps of a bungalow and taking a one-eyed siesta? These are things I might have gone through life without learning, but here in Lilliput I was paid thirty shillings a week to note them down and feed them to the compositors.

Thursday was district day, and I went further afield, recording the same kind of events as earlier in the week but on a smaller scale and by remote control. My approach outside the hub was an indirect one, for here I relied upon a network of tipsters. The goalkeeper of a village football eleven had his chance to explain to all my subscribers why he let three into the net during the semi-final. The local hairdresser told me in a stage whisper that the new people moving into Elm Cottage had just won a third prize in the Irish Sweep and might be persuaded to talk. Sometimes, out here in the hinterland, I fell over a scoop. Famous authors, famous cricketers and band leaders hibernated here in summer and any one of them was worth half a column in my "In Town this Week" section. The source of this kind of information was often a hotelier in search of a free advertisement, or perhaps the second cousin of a national croquet champion. Out here, in the ring of scattered villages, I had a host of informants. Some were paid in beer and others, a majority, spied for the fun of it. District day was pleasant in summer weather, but hell all through in January sleet.

On Friday morning the proofs began to pile up, not only originals but the second and third pulls where I had reduced the risks of libel and common assault by making judicious cuts and alterations. The hardest-worked word in my vocabulary was "alleged." It can steer you through a mile of rapids.

Toward noon on Friday the pace became frantic. There was still a shrinking list of unobliterated appointments and interviews noted down on the brown-papered table top, and time was running out. The supplements were printed and folded. The front and back pages were on the stone. And always, always, with infuriating certainty, something untoward would occur. A fool would fall out of a window. A bus driver would be stung by a wasp and drive his vehicle into a ditch. A gust of wind would fell an elm across a main road. A downpour would cause the brook to overflow and wash stinking sludge into the parlors of sullen ratepayers. It all had to be covered and I did not need to be reminded that printers' overtime was one and sixpence an hour.

All too often there was the sudden or the overlooked death and the hurried visit to the hushed house. Relatives speaking in whispers and the deceased dominating them in silence. "How old was he?" "How long had he lived here?" "How many children did he leave?" "Had he served in the war?" Every question required consultation and when it was done I was ushered, willy nilly, into the presence, and the widow would lift the sheet. "Dornee mind, dear, tiz on'y the young man from the pa-aper . . ." There wasn't even time to ponder the simple annals. Three paragraphs had to be written and keyboarded in fifteen minutes and then the flat-bed would begin to roll.

Five-thirty was the ultimate hour, and at five-forty-five nothing short of the assassination of the Council Chairman could halt the flat-bed. In cases of dire emergency we could use a two-inch stop-press and rubber type, but I only recall us taking such desperate measures once. That was when the local cinema burned down as we were folding the front page and laying in the supplements. It was a proud Northcliffian moment. We headed it *"This Morning's Fire,"* and even Fleet Street could not improve on that.

Folding was the most thankless task of the week, two three-hour stints across a trestle board, one lasting from six to nine in the evening, the other from five-thirty to eight-thirty on Saturday morning. Your back ached, and you wished to God you had never seen a newspaper. You wondered why people bought them. But when the old flat-bed had shuddered to an uncertain halt, its final front page pointing skyward like a flag of truce, you perked up and began to think of tea and cigarettes and ask yourself why the Dock news agent was taking three dozen instead of his usual two and a half this week. Then you remembered why: It was because of Prudence Priddis's wedding and she lived in a Dockland bungalow. You remembered that because she was the lifeboat coxswain's second daughter and had left the west door of the parish church under an arch of upraised oars. The picture hadn't come out too well. The sailor Prudence had married looked terrified on page three.

You went home and washed your smudgy fingers, distributing your sheaf of handwritten contents bills en route. It was all over until next week, apart from Saturday sports fixtures and a religious revival. Lilliput had gone to press.

Four Studies in Black

Of seams mined in search of raw material for the practice of my profession by far the richest were to be found in the enclosed community represented by the subscribing public of a weekly newspaper; and the most profitable of these, so far as I was concerned, ran under the graveyard. In character and atmosphere, its yield was uniquely rare and rewarding, and there is ore still down there waiting to be brought to the surface.

There are those who accuse poor Arnold Bennett of bad taste for using his mother's funeral as a blueprint in a scene for one of his novels. I think they do him an injustice. If professional yarn spinners in the past had been prohibited from drawing upon personal experiences, the fiction of the past three centuries would have been that much poorer. I must admit to having to take my place in the dock beside Arnold Bennett, for, although I daily encounter any number of handicaps in turning out fiction, I am never at a loss to describe a funeral.

In my time I must have attended as many funerals as an undertaker in a modest way of business. For a period of eleven years, when I was earning my living as a provincial reporter, I averaged four a week and double this figure during the undertaker's seasonal crest, that is, the period between late January and early March.

This is by no means as depressing as it sounds. There was a comforting predictability about funerals absent from all the weddings, local elections, bazaars, fires, wrecks, street accidents and foundation-stone plantings with which they were spaced. Most of them had a quality of dignity, and even those that did not were redeemed by a determination on the part of all to give the deceased a rousing send-off, and this, after all, was kindly meant, circulated money, and did not embarrass the deceased.

Like every other event that occurs in the British provinces, a funeral can be precisely classified according to rank and status. There were, as I recall, four main categories, three on a descending social scale and the other, the civic occasion, that had an impersonal aura setting it apart. We are not here greatly concerned with the civic or the town occasion, for even the chilliest funeral starting out from one of the big detached houses in the residential quarter of my beat was a display of grief of a sort. Grief was not present at the civic funeral, for the dismay of near-relatives was moderated by the togetherness of the occasion. Besides, at a public funeral it was always permitted to smile or at any rate grimace, providing of course that one kept a straight face inside the lich gate. This does not mean that we buried our public figures gaily, but simply that grief was spread more thinly, having to serve upwards of three hundred mourners.

There was, of course, another reason for the air of modest relaxation attending all public funerals. It was, to some degree, a convivial assembly. The mourners arrived en bloc, the Masons wearing their sprigs of evergreen, the British Legionnaires their clinking medals. The Boy Scouts and Girl Guides were fortified by their discipline, the local bowlers and golfers by the certainty that at last someone else would have a sporting chance of winning the championship. These groups marched to the service like animals entering the Ark, strictly two by two, paired by the hand of their marshal, or by their inches, or by the claims of comradeship. The few family mourners were on their very best behavior. Their expressions were blank and their upper lips as stiff as brocade. The minimum of tears were shed at public funerals but what they lacked in emotion they gained in spectacle and variety. Toppers and frock coats were often in evidence and the whiff of mothballs mingled, but not unpleasantly, with the heavy scent of the floral tributes. On such occasions (the average age of the "others present" being between sixty and seventy) it was impossible not to speculate who among them would be the next to draw such a crowd and sometimes in the middle of "For All the Saints" or "To Be a Pilgrim," I would look across the aisle and recall that, only a month or so before, I had seen our present host standing there singing as lustily as anybody else. And now, here he was, attending his final public meeting. It was a chastening thought and one upon which I never cared to dwell.

All this, however, was far removed from the mainstream of graveyard ritual. The other categories had an entirely different flavor and a class distinctiveness that death seemed certain to proclaim beyond the grave, beyond indeed the peaks of the Celestial Mountains, so that I soon learned to recognize this and adjust my sights accordingly. Even had I lacked advance information from the undertaker I could have calculated the drift of each funeral in advance, just as a man who has never attended a bell-ringing session in his life can distinguish between the cathedral carillon, the boarding-house dinner gong, and the harsh clang of the town crier's hand bell. Each has a different pitch, a different resonance, a distinctive echo.

At the top of the scale was the strictly private event, where reporters were discouraged and women rarely appeared. They were so discreet that sometimes it seemed as if the deceased had done something shameful by dying and directing unwelcome attention upon surviving relatives. Sometimes my cautious overtures for information would be met by a flat refusal to divulge so much as the date or the whereabouts of the event, much less the departed's achievements. More often the bereaved accepted their cross and facts were dribbled out piecemeal. Then I would be dismissed and the little knot of mourners would go their way, eyes fixed on the middle distance, tearless, emotionally battened down and with guardsmen's measured gait. Commercially their funerals were worthless. The undertaker and *The Times* obituary column were paid, but that was all. Florists and newspapermen were neither received nor encouraged. To these families, all of them well buttressed against everything but Death, the act of dying was as private an act as making love.

Then came what I learned to regard as the In-Betweeners,

family groups who conceded that some kind of display was obligatory but that it must, at all costs, be restrained. Theirs was not
a numerous group. Most people erred on one side or the other
but there did exist a category that had to be accorded its own
approach, and it was usually found in the middle-income group,
in those days people earning between six and eight hundred a
year, who were ready to give Death his due but nothing at all in
the way of a bonus. Clearly they regretted their dead, but a little
of the embarrassment attending their wealthier neighbors had
strayed out of the Anglo-Indian belt and taken refuge in the
small detached house, or the well-appointed bungalow overlooking the sea. These people received me very politely, sometimes
even kindly, but as a family anxious to get things tied up and
sorted out in the manner of people who find themselves the victims of a burglary. They faced up to the necessity of a limited
amount of publicity, but they did not welcome it, and even the
florist was received like a rent collector when he made his deliveries. I sometimes coaxed a quarter column from a funeral of
this kind, but it was hard, unrewarding work, and I only persisted out of a sense of duty to my readers.

How different were the funerals of the poor and the uninhibited. How warm the reception of the reporter, the sympathetic neighbor, the florist's errand boy, and even the gas man
who had called, all unknowingly, poor fellow, to empty the
meter on the day preceding the burial.

The tradition of the wake is supposed to be limited to the wild
Irish but this is a fallacy. Unofficially it still flourishes in many
an English terrace house, or it did in my funeral-going days. It
was always a heartwarming experience and every time it came
my way I felt the better for it and inclined to take a less misan-
thropic view of my fellow men. Death, to these people, was no
stranger, and although greatly respected he was neither feared
nor abused when he came calling. They had come to terms with
him long ago and received him with a little flutter of excitement.
They would, one felt, have addressed him as "Sir," and they did
their best to make a favorable impression on him, not only by

wearing their best clothes and lowering the blinds but by feeding and entertaining him to the extreme limit of their pockets. Nothing was too good for him. Why else would they have insured against the certainty of his arrival?

Yet let it not be imagined that the ritual suffered on this account. On the contrary the observances, particularly those of precedence, were very strictly prescribed; and woe betide the reporter, tiptoeing from the presence of the dead, who wrote down a son-in-law in advance of a son, or a nephew ahead of a brother who had come hustling down from Ashton-under-Lyne and lost two days' work in consequence. Discussion among them regarding the order of precedence in the report was as solemn as a conclave of eighteenth-century noblemen planning a reception for Louis XV, and sometimes there were disputes that I was called upon to umpire.

The undertaker was treated with equal respect, for he was the acknowledged acolyte of death, and it was as well to keep in his good graces. The food at such a funeral was nourishing, and kitchen fires were built up against a chilly return from the graveyard. They were hard work, these funerals, but for the paper I represented they were rewarding. There was no stinting on death announcements, return-thanks insertions, or lists of floral tributes, all published at set fees. The announcement and the list of wreaths were published at threepence a line, the return-thanks notice at the standard price of three and sixpence.

It was part of my duty, of course, to move from wreath to wreath, jotting down the names of the donors and the actual words they had written on the black-edged cards. This does not sound a particularly difficult task, but it often was, for many of the wreaths were collective tributes, and rain or the florist's freshening-up water had made the ink run in all directions. I have known as many as ten people subscribe for a single spray and it simply did not do to omit any one of them, or make a slight error in the wording of the inscription. Thus one found oneself writing "To dear Gran, from Tom, Ned, Nan, Ursula, Marlene, Dorothy and Little Arthur; Always in our Thoughts," and writing it, moreover, in a room already holding twenty people, some of them over fourteen stone, or, worse still, beside an open grave with rain running down one's neck.

For all that these funerals were, as I say, cozy and friendly occasions. Before or after the interment the relatives would surround me and beguile me with anecdotes concerning the deceased. How he had leathered them as children, or played tricks upon them on their wedding days. How toilsome had been his early life in farm or factory and how, by performing an annual miracle, he had always been able to fill their stockings on Christmas Eve. Such occasions reinforced one's faith in family life and in the matchless courage of the overworked and underpaid, and if, during the savage month of February, one was pushed for time and nearing the paper's deadline, it was always possible to publish in two installments, one confining itself to the death and the other, in a subsequent issue, describing the funeral. For the publication of details cash was paid on the spot and sometimes, after a spate of such funerals, I would return to the office weighed down by silver. These people might, on occasion, owe their butcher or the grocer, but they shrank from mortgaging themselves to Death.

Even with the second installment this was not quite the end of the matter. Occasionally, on the anniversary of their bereavement, the family would summon me yet again, this time to deliberate upon the wording of an "In Memoriam" notice, and these sometimes awakened the muse in the breasts of unlikely poets. They would sit down with ruled notepaper and stubs of pencil and sweat out a couplet or even a verse, and occasionally came up with something of striking originality, as when a concert of relatives produced:

> An angel trumpet sounded,
> An angel voice said "Come!"
> The pearly gates they opened wide
> And in walked Mum.

I never forgot this gem, and years later, when I was writing a scene in a newspaper play, I used it in the script. It brought the house down and this surprised and even shocked me, for it had not, as I recall, struck me as amusing at the time but only as possessing a terrible poignancy.

And yet, honesty compels me to confess that these funerals provided a substantial part of the newspaper's revenue. When half a dozen such events appeared in a single issue the circulation leaped up appreciably, for relatives would buy sheaves of papers that sometimes found their way to the ends of the earth.

And there is something else I must not forget. The undertaker paid a fee of one and sixpence for his name at the tail of the report.

Two Studies in White

The range in local weddings was more limited. In those days a Register Office wedding was looked upon as a rather furtive affair, and facts concerning them reached me across the shop counter. They were the mere bare bones of a union—two names, a place, a date. This left me with the big-scale and somewhat formalized event based on one of the isolated houses in what I thought of as the Curry Belt, at the eastern end of the town, and the cozier affair centered on the semidetached or terrace house.

Class divisions at weddings were even sharper than at funerals. The prospect of a wedding in the family—any family—always had an unsettling effect upon local mums, the pace setters on these occasions, but whereas the terrace-house mums adapted as the day approached, the Anglo-Indian mums in the Curry Belt became impossibly arch and often as difficult to woo as their male counterparts at one of those so-private funerals. They were so guarded in their statements that one always had an unworthy suspicion that somewhere behind the young man who had appeared out of nowhere to claim Angela or Gillian was a mahogany-faced dad with a loaded shotgun.

It was never necessary to initiate a meeting with a semidetached mum. With bride-to-be in tow they invariably sought me out, demanding the printed questionnaire and full publicity as of right. The form was carried away in a mood of quiet triumph, together with the wedding-card sample book, and the former was filled in with the rigorous concentration an early nineteenth-century attorney would have brought to an Enclosure Act. Sometimes, such was the wealth of detail, the information spilled over onto additional sheets embellished with a shower of asterisks and broken arrows, directing me to areas where the compiler had run out of space.

In the Avenues I would have welcomed this prodigality, for here I had to make as many as three personal calls if the questionnaire was to be returned in time for the current issue of the paper. Avenue mums were always cavalier in this respect, dismissing the report as a tiresome and irrelevant detail distracting their minds from the mainstream of events. They would sometimes look at me woodenly when the housemaid announced, "The man from the paper, ma'am," as though I had no more business there at that time than a man who had called to ask if he could cast away rags and bones.

On these occasions I always stood upon my dignity, reiterating that they were under no obligation whatever to publicize their daughter's nuptials and usually, in the end, they capitulated but without grace. They would forage among mounds of wedding litter in a halfhearted attempt to unearth the questionnaire and for a time I would let them forage. It did not do to allow such people to make light of the Fourth Estate. Then, like a patient debt collector, I would produce a spare copy and we would go to work on it together, names, parentage, bridal gown, bridesmaids' gowns, bride's mother's ensemble, best man, ushers and so on, down to the patent-leather shoes of the page. They were remarkably ignorant concerning the strict protocol of wedding accounts and awareness of this would blunt the edge of their conceit and enlarge me a little, so that when one of their tweedy menfolk appeared on the threshold they would say, sharply, "Don't bother me, Angus! Can't you see I'm busy with the press? Attend to the marquee!" And the tweedy one would drift away and presently, through an open door, I would hear the chink of decanter on tumbler, and the soft hiss of the soda siphon, followed by a guttural command addressed to shirt-sleeved natives at work in the compound.

I never enjoyed this kind of wedding. It was dehumanized and dehydrated, bereft of the panoply and spontaneity of the wed-

ding in the semidetached or terrace house, where the union of
Jill and Arnold was an event that took precedence over anything that could possibly occur in the world outside.

Here I was always received with cordiality and gusto. Drinks
were poured and wedding presents displayed with pride and
sometimes a semijocular aside—"The fireside set is from Auntie
Bessie. I don't mind saying Jill expected blankets but after all,
she *is* the third in less than two years . . ."

Sometimes I would call on the day itself in order to clarify a
garbled paragraph or collect the questionnaire in time to meet a
deadline, and on these occasions I almost always returned to the
office the worse for wear, with liquor on my breath and the
broken shards of wedding cake in my pocket. How cheerfully
Dad dipped into his pocket for Jill, even when she was "the third
in under two years"! It would not be true to say that Cupid took
precedence over Death, but he ran that spendthrift a close second
to the top of the family budget. Jill had her ivory-satin gown
(soon to be downgraded into a dance frock), her lace veil, and
sometimes as many as four bridesmaids, all outfitted by Dad, in
apple-green organdie. There was always a photographer, a three-
tier wedding cake and so much to drink that the living room,
over the period of the celebrations, looked like an off-license
where half the week's customers had dumped their Christmas
shopping. Sometimes I had to make a list of these gifts for publication at sixpence a line, but this was reckoned an extravagance
and rarely occurred more than once a week, even at Eastertime.
For, just as boomtime for funerals came in late January, so Easter
was high tide for weddings. It was not unusual to feature a dozen
or more in a single issue.

Often the family was glad to see me an hour or so before they
left for Church, using me as a diversion on which to rally their
nerves. Nerves were much in evidence on these occasions. Mums
had a habit of going to pieces so that they had to be petted by
half-dressed brides. The brides of the semidetached and terrace
houses never wavered, displaying nerves of proofed steel. I never
encountered one who gave way to anxiety, much less panic, and

their serenity was intimidating. They would whisk around the house in their dressing gowns, answering the door, opening last-minute presents, and freeing the jammed zip of a bridesmaid's dress, and I wondered at their repose the more because I sometimes had occasion to call upon their grooms at about the same hour. To do this, however, was to risk personal involvement, for grooms were often in desperate need of male reassurance and whenever possible I kept clear of them. I had never forgotten helping a terrified sailor to empty a bottle of rum an hour or so before the ceremony and then being conscripted by his bride and her mother to sober him before the taxis arrived. It was a painful incident and went some way toward proving the validity of the superstition that prohibits bride and groom from meeting on the wedding day until they stand together at the altar.

When there was a rush of weddings of this kind I was sometimes unable to call at the house until the ceremony was over and would arrive in the middle of the reception. This was not conducive to coherent reporting, for once the champagne was uncorked, and a house built to accommodate five was sheltering upwards of eighty, it was difficult to assemble accurate information. The elder women would involve themselves in complicated discussions on technical details, bishop's sleeves, flared panels, Medici necklines and the like. When this happened I would steal away and locate Dad in one of the bedrooms, where he would be easing his ecstatic feet out of shining pumps and into plaid slippers. Adrift on an ebb tide of champagne and anticlimax he was often a prey to the same nameless anxieties as those that had assailed his wife before the magic words were spoken. Now that the knot was tied he needed convincing that Arnold would not resort to beating Jill with a razor strop, that Arnold was indeed Mr. Right and was therefore unlikely to saddle his daughter with a long family and disappear into Central Australia. Dad would brood about these contingencies for a spell but when somebody below shouted, "They're leaving! Where's Dad? Somebody find Dad!" he would force a smile, straighten his Moss Bros. vest, and make a spectacular descent of the narrow stairs just as if he and not his daughter was the star performer.

His appearance would always be greeted by gusts of drollery, by long "Raahs" and cries of "Good old Dad!" But it was a moment he would share with nobody, not even the beaming groom. For a splendid moment, as father and daughter embraced, the revelry would be hushed and then, reignited by somebody's bawdy jest, it would begin again as the car drove off, trailing its traditional strings of old boots and dustbin lids, flaunting its "Just Married" sign and its enormous red "L."

It was a moment for which I always looked after a semidetached- or terrace-house wedding, for it seemed to me to have more human dignity and significance than the sense of occasion one witnessed, but was never invited to share, in the Avenue marquees.

The Left and the Right of It

Notwithstanding his colorful and exceptionally dominant personality, my father's fiery radicalism did not rub off on me, and this was not because I inclined toward an alternative political faith. It was because, by the time I was about twelve and Labour was making its presence felt at Westminster, my father's Gladstonian Liberalism petrified. By the mid-twenties his views on how the country should be governed seemed as archaic as Peel's or Palmerston's.

Something like this happened to many of the old radicals who swept their party to power in the famous 1906 election. Most of the issues that agitated them were either settled by the time war broke out in 1914, or had become irrelevant under the fearful pressures of four years' nonstop slaughter. I see my father's political development as stopping in December 1916, when Lloyd George, until then his hero, neatly disposed of Asquith and took his place as leader. It was too much for my father to swallow in one gulp. He dropped away and was left floundering in a hotchpotch of outdated controversy composed of Free Trade, Irish Home Rule, Disestablishment of the Welsh Church, and all the other issues that bedeviled his generation. He distrusted the New Left as much as he distrusted Welsh Wizardry but his indoctrination against the Tory party in his youth prevented him from moving, even slightly, to the Right.

Right and Left were labels not often displayed in the shires until the early thirties, and they emerged, strange to relate, not from the Slump, and the terrible social inequalities of the postwar period, but from the postures adopted by the dictators in Europe. The real watershed in British politics was not the Spanish Civil War of 1936, as is generally believed, but the invasion of Abyssinia in the previous autumn, resulting in the collapse of the League of Nations, until then the Holy Grail of the British Socialist and Liberal. After that, consciously or not, almost every elector found himself or herself enlisting with one side or the other, and the interesting aspect of this from my standpoint was to see it happening on my own doorstep. For this was something quite new, owing little to the conventional political loyalties my neighbors had held throughout the twenties. For the first time, or so it seemed to me, provincials began to sense rather than inherit their political affiliations, and almost overnight the words "Blimp," "Diehard," "Red" and "Bolshie" lost their jocular opprobrium. What really occurred, I think, was that the arrogance and menace of the two dictators compelled the local Left to mature, and maturity on their part caused the local Right to take them far more seriously than during the seventeen years that had passed since the Armistice.

Something along these lines was happening all over the country at that particular time. Until then the small but always vocal Left of provincial Britain had been obsessed with domestic issues. Foreign affairs did not figure predominantly in their pamphlets and speeches. They had as much as they could do to broadcast their views on matters like bad housing, unemployment and, later on, the Means Test, whereas, deep down in almost every Socialist, was a furtive imperialist, secretly proud of all that red on the map and believing implicitly in the infallibility of the British Navy. He never let his loyalty to the flag show and would inveigh glibly against imperial exploitation on the part of the wicked capitalists, but it was there for all that, as was soon revealed when the Spanish Civil War caused the entire political scene in Britain to turn a somersault.

I have always seen this General Post as one of the most astonishing processes in the history of democracy as it evolved in Britain over a period of seven centuries. It was so sudden and so complete that it left most people breathless and bemused.

I make no attempt to describe it from the national standpoint. At that time I never spent more than the odd day or two far from my local beat, and I had very little opportunity to study the political scene as a whole. The nature of my work, however, gave me a grandstand view of how it affected all the people I knew, mostly by their Christian names, whereas, for my part, at the age of twenty-three, I could not help but be influenced by their apostasies.

Until then—until the autumn of 1935, that is—the small group of Liberals and Socialists on my beat were passionate devotees of the League of Nations. In addition, many of them were paid-up members of the League of Nations Union and the Peace Pledge Union, a group led by men like George Lansbury and Canon Dick Sheppard. Regularly, at least once a week, they attended peace meetings pledged to promote international fellowship, or distributed leaflets attacking men who trafficked in the sale of arms. Day after day they declared war on war, any kind of war, in whatever cause.

The local Tories, for their part, sometimes paid lip service to the League but they did not put much faith in it as a means of settling international disputes and were contemptuous of more extreme forms of pacifism. As the thirties passed the halfway mark, however, the metamorphosis occurred. The local Right shed its traditional belligerence and became almost plaintive in the cause of peace. I attended, with poised notebook and pencil, most of these political or quasi-political meetings and was thus well placed to notice what was happening on local platforms. Books published on the period have since confirmed that the same *volte-face* was happening simultaneously in every town and village in the land and a very curious spectacle it provided. By mid-1937, less than two years after the sad-eyed Negus had quitted his conquered realm, and come to lodge at the Ritz, political attitudes in the towns and villages where I peddled news were utterly reversed. The Left put on the costumes of Edwardian Jingoes, howling for arms and a bloody confrontation with Fascism, whereas the Right, the people one had always thought of as militant, flag-flapping reactionaries, were advocating policies of the kind local Socialists had used to build their platform five years before.

It was all very confusing and took a little getting used to. A man cannot suddenly come to terms with reckless extravagance on the part of the local miser, or the advocacy of milk by the town drunk, especially when he knows the miser as Fred and the drunk as Albert. One did get used to it, however, and by the time Chamberlain flew off to Munich and Franco, with the active help of the dictators, had conquered Spain, left-wing militancy and right-wing pacifism had become accepted local attitudes, fixed until the moment in 1940 when Churchill succeeded in polarizing the two.

It is interesting, looking back, to isolate the events that brought about this all-change on the part of one's neighbors. I can recall some of them vividly.

The first, I think, was the burning of the Reichstag and the mock trial of the Dutch half-wit van der Lubbe. The second were newsreels showing elderly Jews scouring the streets of German cities, with arm-banded young thugs looking on. A third was Hitler's Night of the Long Knives, that warned some people, even those living in remote Devon villages, that we were now confronted with a Continental Al Capone. A fourth was the murder of Dollfuss, the little Austrian Chancellor. Then came Mussolini's invasion of Abyssinia and the tacit acceptance of naked aggression by the democracies, and after that the outbreak of the Spanish Civil War and the policy of nonintervention.

It was at this point that shame began to invigorate the local Left. Meetings on behalf of the Spanish Republican cause were organized and some of the speeches made at them by former pacifists might have served Joe Chamberlain at the height of the Boer War, in 1900. The reverse was true at right-wing meetings, where speakers hammered away at the theme that what was happening on the Continent was none of Britain's business, and that elected governments in Germany and Italy were at liberty to pursue any policy they chose so long as British interests were not threatened.

220

Statements like this, often made by responsible people, maddened the local Left, who by now were convinced that the intervention of Germany and Italy in Spain was nothing more than a dress rehearsal for the conquest of the world. This, in fact, soon became so evident, even to neutrals in the debate, that the local Right began to put it about that appeasement was a cunningly conceived policy designed to buy time in order that we could re-arm for the fight—if there was a fight. This justification for the craven behavior of government did not fool any local Socialist or Liberal I interviewed during this hectic period. Their heroes were men like "Potato Jones," a Welsh skipper who ran the blockade into a Spanish port with a cargo of potatoes for the Basques, and we even had a local celebrity, Dougal Eggar, who enlisted in the International Brigade, was taken prisoner by the enemy, and spent months in one of Franco's crowded jails.

Things now took a more serious turn in and about the hustings. For the first and only time in my experience political violence erupted on the streets of the little town. A local Blackshirt group was formed, and local policemen, hitherto occupied in checking on reports of adulterated milk and collecting cattle straying on the highway, were called upon to intervene between jack-booted Mosleyites, self-consciously standing on Chapel Hill with Mussolini glares and folded arms, and their less organized opponents of the Left, who pranced around the speakers, howling abuse and sparking off little scuffles. It gave one pause to see young men one had known throughout one's entire adolescence striking out at one another on their home ground, and accusing one another, over the shoulders of a sandwiched policeman, of using knuckle-dusters; but this actually occurred one summer evening, and I wondered, rather wretchedly, where it was likely to lead; wretchedly because I felt myself, to some small degree, personally responsible for the sorry state of affairs.

I wonder how many peace crusaders of that period examined their consciences as attentively as I did as the Nazi menace across the Channel enlarged itself, in a matter of seven years, from malevolent dwarf to fire-breathing dragon of monstrous proportions? Perhaps a majority, for I was to encounter many ex-pacifists as enlisted airmen, sailors and soldiers in the next five years. Like me, most of them still felt a little foolish whenever they recalled their fervent convictions of the recent past.

The wave of violent reaction against war as a means of settling international disputes did not reach the remoter provinces until the end of the twenties, and for my part I was not fully aware of the horrors of the Western Front until I read Remarque's *All Quiet on the Western Front*, in 1929. It was about then that the books of survivors of the holocaust in Flanders began to attract serious attention, ten years having had to elapse before the general public could brace itself to take an objective look at the years 1914–18. *All Quiet* made a very deep impression on British youth. For the first time the German infantryman was seen as a fellow victim and not as the baby-crucifier and rapist of wartime propaganda, but British and French writers were also trumpeting their abhorrence of war in plays and novels, some of which made a considerable impact on young people at that time. Aldington's *Death of a Hero* was one that impressed me, and Sherriff's play *Journey's End* was another vivid reminder of what had happened to the previous generation. Translations of the French novels *Under Fire* and *The Paths of Glory* told the same story, and a popular newspaper made a unique contribution to the peace campaign by publishing a horrific pictorial record of the First World War called *Covenants with Death*. I joined the local League of Nations Union on the strength of these books and became a conscientious and rather smug leaflet distributor, alongside the local Liberals and Socialists. The fact that I was a member of the local Junior Imperial League at the same time does not imply that my convictions were suspect. The "Imps," as the League was called at that time, was a social movement with mild Conservative undertones, so mild that few local members took them seriously. Some of us even attended local Cooperative Youth Group gatherings, determined, socially at least, to enjoy the best of both worlds.

In our area, however, where Conservatism was very deeply rooted, the Tories had practically cornered the youth market and down at the Imps headquarters we had high old times, so long as the local Conservative agent kept out of the way. Conservative policies were not discussed there. The talk was of dance bands, the recently arrived talking pictures, and who had the best legs among the new members.

By the time Hitler took office, however (it was shortly before my twenty-first birthday), I was forced to reconsider my position. Not long afterward, in order to ensure that my renunciation of war went on record, I signed Canon Dick Sheppard's peace pledge, but it seemed to me, as it must have seemed to many young men at that juncture, that one could not really expect to have it both ways for much longer. Driblets of news concerning the concentration camps reached the town (I was subsequently amazed to learn that conditions in these camps do not appear to have been generally known in Britain until we captured Belsen, in 1945), and I interviewed several Jewish refugees, who confirmed the frightful truth of what was happening in Germany after 1933. Then, with the failure of the League to stop Mussolini's invasion of Ethiopia, I moved over, resigning from the Junior Imperial League and writing for the return of my peace-pledge card. It came, with a letter of regret, and I celebrated its return by joining Victor Gollancz's Left Book Club.

By now the pattern of Fascist intentions was becoming clearer day by day, and after I had digested Koestler's *Spanish Testament* I no longer had any doubts about the future. I executed my private somersault. From advocating disarmament I moved on to write banal leading articles urging the policy of rearmament upon the dithering government, and I did not blame some of my local Conservative friends for thinking me weak in the head. After all, I was in good company. All but one of my fellow pacifists in town had similarly recanted but we had little to boast about. We had bleated down the years, first to convert swords to plowshares, then to convert the plowshares back into swords, and the only excuse I can find for us is that we had grown up in the aftermath of the Somme and Passchendaele and had been in common with most of our generation, the victims of a gigantic confidence trick. We had honestly believed that the 1914–18 war was a war to end wars. Nobody had told us that the Versailles Treaty was a blueprint for its successor. Yet I do not know that we were any more fatuous than the Americans, or our friends who held to the Right. The disengagement of the one, and the bad faith of the other, brought about the stillbirth of the League of Nations at a time when it had a fair chance of survival, whereas the British Government's policy of appeasement was a direct encouragement to the men holding the world to ransom. It was a sorry picture and everyone involved (with the exception of Churchill, who never moderated his Jeremiad) could have been said to have made a contribution to the situation in which the democracies found themselves in 1938.

Yet perhaps I overlook one factor, at least as far as the British electorate was concerned. Perhaps there was something in the very air of Britain in the period between the Armistice and the end of the Slump, that made the cavortings of Continental dictators seem so grotesque that it could be watched for entertainment value alone. God knows, we had enough to occupy us, with three million unemployed, and over seven hundred in our town in 1931, a town with a working population of about four thousand. Aside from that, however, there wasn't one of us, high Tories included, who had not been touched in some way by the great liberal upsurge of ideas that changed the face of Britain in the last years of Victoria's reign and in the first decade of the new century. It was very difficult, growing up in an English shire, watching how our sober elections were conducted, and how an unarmed police force went about their work, to conceive of whole nations succumbing to hysteria on the German and Italian patterns. No one had ever knocked on our doors in the middle of the night and if, perchance, a neighbor was missing from his accustomed place without a satisfactory explanation, the entire district, supervised by polite policemen, joined in the search until he was accounted for.

I suppose, like everyone else in Britain then and now, I took social stability for granted until I had a conversation with a Polish student, a Jew over here on a short holiday in the spring of 1938. He happened to be with me while I was collecting information about a murder and a suicide in one of our surrounding villages, and the nature of my inquiries amazed him. "Why, in the name of God," he said, "should anyone want to murder or kill themselves in Britain?" He told me, shortly before his return to Krakow that he was living on borrowed time. "I shan't live to be thirty," he said. "That man will come for us soon." I heard from him once in the summer of Munich, and after that, silence. Very few young Polish Jews survived the war.

I think of the democrat's dilemma when I see today's demonstrations against the war in Vietnam, and watch films on the Russian rape of Czechoslovakia. Where, exactly, does one draw the line between the renunciation of war as an extension of policy, and tame submission to tyranny? That particular 64,000-dollar question is still unanswered.

2

I have said that international politics did not preoccupy us much in East Devon, and this is true, at least until the mid-thirties. For a majority it remained true until September, 1938, but Munich demolished the last parochial railings that had isolated us through the years, when I was growing up in the little seacoast town of Exmouth. After the ecstatic post-Munich honeymoon (a brief and very uncomfortable interval for most of us) we knew, with complete certainty, that the roof would fall on us in one year or two.

So few people have been frank about their personal reactions to Munich that I intend to be, admitting that I shared in the general relief when Chamberlain stepped down from the plane, smiling his rabbit-toothed smile and waving his famous piece of paper. I was relieved, but by no means reassured. At best it meant a chance for someone to shoot Hitler. At worst it was a respite, one more spring and one more summer perhaps, for the history books told us that wars do not begin until the harvests are in. But when the town clerk asked for volunteers to make out billeting lists for children likely to be evacuated, when an exceptionally courageous local Liberal candidate named Halse stood up in our church hall within a week of Munich and told his audience that they had been duped, and that Hitler would occupy Prague in a matter of weeks, I think I resigned myself to Armageddon.

I had been writing plays then for ten years without ever having had one produced by professionals. That summer, the last summer of peace, I had two presented, one by the Birmingham Repertory, the other at Q Theatre, in London. Both were well received, and I was offered eight hundred pounds for the film rights of *Printer's Devil*, to appear after the war as *All Over the Town*. I had broken out of the cozy circle at last but my timing could not have been worse. *Printer's Devil* was produced in July. In August the Hitler–Stalin pact was signed. On the first day of September, Hitler went looking for that Krakow friend of mine, and Wardour Street, hub of the film industry in London, was evacuated. "It was so quiet." said a wit, "that you could hear the options dropping." Mine was one of them. On September 3 all the theaters closed and I started a new local column called "With the Forces . . . "

I volunteered for the R.A.F. and stayed on the job awaiting a call-up until the spring of 1940, and bad as things were for everybody after that, I don't think they were nearly as depressing as the eight months of the Phony War. I would choose to relive any period of my life in preference to that interval of gloom, frustration, doubt and yammering boredom.

It was as though we had all died and were waiting in a blacked-out railway siding for the undertaker to come and bury us. Nobody who did not live through this period as a young and ambitious person could possibly imagine its overriding sense of futility, for all the time one had depressing doubts about the possibility of a new lease on appeasement and nonintervention. When, at last, the Panzers began to roll westward, when Churchill took Chamberlain's place and the epic of Dunkirk was followed by the Battle of Britain, everything was changed utterly. Then it was as though we had not survived a chain of frightful disasters, but had won a brilliant victory and in a way, I suppose, we had. The alchemy of Churchill, months of brilliant sunshine, and the whiff of Gestapo breath in our nostrils, fused Left and Right in a way that would have seemed unimaginable a year before. Middle-aged men who had been calling one another rude names ever since the invasion of Abyssinia nearly five years before shared an amiable cliff patrol in the Local Defence Volunteers, forerunner of the Home Guard. Younger men, who had been dragged apart by policemen at the Blackshirt scuffle on Chapel Hill, joined the same unit and traveled in convoy to military depots. People hoped and people grinned. People didn't give a damn about standing alone and fighting it out on the beaches. And (with one exception) nobody I met that summer had the least doubt but that we should emerge not merely intact as a nation but cockier and more self-assertive than we had been for twenty years.

There was something else, too. Whenever I returned to Devon on leave I never once heard the words *Left* and *Right* bandied about. They cropped up again, of course, but not until around July 1945, when we all trooped off to the polls.

227

Budleigh Salterton and
Mrs. Simpson

One of the most profound social changes that have occurred in Britain over the last quarter century concerns the public attitude toward divorce, particularly divorce in high places. If anyone denies this, let him reflect upon the tremendous impact caused by what has become known in history as the "Domestic Crisis," leading up to the abdication of Edward VIII, in December, 1936.

It was a mere thirty-four years ago, less than what passes for a generation, and yet the heat it generated, the fury and self-questioning it occasioned at the time, was stupendous, dividing as it did any number of families, and splitting the country into two camps, who for a month or so glared at one another as though on the verge of carrying the issue to the point of physical violence.

I touched on this in my saga of the suburbs, *The Avenue Story*, where an elderly spinster, who had revered Edward through his long period as Prince of Wales, assaulted a neighbor with her shopping bag during an altercation on the subject in a grocery store. I do not think I exaggerated. People did get tremendously steamed up about it, and the emotional wounds caused by the abdication, that came as a great shock to a British public almost completely in ignorance of the mounting crisis, were not healed until George VI and Queen Elizabeth had restored public confidence and won international respect by the tactful way in which they set about filling the vacuum. As a journalist pounding a small, provincial beat I was probably more aware of this than Fleet Street men, who were naturally more concerned with day-to-day headlines and were thus able to put the abdication behind them in a week or so.

One of the main reasons why the crisis generated so much controversy, I think, was the action of the British press in contriving, with remarkable success, to keep the public in ignorance of the situation long after it became general knowledge elsewhere. This, of course, was done in good faith and was designed to spare the parties concerned acute embarrassment, but it was folly for all that. It had the effect of multiplying the force of the explosion many times over when at last the silence was broken, and those members of the public who had seen saucy references to Mrs. Simpson in American and Canadian papers, could no longer dismiss them as examples of transatlantic fantasy in bad taste.

I can recall the circumstances in which I came to hear about it, some time in the early autumn of that year, when a friend sent me a Canadian newspaper with a headline that ran, *Will Teddy Marry Wally?* Until then I had never heard of Mrs. Simpson, and when I showed the newspaper to friends they regarded it as so nonsensical that it hardly merited perusal.

In ordinary circumstances, I suppose, a story as sensational as this would seep into the public consciousness, and perhaps it did in more sophisticated circles. But nothing like that happened in places like Budleigh Salterton, the town on our eastern border, allegedly populated by scores of retired admirals and major generals, with a sprinkling of mahogany-faced Indian civil servants who had migrated there at the expiration of their service abroad. Budleigh Salterton, I'll stake my wig, had no inkling of what was brewing. It went right on preparing for Edward's coronation in May of the following year, and Wally—whoever she was—was not spared a thought, even by the tiny minority who read overseas newspapers.

Then, like a thunderclap that strips every slate from the roof and brings out all the local fire brigades, the story broke and we were plunged into a mad welter of rumor and counterrumor, involving not merely the King and Mrs. Simpson, but Mr. Ernest Simpson (whoever he was), the Queen Mother, the Prime Minister, the Archbishop of Canterbury, the Bishop of Bradford (who unconsciously leaked the news in a sermon) and the entire British establishment.

It was appalling. Nothing remotely like it had occurred since George IV had refused to admit his wife to the Coronation over a century before. People went about their business with dazed, incredulous expressions, exchanging views about what was likely to happen and half believing, *wanting* to believe, that it was all a gigantic hoax on the part of Fleet Street and the BBC. Lesser scandals had always been relished to some extent, the subject of sly innuendos in the bridge clubs and on the golf course, but there were no fringe benefits to be extracted from this fantastic sequence of events. It was all far too personal, for most people living in the British provinces in 1936 had come to regard Edward, Prince of Wales, as a kind of Sir Galahad who used a sports car instead of a horse, someone they saw as the very embodiment of British tradition, with a pleasing dash of modernity about his temperament.

It is difficult, at this distance, to convey to a later generation the extent of the popularity Edward enjoyed as Prince of Wales. It was more embracing than that enjoyed by any member of the Royal Family today, much as the Queen, Prince Philip and the present Prince of Wales are liked and respected by a vast majority of the British people. He was at once a fact and a legend. Young and old identified with him, were interested in everything he did and said, and saw him as someone endowed with the ability to blend past, present and future. He was a symbol of continuity to the elderly and a lively promise to those of his own generation. He did everything and went everywhere. He hunted, and came an occasional cropper over a hairy fence. He traveled by air. He walked bareheaded in London. He knew, from personal experience, every corner of the Empire. He showed a very real concern for the plight of the unemployed. He was known to dislike protocol and flunkydom and would run contrary to it whenever he saw an opportunity. He dressed informally, used slang, danced well, enjoyed visiting nightclubs and somehow, to those who remembered his amiable face on toffee tins during the First World War, he never stopped being young. Those among us born during his father's reign looked to him to occupy the throne for the rest of our lives and were not in the least concerned whether he married or went through life as a bachelor. He had plenty of brothers, the line of succession was secure, and we liked him for his vitality and informality. He was a fixture, like the Houses of Parliament and Westminster Abbey and at that time, with Hitler and Mussolini rampaging across the Channel, we were in sore need of a fixture.

All this blew up in our faces overnight. One morning he was there, as rooted as the oak in which his Stuart ancestor had hidden, the next he was a royal cork, tossed about by people we didn't much like or hardly knew. It was all very chastening and uncomfortable, as though we had come down to breakfast one morning and learned, via the milkman, that the head of the family has absconded with his blond secretary and was said to be making for Buenos Aires.

2

My own family was split on the issue. My father, a great traditionalist despite strong radical convictions, was outraged by the whole sorry business, whereas my brother and myself, whose job it was to present a local interpretation of the crisis to *Chronicle* readers, were King's Men from the outset. We took the view, a view upheld by a small but vocal minority, that, Mrs. Simpson notwithstanding, we did not want Edward to stand down, and that Parliament and the Dominions would be well advised to find some kind of compromise. My mother, another traditionalist, took my father's side in the argument, and I imagine acrimony of this kind was present at millions of breakfast tables from Pentland Firth to the Longships Lighthouse. I would not like to give the impression, however, that the battle was joined between Victorians and Edwardians on the one side and Georgians on the other. This controversy was unique. It had no kind of precedent, and protagonists were left to sort themselves out and align themselves as best they could. Churchill and Beaverbrook, of course, were regarded as potential champions of the King's faction, whereas the ubiquitous Baldwin, and His Grace the Archbishop, emerged as the figureheads of the King-Must-Go faction. It seemed at first as though the King's Men were holding on to the initiative during days of mounting confusion and they found themselves in strange company. Mosleyites (and left-wingers who abominated Mosley) were seen bearing placards that read "*We want the King and not Baldwin*" parading up and down Whitehall, and every point of view put forward by leader writers was solemnly debated in saloon bars, public vehicles, shops and on the curbside. The most extravagant forms of compromise were mooted but in the end they crystallized into that of a morganatic marriage. It was this, however, that succeeded in widening the gulf, for that section of the public siding with Baldwin could not swallow the fact that Mrs. Simpson would have not one but two divorces behind her if she became the morganatic wife of a man ruling over the largest empire in the history of mankind and who was also, through no fault of his own, a royal Peter Pan.

I first became aware of the strength of this undercurrent when I elected to take a sample public-opinion poll in one corner of my beat. I should have known better than to choose Budleigh Salterton, but it happened to be a Thursday and Thursday was my day for visiting Budleigh Salterton.

I must admit to being shocked by the reception I received from this section of my regular subscribers. By merely asking the question—were they for or against the King—I somehow converted myself into a target for the abuse that would have been directed at Mrs. Simpson had she taken refuge in Budleigh Salterton instead of Fort Belvedere, the mock-Gothic retreat of the King at that time. Mrs. Simpson herself tells how, during her flight to Cannes, a man seeing her car pass down a street in Lyons screamed, "*Voila la dame.*" I am persuaded that the arrival of Wallis in most parts of the English provinces at that time would have provoked similar epithets and possibly demonstrations.

As an opinion sounder, designed to test the local strength of the Churchill-Beaverbrook faction, my private poll was a failure, but it taught me something important about the worth of popular adulation. Budleigh Salterton, at that time, was probably the most throne-loving township in the country, with the possible exceptions of Sandringham, Windsor and Cheltenham, but I can see now why its verdict was so unanimous. It considered itself, collectively, to have been the victim of an outrageous practical joke. Its older inhabitants (long since laid to rest alongside what the brash newcomers to Budleigh Salterton describe as "The Curry" of earlier generations) never forgave Edward or Wally and would growl when their names were mentioned, but the middle-aged and younger sectors soon mellowed. If the Duke and Duchess of Windsor appeared in the High Street now they would probably be greeted with respectful hurrahs.

For my part, however, I was equally unforgiving. It seemed to me at that time, and still does for that matter, that the British did not emerge very creditably from the Domestic Crisis, demonstrating as they did a most uncharacteristic vein of hysteria. Up to that moment Edward's life had been devoted to public service, and it has since been admitted by historians that he made a spectacular success of his job. His postwar imperial journeys alone were of very considerable value to the economy. He had always seen himself as a bridge between the sedate but hypocritical era of his great-grandmother, and the more relaxed era of the twenties. I never recall hearing a slighting word spoken of him until December, 1936, if one excepts an unemployed Welsh miner's refusal to sing "God Bless the Prince of Wales" at a local concert. Yet the things said of him during the ten days of the Domestic Crisis were not merely critical. Many were spiteful and some were scurrilous. Men and women whom until then I had always looked upon as tolerant and kindly neighbors, talked of him in a way they might have referred to an infamous scoundrel caught in the execution of a shabby crime. To live through it all was an unpleasant experience at the trusting age of twenty-four. To record it, as I did in the course of my work, was to understand that there are times when British moral righteousness deserves the cynicism of Continentals. The historian Macauley was very discerning when, in the middle of the last century, he drew attention to this curious quirk in the national character, this sudden and inexplicably violent access of puritanical rectitude that is capable of flaying a man alive and enjoying the exercise. For a week or a fortnight the British public dance on the corpse and then, feeling rather foolish, they return to their cricket and their crumpets beside the fire and promptly forget all about him. Such a demonstration helped to send Edith Thompson to the gallows. A little more than a decade later another moral explosion (this time spiced with leeriness) delivered the Reverend Davidson, sometime Rector of Stiffkey, to the lions. In the early sixties we saw it again in the Profumo case, but on each of these occasions there was some kind of justification for a public outcry. We know that Edith Thompson played around the edges of murder, even if she had no real intention of committing it, whereas Davidson, guilty or not, behaved like a fool over a long period of time. Profumo made the mistake of deceiving Parliament and the nation. But Edward VIII deserved, to my way of thinking, something better of the people he had served so well and for so long. At the very least he should have earned their spontaneous sympathy and not their execration. Unwise and headstrong he might have been, but his own account of his life, up to the moment he left these shores on the appropriately named *Fury*, makes it abundantly clear that his patriotism and his deep regard for his heritage and what it entailed in terms of duty were never in question, then or later. A majority of Saltertonians of that time thought otherwise, and their attitude was not singular. You would have found the same sentiments in any market town or resort, and even in the cities. A few people openly championed the fallen idol, and rather more sympathized and held their peace. But a majority fell over one another in their eagerness to cast the first stone. It is curious that all this occurred less than four years before the period Churchill described as Britain's finest hour.

Tweedledum and Tweedledee

I

The British are an exceptionally conservative race. They display a deep distrust toward change in their national way of life, and although their history is studded with eccentrics they are, at bedrock, suspicious of displays in public places. In view of this I find it extraordinary that so many of their prime ministers over the last century should have been clowns.

There was Palmerston, whose strident chauvinism was a non-stop harlequinade; Disraeli, who never once took his tongue from his cheek; Gladstone, who came to identify himself with an Old Testament prophet; and the donnish Asquith, who could find time to write a daily love letter to a young girl whilst directing Britain's contribution to the bloodiest conflict in history.

Nearer our own times there was Lloyd George, possibly the most accomplished entertainer who ever trod Westminster boards, and after him Baldwin, who was rarely seen without a cherry-wood pipe, and liked to lean over a sty and scratch his pigs with a stick, concealing his astute political brain under the motley of a kindly, unimaginative English squire.

After Baldwin there was MacDonald, whose clowning took the form of kissing duchesses and making long, rambling speeches that not even the faithful could understand.

By then, of course, the British voter was aware of the inherent weakness in his political system and, accepting the fact that the real business of government was carried on by the Civil Service, resigned himself to buffoonery in high places, even bestowing an affectionate nickname on the reigning clown. Lloyd George became the "Welsh Wizard," Baldwin "Honest Stan," MacDonald "Ramsaymac." By the time Neville Chamberlain appeared, with his ragged mustache and his umbrella, one began to feel that these people should forgo election addresses and resort to circus billing. "Roll up, roll up and watch the Umbrella Man vanquish the Ugly Sisters" would, I think, have been appropriate billing for the election that should have taken place around 1939–40 but was bypassed, the British electorate having rather more pressing affairs in hand at that time.

By then, of course, Churchill was in power, and in some ways he proved the most electrifying clown of them all. He cleared the ring of rivals, roared defiance at hecklers, went everywhere with a half-smoked cigar in his mouth, and wore a succession of funny hats. For years the British delighted in him, and then quite suddenly they tired of the performance and longed for a bit of peace. That was how they came to elect a quiet little man like Clem Attlee, who had no pretensions whatever toward buffoonery.

In the period between 1938 and 1955 my work as an airman, journalist and dramatist brought me into contact with these two prime ministers, whose personalities were so opposed to one another. This contrast seems to me to reveal something fundamental in the British character, an assertion that compromise between two extremes is the only thing that is important in the art of government.

2

I met Attlee twice and had two conversations with him, one of them in private.

In 1937 he came to the West to rally the cause of Labour and as a newsman I attended a small private tea given in his honor. As there was no other journalist present I was able to talk to him for perhaps thirty minutes, and from the first he made a deep impression on me, so that I never shared the public view that he was a nonentity.

I was aware of his record, of course, up to the time when he appeared in the lounge of a prominent local Socialist and sat sipping tea, looking like a patient Chinese mandarin presiding over a trivial lawsuit. I knew that he had fought on the Western Front as a tank officer at a time when the Top Brass regarded tanks as clumsy toys, and how, throughout the twenties, he had worked in the East End as a social reformer. He seemed to me at that time, and does in retrospect, the very best type of Englishman, a man whose dominant characteristic was compassion and concern for the unfortunate, and who considered it a privilege to spend himself working for them, a man without personal ambition of the kind one associates with every professional politician, someone with deeply rooted convictions based on Christian ethics, but the good manners not to wave them like banners. I envied him his quiet but fluent command of the English tongue when expounding an idea or propounding a policy. He never raised his voice or allowed himself to be carried away and remained, in essence, a man of tremendous restraint. One knew, somehow, that he had never willingly misled anyone in his life, that he would make a good friend and a forgiving enemy. In this sense, I think, he was unique in politics, and Britain is the poorer for his not having taken office in the early thirties, when our leaders were first confronted with the menace of Fascism and responded to it with that most craven of all policies, nonintervention.

Ten years later when he had grown considerably in political stature, I had the very real pleasure of meeting him again. He brought his daughter to see my comedy, *Peace Comes to Peckham*, on her twenty-first birthday, while the play was running at the Princes Theatre, and during the interval he came down into the foyer and told me gravely that he and his family were enjoying the entertainment. I asked him whether he would like a drink. After a brief hesitation he asked for a gin and lime, and we carried our drinks into the box office, where I reminded him of the occasion we had first met. He recalled it in detail and this surprised me, for so much had happened in between, and it struck me then how lightly the years, and the fearful responsibilities that had pressed on him as Churchill's deputy, had dealt with him. He still looked like a kindly mandarin pondering a judgment. He still talked like the middle-aged man next door commenting on the headlines in the evening paper, the kind of chap whose hedge clippers you would borrow on a Saturday afternoon. But on this second occasion I detected something new about him. Outwardly undistinguished, and without displaying any of the apparatus or shadow play of power, he yet projected a kind of dynamism. One had the impression that he was possessed of an immense store of wisdom, emerging as common sense. I was to see him once again.

3

I never met Churchill, but I stood close to him on three occasions, and those occasions, seen in retrospect, remain in my mind as three stages in a career of astonishing variety. They could be signposted failure, triumph, and death.

In the very early thirties he too came West to address a Conservative garden party, at a time when he was in the wilderness, without the least prospect of finding his way out again. His long series of personal adventures were behind him; but, far from trailing the glory of an imperial past, he looked as though he had already conceded defeat, accepting it with a crustiness that would have put any experienced reporter on guard, encouraging him to tread softly on Churchillian corns. There was nothing about Churchill's manner or appearance at that time to suggest that, in less than a decade, he would rank with Pitt, or that his name would pass into the language as the embodiment of dramatic leadership and truculent oratory. I am inclined to the view, however, that he was conserving his stupendous energies and, as time went on, and he warned repeatedly of the growing menace of Germany, he addressed a small part of those energies to the task of preparing the British electorate, particularly the part of it inclined to the left, for his assumption of power in the spring of 1940. If this was not so, why did we turn automatically to Churchill after Chamberlain's egregious Hitler-has-missed-the-bus speech?

Churchill was in and about the Air Ministry all the time I was based there in the spring and early summer of 1944 and later when the war was drawing to a close, but I did not see him again until V-E Day, when I had the luck to walk into an office on the first floor that adjoined the balcony on which he was to announce the Allied victory. Naturally I remained there, despite the bleats of the officious civilian clerk on whose chair I was standing. By leaning out over the stone balustrade, and craning my neck to the right, I could see Churchill's famous profile a few yards away. It would have taken ten clerks to drag me away.

It was a tremendous moment. Down below, Whitehall and the adjoining square were densely packed with people, all staring upward, and when Churchill began, "This is *your* victory . . ." the roar that echoed across the capital was like that of a thousand jets breaking the sound barrier at treetop level. I remember thinking back to that sad, slightly sagging figure of the early thirties, and my father's wry comment, "He's been drinking brandy . . ." and wondering at the curious shifts in human destinies. For here was a man who had been written off by every political pundit in the world, but had finally emerged as someone who could set London in an uproar with six syllables.

A few weeks later he was toppled, and the quiet mandarin took his place, to occupy it for six years before their positions were reversed once more. Until then, I think, one had never credited Tweedledum or Tweedledee with such resilience, and the grandee must have been astounded to find himself shown the door by the mandarin. He was only the first to be astonished. Nobody, it seems to me, has yet explained how Attlee held together a team of lieutenants that would have daunted Cromwell. Bevan, Bevin, Herbert Morrison and Stafford Cripps were all big men in their own right, and there was unquestionably a galaxy of talent in the postwar government, but Attlee controlled them all effortlessly, without resort to the wiles of Lloyd George, the flattery of Disraeli, the thunder of Gladstone and Churchill or the butchery of Macmillan.

He slipped away in the nineteen-fifties without fuss, the way he did everything in his public and private life, and it was a very frail little man I watched mount the steps of St. Paul's one bitterly cold day in 1965, as one of his rival's pallbearers.

Until that moment I had never seen Tweedledum and Tweedledee together, as so many people present must have done, but it seemed fitting that Attlee, whose walk was beginning to develop into a stumble, should stand there bareheaded behind the enormous coffin resting on the shoulders of six panting Guardsmen.

Almost everybody who had played a part in that curious wartime alliance was there to see Churchill honored, as no Englishman has been honored since Wellington was borne to that same spot more than a century before. At the rear of the cathedral, near the great doors that opened and closed to admit distinguished mourners, one's attention fluctuated between the arrival of the Royal Family, the Churchills, De Gaulle, Eisenhower and a score of others, including one reigning prime minister and a band of former prime ministers, of whom Attlee was the smallest. But it was Clement Attlee I watched as the cortege left, and he followed it into the near-freezing atmosphere beyond the great doors. And here, approaching the steps, a rather touching thing happened, for Attlee did stumble and Eden, who seemed to be anticipating the falter, reached out and steadied the little man's elbow. It brought into focus the party truce of the war years, and I wondered then whether the Tweedledum and Tweedledee routine is anything more than a game the British like to play between crises.

One Man Went to

The Even Sadder Truth About
Me and the Footlights

The fact of the matter is, of course, I never was stage-struck, not even temporarily on the night I came home from my first pantomime.

I was entertained, and occasionally excited, but never captivated. Neither did I envy actors their incomes, their fame, or their domination of an audience, for I always had an unworthy suspicion that behind the back cloth there was a dank passage giving access to numerous untidy little cells that stank of grease paint and housed bagging chairs and fly-spotted mirrors, where the motley was shed and the bill had to be settled. I was quite right about this as it happened, although it took me something like thirty years to prove.

I have often wondered what first warned me of the fallibility of glamour projected across the footlights. I never found it echoed in any one of my associates who also earned their living on the stage. One and all had fallen victims to the mystique in earliest childhood, and most of them are still enslaved and bravely admit as much, even when resting. Did I inherit my profound mistrust for professional buffoonery from my Puritan ancestors? Or did I, in some Freudian way, associate backstage with the horrid risks of poking around a fairground, being abducted and having my face stained with walnut juice? I don't know and I never will know, but in the end the vague suspicions of infancy were triumphantly confirmed. After writing more than a score of three-act plays and seeing them performed in theaters of every grade, I can think of no worse fate than being born on Boxing Day in a basket of tights at, say, the Hippodrome, Dudley, or the old Royalty, Newcastle-under-Lyme. The advertisement columns of *The Stage* still make me shudder and hurry away, as from a scene of degradation, and the people who spend their lives in this half world I regard as desperate, gallant, bedeviled creatures, half mountebank, half mercenary freebooter capable of sacking cities. I have a great affection for some of them, but I cannot bring myself to believe that they are of the same species as, say, a bank manager, a postman, or even a steeplejack. They are a race apart, doomed to go through life pretending to be somebody else, Flying Dutchmen and Wandering Jews with no prospect of repose or privacy save that which they find sitting before their spotted mirrors awaiting the summons of the callboy. Naturally, in these circumstances, they tend to marry one another, so that the families perpetuate a protocol as bizarre as that practiced for seven centuries by the Hapsburgs.

This attitude of mind would be odd, I feel, in a man who earned his bread as a solicitor or an estate agent. In a playwright it is heresy.

To enjoy a live stage show one has, of course, to suspend disbelief and to do this much more wholeheartedly than in the cinema, where players are shadows, when one can see round corners, and where there is no necessity for strict continuity of scene. Perhaps this was my initial handicap. I could never do it, not even as a child and not even in the presence of the world's finest players capering about the most lavish sets. For me Robinson Crusoe was never, for a single moment, the village ne'er-do-well cast upon a desert island, but just a saucy girl with plump thighs who had a false and hearty ring to her voice and was unable to utter a word that was not bracketed in rhyming couplets of appalling banality.

When I grew out of pantomimes and my mother took me to

see a spate of three-act plays suspension of belief grew even more difficult, for here the actors and actresses were not even laughing at themselves, as I felt sure was the case among the Principal Boys and Widow Twankeys. Obviously they intended you to take it for granted that they *were* an assortment of wronged women, fumbling blackmailers, bumbling detectives, lean students, star-crossed lovers, butlers, alcoholics and starving musicians. It made no difference whether the play I saw was an acknowledged classic or a three-act farce, a musical or a "nudger," a straight comedy or a thriller, a tragedy or a dramatized biography of someone I had encountered in my history lessons or in the public library. I simply did not believe a word anyone up there was saying, and all the time they were simulating, in many cases very expertly, moods of grief, passion, jealousy, drollery or even curiosity, something kept reminding me that they were only doing this for money and that as soon as my back was turned they would transfer their makeup to a soiled towel, put on their proper trousers, swig a bottle of beer and go home to cold lamb in Ma's digs, where—as actors were informed in other days—there was a "pub. op. and a lav. in." It seemed to me an agonizing way to earn a living, and I was relieved to know that the professions of engine driver and deep-sea diver were still open to me.

How then, one might ask, did I ever become professionally involved with the stage? In the light of my earliest convictions about it, involvement with counterfeiters and white-slavers would seem to be more likely. How was it that, from the age of eighteen, I spent almost every moment of my spare time writing plays and sending them off in large buff envelopes that contained, besides the manuscript, another buff envelope addressed to myself?

I have asked myself this question many, many times over the last thirty-five years but have never produced a satisfactory answer. Primarily, I suppose, it sprang from motives of greed and the yearning that all of us have in one way or another to earn the plaudits of our contemporaries. But also it was a response to a challenge, for by that time I had sat through so many straight plays, and seen so many changes rung that it occurred to me I must be a complete idiot if I couldn't produce something at least as compelling in the way of arranging words.

I suppose the itch began a year or so after I became a reporter on a weekly newspaper where my duties included attending, and commenting upon, the bread-and-butter plays of several amateur societies, presenting what is now known as who's-for-tennis entertainments. Many of them were well-constructed pieces by professionals like Stanley Houghton, H. F. Maltby, John Van Druten and Dodie Smith. They all ran about two hours and ten minutes, and most of them had one change of scene. They all used from nine to thirteen characters, and graphwise they followed an identical course—that is, Establishment, Conflict, and Tying of Loose Ends, in acts one, two, and three.

I watched these plays in the way George Stephenson watched his father's pumping engine when he was a boy. It interested me to see how they were put together and projected, but as for believing in them that was impossible, and even more impossible than at the professional theater. How could one conceive of Fred Vetch, chief of sales of the local outfitters, as Robert Browning? Or Mollie Young, whom I had kissed last night on her doorstep after the Licenced Victuallers' Ball, as the ailing Elizabeth Barrett? One couldn't, of course, any more than one could accept Mr. Baines, the undertaker, as an apprentice pirate in *The Pirates of Penzance* that had been performed on this very stage the previous Wednesday. Mostly I just sat there and pondered, making guesses at when Fred was due to reappear from down right, or Mollie make her exit up left. I noted the kind of line that coaxed a murmur from the audience and the quip that drew laughter or applause. Then I went home to my bedroom and set to work on plays of my own, parceling them up with painstaking persistence and dropping them into the gaping letter box of the G.P.O.

They always came back. Day after day, week after week, year after year, they came back, producing the familiar plop on the mat just inside the front door. Sometimes they were accompanied by a short, typed note that began: *"Dear Sir, I have read your play . . ."* and sometimes they came back without a note, but liberally spotted with tea. By the time I was twenty-four I had a wardrobe drawer crammed with manuscripts, rejection slips clamped to their outer covers by rusty paper clips.

Then it happened, and it all came about in the way I had half anticipated because one naturally associated the stage with muddle and disorganization, with indecision, false assurances, fair promises, flatteries and strings of bare-faced lies.

I met a strolling player earning an uncertain living with a small touring company and told him the plot of a comedy I had written two years before, a play set in a garage on the South Coast and run by a former Australian goldminer and his daughter. He seemed interested and asked to see a script, but when I searched for one I discovered that the only copy I could trace was at the Birmingham Repertory Theatre and had been for close on two years. I had written a dozen plays since then and who could keep track of so many disappointing children? I wrote to Birmingham and asked for my manuscript, taking care to enclose the usual stamped addressed envelope. By return of post I received a wire from the resident producer. It read, "Don't ask for it back now, we're doing it next week." I must admit that, for all my built-in mistrust of the theater, this information surprised me so much that I made up my mind on the spot to travel to Birmingham and discover whether in fact it was true.

It was true. For the first time in my life I saw my name on a billboard, and the shock was so terrible that I almost collided with it. It *had* happened, then, and I was one of them. Before me was the prospect of money and fame, certainly, but what else? Theatrical digs, with a "pub. op. and a lav. in"? Grease paint, and a bagged-out chair in a gaslit dressing cell? Years and years of walking about between flimsy flats of lath and canvas pretending like mad to be somebody else? I didn't necessarily have to act, of course, but it was a salutary reflection all the same for it seemed to me then—indeed, it does still—that a man who writes for the theater is, of necessity, part and parcel of show business and has turned his back on the sane and civilized world.

Nothing I saw that night reassured me. Strangers addressed me as "Darling" and rubbed cheeks with me; the backstage smell of dust, grease paint and pinched-out cigarettes confirmed my worst fears about what went on down there, and as for the people I had created, they looked just as incredible as the characters in every other play I had witnessed. I was amazed when, in the *Birmingham Post* the next morning, Mr. Maurice Wiggin, then critic of the paper, headlined his notice, "More Please, Mr. Delderfield!"

I was paid for my services, slunk away and went on writing. A few weeks later Q Theatre, one of the many tryout centers that existed in London in those days, staged another play of mine called *Printer's Devil*, and watching it I had my first lesson in the supreme folly of last-minute revisions. When a line the company had greeted as "a belly-laugh worth two hundred pounds to the box office" failed to get more than a simper I trimmed it and threw the emphasis onto a subsequent line that had, for no reason whatever, produced loud cackles. At the following performance everybody laughed in the right place so I had to put everything back as it was. The tension behind stage was terrible. All the leading characters were hard at work persuading me to give them the laugh lines of the character players, and all the character players wanted their parts enlarged. It was like presiding at the counter of a January bargain sale, besieged by clamoring housewives who had been queuing outside the shop since dawn. There was no pleasing anyone. Even the then-famous critic James Agate wrote, "Good enough to fail instantly in the West End!" Mercifully, World War II broke out and I slipped into the anonymity of uniform, but the theater is like drink and degradation. Once launched upon the slippery slope, you tend to lose control of circumstances, and I was soon involved in unpaid stage writing on behalf of the R.A.F., and ordered to write a service pantomime for Christmas. The C.O., a very practical man, asked how many acts it was likely to have. I told him that most pantomimes had two, so he gave me two days off to write the piece. In the meantime my real work accumulated in the in-trays and to cap it all a bomb fell on the Birmingham Repertory just as I was about to return the scenery I had borrowed.

Reduced to five and sixpence a day, and marooned in a cheer-less Blackpool billet, I made yet another attempt to coax a profit from the theater and wrote a play about Florence Nightingale. It was carried away in triumph by a manager with long hair and fanatical eyes who prophesied a smash hit and a fortune. I have never seen him or the script since.

Years of postings followed, and now and again I wrote parts of plays in service notebooks. One day, firewatching at the Air Ministry, I was scribbling away when I looked up and saw a manager I had known in my Birmingham days. He said, "I'm looking for a comedy. Have you got one?" He said it as though he was out of matches and wanted to smoke. I told him I was writing the first act of a comedy about R.A.F. men in a billet, and he said he would read it and tell me if it was promising.

The next day he came back and gave me thirty pounds for an option, and the day after that I wrote the second act. I had to think hard about the names of the characters, because it hadn't occurred to him to return Act One. On my next day off I wrote the third act, sitting on a seat opposite Marble Arch. It seemed an appropriate place to traffic with the theater, for Tyburn Tree had once stood within yards of my perch. Then a V-1 descended, and I hurried away, promising myself that I would assemble all three acts and touch them up when I was firewatching but I never did, for that week I was sent to France, forgetting all about the comedy and the manager to whom I mailed the rough draft just before boarding the Auster. It was only one of many such manuscripts bearing my name and now gathering dust on the open shelves of managers' offices. I had seen some of those shelves, stacked with the dead and dying brain children of people like me and had recognized them as the graveyards of plays. After all, plays were expendable, the work of the lowest form of ani-mal life in the theater—authors.

I do not think I gave a single thought to this play about airmen until I called in at the American Express in Paris some months later and asked if there was any mail for a Flight Lieutenant Delderfield. The officer in charge looked at me with distaste. "In there," he said, and he pointed to the bottom drawer of a file cabinet under the window. In the drawer I found fifty-seven letters, nearly all from airmen and W.A.A.F.'s serving in the Midlands. They had all, they declared, seen and enjoyed a play of mine and were asking if they could have free tickets when it went to the West End. This was another lesson I learned about the theater. You don't have to have a play actually running in London before your mail is spiced with demands for complimentary tickets. It happens the moment you get a play on anywhere.

It was through this particular comedy that I met Ronnie Shiner, then playing an S.P. corporal in *Something in the Air* at the Palace. We were introduced in one of those awful dressing rooms, Ronnie leering at me through a thick coating of custard pie, thrown at him as he left the stage by Cicely Courtneidge, in the role of a mutinous W.A.A.F. Ronnie believed in the play from the very beginning, and eventually, between us, we managed to get it on tour. Its reception was very odd. At three of its six dates it was a sellout. At the other three a flop. Then it lapsed and I was demobbed and went home, happy to return to the comparative sanity of the newspaper world.

But, as I say you can't control these things. Pick up a stick of grease paint out of curiosity and before you know where you are you find yourself with a black mustache and blue pouches under your eyes, and it was this way with me. The play shared a bill at the Embassy, another tryout theater, and after Beverley Nichols had kindly announced that it made his ribs ache it was transferred to the Whitehall, again on a double-bill basis. Unluckily I had the earlier half of the evening, and the first week the takings were £148. I believe the rent at that time was about £900, but like everything else about show business the economics of the theater is crazy. We were told that if we didn't top the £1,000 mark in a month we would be out on the pavement, and when, at the end of the third week, we had climbed to about £800, our backer bought enough tickets to retain the lease. He must have kicked himself hard that Saturday night. We had taken about £1,500 without his contribution.

By now the play was a success and people who had sat through it on tour and at the Embassy in glum silence paid it a second visit and howled with laughter. I used to slip in sometimes and listen to them. It was always entertaining, because I saw and heard so many variations of the script as the cast fought madly for more laughs, clutching at lines and situations like men making their way down a steeply angled roof, or women almost within hailing range of the approaching lifeboat. Nobody took the slightest notice of me, and sometimes the booking-office people said, "Full up, try again next week!" so I slunk round to the stage door, where occasionally a member of the cast would recognize me and ask me what I was doing backstage and did I want to see anyone special? One day, getting out of the stage manager's way, I bumped against a Canadian reporter, who asked where he could find the author. I told him that I was the author and he seemed incredulous, but just then one of the cast bustled up and confirmed my identity, whereupon the reporter asked me to tell him about the earliest days of the play. I said he had far better ask the players, who were so much closer to it than I was, but the actor who had confirmed my authorship then put his arm round my shoulders and said, gaily, "Now then, now then, we couldn't have done much without a good blueprint, Ronnie!"

God forgive me. I went to work on another play about the reunion of a London family after the war, and this too went to the Embassy where it was bought by Mr. Firth Sheppard, the well-known impresario. Under his sway my life became even more unreal, for he had two big henchmen with whom he discussed the play in detail over my head and as though I wasn't present. He even took the bow on the first night and when a lone voice shouted "Author" he sent someone to fetch me and propelled me onto the stage, where I mumbled and grimaced until I was enveloped in the falling curtain. We played to what

I thought was excellent business, but for all that we lost the
lease of the theater, and when the manager booked a smaller,
more central one, we discovered that the leading character
wasn't available. He had just signed on with a film company. So
we found another lead and took the play on tour.

This kind of thing went on for years. I continued to write
plays and travel to and from London, but somehow, the moment
I was caught up in the swirl of rehearsals, I lost touch with the
piece, and everyone associated with it seemed to go off their
heads, quarreling with one another over those exit lines, cornering
me in the Gents' in the hope of persuading me to rewrite their
parts, add new scenes, or take four pages of Act Three in order
to lengthen Act One. In the end I hardly knew what the play
was about, and always, when pressures became intolerable, I ran
away and went home to Devon. They used to phone up and ask
if anyone had seen me, as they wanted a better joke in the middle
of Act Two, and when I came to the phone they refused to believe it was me and said I was to stop pulling their leg and find
the author.

I once had three plays running up there at one time, and
everybody thought I was making a vast fortune, but I wasn't;
and soon even the income-tax man began to take my denials
seriously. The income from the plays shredded away, like puff
clouds scattered by a southwesterly gale. Curious percentages
were clipped off here and there, and when we transferred from
the Whitehall to the Comedy the management told me they
couldn't pay me anything until the takings had climbed to over
a thousand a week. My constant trips to London proved ruinous.
Actors and actresses would run me down and order champagne,
and sometimes, when we had all had a jolly lunch together, they
would say, "Darling! So lovely to have seen you!" and disappear
in a body, after which the headwaiter would bring me a bill for
£14 16s. 9d. All actors and actresses have schoolboy appetites.

Sometimes I would sulk and not appear in London for weeks,
and then everybody would write or phone telling me I was dis-
loyal and undermining their confidence in themselves. This, of

course, was said in jest, because it isn't possible to undermine the confidence of anyone who earns his or her living on the stage. People have been trying for hundreds of years and nobody has ever succeeded.

By 1955, about a decade after my arrival as a playwright, I had had enough. I began to make wide detours round the capital when it lay on my route, and I also began writing historical plays for a Scottish festival hundreds of miles to the north. Here, for a spell, I was lulled into believing that some theater folk took authors seriously. The festival people booked rooms for me and gave me cups of tea, and held up rehearsals if I was late, and found me parking spaces outside the theater, although they still approached me warily, as though I was a close relative who, to everyone's embarrassment, had just been released on license from the county jail. Then I realized they were just as mad as everyone else in the profession, for I was summoned to a rehearsal of a play I had written about Napoleon, and the producer had made Napoleon go to bed, wrapped in his cloak, on the uncarpeted floor of the Tuileries! When I protested that this was most unlikely, and that I had actually seen the bed in which the Emperor slept, the producer was very upset and went away muttering that authors could be terribly difficult.

I think it was that cat nap of Napoleon's that snapped the long, snarled cord that bound me to the theater. I decided that there must be easier ways of earning a living and professions where one did not necessarily have to live cheek by jowl with talkative madmen and madwomen who were either wildly gay or threatening to throw themselves off Westminster Bridge on account of someone telling them to say the words that were actually written into the script. I began to write novels and at once put on weight. The telephone rang no more than twice a day, and even then one of the calls was from my bank manager asking about the overdraft. It was very still and peaceful in the study, tapping away on the typewriter and creating characters safely imprisoned between two hard covers, who were not in a position to dispute their exits and entrances. The moment I realized this I began to enjoy exercising my despotism over them and would sometimes kill them off by bombs and electric shocks just to prove who was boss. I was happily engaged doing this one morning when I had a shock myself. The postman arrived with a letter from my publisher asking, in courtly terms, if he could change one of my commas into a semicolon.

I sat and looked at that letter a long time, mourning my wasted years among the savage hill tribes when, all the time, civilization had been beckoning from the plains. I have stayed on the plains ever since. If you want to scare the hell out of me suggest I visit the theater.

The Butterfly Moments

Disregarding that cynical if resolute minority who are content to accept death as oblivion, I imagine that most of us have a very personal and private notion of Paradise.

To those growing up in the first two decades of the century, Paradise was strictly prescribed. It was a vast (and even then improbable) housing estate, spacious, well appointed and built entirely of marble. It was populated by millions of winged choristers wearing spotless night shirts. The only variation of scene one could expect up there was the splendor of the throne room. The only permissible musical instrument was the harp. It was enclosed by a huge, circular wall, broken by a single gate, where Peter was permanently on duty, and that, it would seem, was that. No excursions and no occupations apart from singing, and presumably rehearsing, songs of praise. No boon companions, apart from identically attired and harpist neighbors, no flowers save lilies, no pubs and certainly no girl friends—there was Holy Writ for that bit.

Even at five years old it struck me as insufferably dull, and I had no wish to qualify. By the time I was eleven it was a place to avoid at all costs, a clinical jail where good behavior earned one nothing but extra time.

As I grew older I discovered that I was not an isolated challenger of conventional bliss. For instance, I once met a boy who delighted in eating well-made porridge and he told me that he pictured a heaven where he was endowed with an appetite to devour plate after plate of rich, warm, glutinous porridge. Nothing else, just porridge. I remember that the stark originality of this vision made a deep impression upon me, for porridge was something I could always accept or decline.

It set me thinking, however, on the nature and substance of personal heavens, and some curious speculations resulted. I supposed that the men against whom my father inveighed, as they reeled singing from bar to bar, would expect an eternal drinking spree, that sinners addicted to gambling would want a nonstop race meeting, with an endless succession of winners at long odds, and that the professional politician would be disappointed if he was balked of a succession of passive audiences, enslaved by his oratory and believing in all his electoral promises.

In the meantime my own ideas of heaven began to moderate, adjusting, as time went by, to successive enthusiasms. There was a heaven like a library crammed with tooled-leather books, a pastoral landscape populated by troops of bobbed and shingled brunettes, a sunlit forum where I could engage in endless conversation interesting chaps like the Tolpuddle martyrs, or even a bustling Valhalla where I might have an opportunity to inquire of Simon de Montfort why he was such a fool as to let himself be trapped in the loop of the Avon at Evesham, or why Marshal Grouchy did not march to the sound of the guns at Waterloo. Like many another who prefers moonshine to neon lighting, I shaped Paradise to my own requirements and at fifty-plus the job is done. My private heaven is simply a permanent extension of all the moments in my life when I have heard myself saying, "This is *it!* This is delightful! This I should like to continue indefinitely!" For these are our butterfly moments, rare and fleeting intervals, most of them living no more than a few seconds, when we can trap delight in the net of awareness and spread-eagle it in the memory like a butterfly.

Ruskin was on the track of such moments when he urged us "to build ourselves nests of pleasant thoughts, that care cannot disturb nor pain make gloomy," but you cannot build yourself a butterfly moment and perhaps one way to ensure a lack of them is to go in search of them. They are fleeting, fragile things that fly out of nowhere into nowhere, and it is only rarely you can reach out and catch one. They come unbidden, and most of them are so elusive that they are gone before they can be netted, much less classified. But a few are slow to take off, and once trapped they appreciate in value with the passing years.

There are many categories and I classified my trophies long ago. Most of them, alas, belong to distant childhood and almost as distant youth but the middle-aged need not despair. A man is never too old to add to his collection, provided that he keeps a sharp lookout. Let me make shift to open the case and exhibit them in order of precedence.

There are the butterfly moments of repose that fly close to the earth and identify themselves with scent, sound and landscape. They flit across the sun-drenched hours of infancy, when the faculties are razor-sharp. My prize specimen in this category was trapped early one morning when I was seven and had wandered out across midsummer meadows on the Kent-Surrey border.

In those days it was possible to do this twelve miles from London Stone. The spoilers had not reached out that far, and in a long, winding lane two hundred yards south of our suburb, elms still grew to over a hundred feet, and Chalkhill Blues still flirted in dappled sunlight under enormous oaks. Cow parsley, that country folk still dignify by the name of ladies' lace, grew in umbrellas taller than a man. And overhead, under armadas of puff cloud, the larks sang. Less carefree birds rustled in the thickets and the lightest breeze, bending the buttercups, reached the south-sloping fields as a long sigh of content.

I remember settling down to listen, for it was an aural rather than a visual moment. The murmur of summer was like a quiet sea, infinitely distant but engulfing, and the weight of the orchestra came not from birds but from insects, a low, melodious, humming, exclusively English sound. That was how I thought of it then and how I think of it now, the *sound* of English summer, runic, magical and unforgettable.

This was a moment of stillness, but one does not necessarily have to associate such moments with repose. There are butterfly moments of ardor, laughter, achievement, relief and expectation. I was about fourteen before I caught and held one of these, and it had subdued undertones that linked it to the magic moment of infancy. But the setting was different, a darkening February afternoon high up on the Exmoor plateau, where we waited, two hundred strong, for the starter's orders to run for home.

Home, at that time, was school, a murky orange blur in the middle distance, and in the uncannily silent moment as we stood with one leg through the boundary fence of the Fortescue estate, the last light of the winter's afternoon centered over Barnstaple Bay revealing everything that seemed important just then—the moor, the school buildings, one's companions and, above all, one's hopes and fears to be among the first forty into the quad and qualify for points. I trapped that moment just in time. A second later we were off, a slipping, stumbling shouting avalanche of mud-splashed boys descending one of those steep, testing gradients that are rarely found on cross-country courses outside Devon or Cumberland, but the moment itself, the frozen tick of time before the "Off," was a captive, and I have it still, a rare and comforting specimen.

I caught another rather like it thirty years later, but here again there was a difference.

We had been hunting all morning over difficult, broken country, steep down-slopes bordered by thickets, with any amount of obstacles that a seasoned rider to hounds would take in his stride, but which presented nightmarish hazards to the beginner. And then, in full cry, we emerged from a copse and saw a long up-sloping field immediately ahead, with riders strung out like fugitive geese, thrusters in the van, plodders in the center and the stragglers, myself among them, in the rear.

The opponents of blood sports, bless them, are for the most part sincere and worthy folk, but how many of them have ever been involved in a hell-for-leather gallop over an English countryside on a frosty autumn morning? How is it possible to explain to them that blood lust has nothing to do with the exhilaration of violent exercise plus risk, of scenting and seeing half a hundred rare scents and sounds as the field pounds through open gates, passes a harrow safely tucked under the hedge, and settles to a blessed incline that will take some of the furious energy from one's mount and ensure a firm seat in the saddle for another five hundred yards? It was halfway up that slope, as my foot found an errant stirrup iron, that I had my moment and held on to it, no more than a swift, over-all absorption of the sight, sound and smell of faded green hedgerows, glistening briars, the thrum of two hundred hoofs on flint and wet soil, the squeak of leather and the imperious toot of Arthur's horn, the raw and pungent whiff of sweat, turned earth and hoarfrost. It is curious how vivid are the images that stamp themselves in the memory at such a moment, and I see them now as clearly as in a colored print. The narrow-faced major, seventy-seven and riding with a cavalry seat he acquired at the Dragoon Guards riding school and on the Veldt some half a century before; the country doctor, no longer bland and genial, but grim of visage as he cantered round a wicked-looking gatepost; the riderless horse who had shed her twelve-stone owner; the pigtailed farmer's daughter, stirrupless but unable or unwilling to ride against the stream and retrieve her irons; and finally the rump of Arthur's gray disappearing over the blind side of the hill. A colorful butterfly this, with the hint of lusty flight in rigid wings.

There is, however, a case of rarer exhibits and some of them we are reluctant to display, for they are shy, fragile specimens caught long ago in the company of another, and we remember, when we look at them, that clocks do not really stand still and also that some species we have trapped are not butterflies at all but moths that flew by night. I have one such specimen and you can take a quick, patronizing peep at it. It is no great shakes to a sophisticated collector, but it is to me. I caught it when I was seventeen, and sometimes, when I contemplate it in private, it still seems to me the one flawless trophy in the collection.

Her name was Muriel. She was dark-browed, petite, outwardly modest and inwardly devastating. She walked alone, with downcast eyes that, once raised, were full of promise. She had a trim figure, chorus-girl legs, and a quality of repose that set her apart from girls who resorted to artifice all the way from coquetry to the honest giggle. Muriel had outgrown all this by the time she was fourteen and was already a woman, with a woman's ability to put a realistic price tag on her favors.

I was aware of this the moment I set eyes on her, but so, alas, was every other boy in town. Muriel's popularity was daunting. It would have daunted Don Juan and Benvenuto Cellini, for all through the fourth and fifth forms she maintained a court of gangling, spotty suitors none of whom, so far as I could determine, gained the slightest advantage over a rival. Muriel was like that. She didn't believe in playing one swain against another. To Muriel the equilibrium of existence rested on a diabolically judicious balance of power. She would sometimes reward the eager and original with one of her soft, inexpressibly tender glances, but whenever she did she qualified it by a knowing, Gioconda smile. In that smile was certitude that she could read the minds of men as easily as she read the hockey notices on the school notice-board.

I watched all this from a distance when I was attending the co-ed school, and when I left she was still holding court. What surprised me, I think, was that she continued her reign into her late teens, when we all thought of ourselves as sophisticated men of the world equipped to advance against her on equal terms. We were not, of course. Muriel had the edge on every one of us, assessing male vanity to the thousandth of an inch and continuing to maintain that wonderful balance of hers so that she demented and belittled every one of us, tormenting us with longing when she left us at the little iron gate that enclosed her pint-sized front garden and murmuring, in that self-effacing and slightly husky voice of hers, "*Thank* you for seeing me home. It's been *so* nice.

I've had such a *wonderful* time." And then, with downcast eyes and modest mien, she would walk up her short garden path and the green front door would open and close, very quietly, but with a finality against which there was no appeal.

To cross that threshold one day became imperative, a condition of attaining manhood, a full extension of our personalities. Without achieving it we were not men at all but poor, disembodied things, obliged to make shift with dates and dances among the responsive and attainable.

And then, one dank November evening, I had an unlooked-for piece of luck. I was reporting a lantern lecture on Florentine art, one of a series arranged for us in those pre-telly days by one of those bodies of mind improvers who flourished in all small towns during the twenties, and when the lights went up there was Muriel, in the capacity of student teacher, one row away.

The sight of her stirred me more deeply than ever. Fresh from the company of all those Venuses and Andromedas and Renaissance Madonnas, I was overripe for romance. It was as though the Arno had taken to following the course of the Exe, but what was more uplifting than the mood was the realization that she was alone. All the courtiers seemed to have conspired to take a night off, neglecting Beatrice for the more plebian delights of Mae West at the cinema, or living it up at the Wednesday hop in the Institute, or at a game of billiards in the Y.M.C.A. I said, cautiously, "What did *you* think of it, Muriel?" and she replied, "Lovely! Quite lovely! So different, so exciting, so *edifying!*"

It was the word "edifying" that provided the clue. Somehow it relegated all my rivals to the status of chawbacon. Alone among them I was a man of cultivated and civilized tastes, a fit consort for a queen ruling a horde of ignorant rustics. I said, eagerly, "Leonardo—what a man, what a mind!" and tried to make it sound as though I had sat at his feet. My instinct was not at fault, and I was instantly rewarded with one of those soft, melting glances, and I noticed something else too. In her eyes was abstraction, as though the inspired commentary and colored illustrations of the beak-nosed lecturer had transported her into a world infinitely remote from and infinitely preferable to the one we shared. It seemed to me a set of propitious circumstances, to be exploited on the spot.

We walked home through trailers of sea mist along gleaming pavements. She didn't say much, but there is no record that Beatrice indulged in small talk. It was enough to be there beside her in the slanting rain and to know somehow that her senses had been attuned to dalliance by the splendor of fifteenth-century Florence and that I was on hand to consolidate my unique advantage over all those who had listened, inwardly quivering, whilst Muriel had declaimed *amo, amas, amat*, across the years.

She was aware, of course, precisely what was passing in my mind. Her birthright ensured that. From the moment her fairy godmother had decreed that she should receive a bonus gift of intuitive awareness of the male she had been familiar with all the devious approaches of the hunter, but tonight she was obviously at a disadvantage. She said, as we reached her iron gate and I hesitated, "It's all dark. They've all gone to bed."

"Yes," I echoed, glancing up at the blank windows. "No lights! They're all in bed!" It was more of an incantation than a response. A few seconds passed, agonized but also enriching. Somewhere down the road a man coughed behind an open window, and a bedside light went on and off again. "Poor deprived devil," I thought, "he's never lived! Only those who have stood at Muriel's gate hoping have lived!" She said, slowly and carefully, "If we were very quiet . . ." and then stopped. Her fairy godmother had taught her to do that when she was a day old.

I said, with the closest I have ever come to bravado in Muriel's presence, "We'll *be* quiet!"

She went in, feeling her way, and I followed strangely blind in a world exploding with golden rain and arching rockets. In Muriel's front parlor the gas still burned but very low, so that her mother's collection of Goss china was in deep shadow and the sheen on the aspidistra leaves converted the window alcove into a bower. We sat down on Muriel's shiny, horsehair couch, gently adjusting our weight to offset its glacial insecurity. On the marble mantelshelf, under the enlarged photograph of her dead, Kitchener-army father, the pendulum of a French clock spun, but not so majestically as my senses. Then the butterfly moment surrendered itself into my lifelong keeping. With a soft puff, and after faithful and overlong service, the gas mantle died. I turned off the tap and the red glow lived on a moment or two, long enough for me to absorb the portent of this tremendous benediction. Then Muriel and I were in comforting darkness, and darkness, as any fool knows, is the ally of the bewitched.

There were other butterfly moments. In the era of false dawns between seventeen and coming-of-age there were even somewhat similar moments, when all the clocks in the world ceased to tick, but it would be profitless to elaborate on them. There was Edna under the apple blossom, Gwen and her upright piano, Margaret and the one day my elderly Austin Seven did not require running repairs, any number of moments about which Leigh Hunt might have written his "Jenny Kissed Me" verses, but they are cabbage-whites alongside the first of them beside Muriel's mother's Goss china and the aspidistra. It all took place nearly forty years ago, and in four decades a good deal happens to all of us. A little of what occurs is distilled, bottled, and set aside to await privately proposed toasts to someone somewhere. In my own case the bottle has been uncorked once or twice a year—a first night, a day of publication, an unexpectedly kind notice, bills paid, bargains bought, the copper change of creative and commercial endeavors. But these are not bona fide butterfly moments, for they are triumphs pursued and striven for. Butterfly moments are rare and elusive as the scent in that Kentish meadow and in Muriel's Gioconda smile and if you sense one approaching, stop whatever you are doing and catch it. It yields the kind of percentage that causes stockbrokers to stammer into telephones. And something else. Like Georgian silver its market value increases with age.

Five Traveling Companions

Most people seem unable to remember the magic moment when they realized that they could read. I find this astonishing. I can remember it clearly as one of the most exhilarating moments of my life, the actual tick in time when I made the breakthrough and was transported from the shopwindow, represented by book illustrations, into the shop itself. It occurred during a period of convalescence, and the key I used was a Victorian tear-jerker called *A Peep behind the Scenes*. It made me sniffle, and has left within me an irrational distrust of Gypsies and fairground folk but even now, half a century later, I respond to the title as readily as a man responds to his own surname.

I went on to read a thrilling adventure story, *The Phantom Battleship*, but after that my memory of the paths I trod is hazy, some kind of aimless journey across a vast countryside, I fancy, in warmish weather, with here a steep ascent and there a pleasant, wooded valley, with wrong turnings that led nowhere, and occasionally a signpost pointing the way to a populous city. One such signpost, I recall, was *Oliver Twist*, beckoning me into the malevolent London of Dickens. My mother was a great lover of Dickens and would talk engagingly about all his characters. She simplified her directions by getting hold of his abridged versions and performed the same office for Scott, Kingsley, Bunyan and Harriet Beecher Stowe. Thus, at a very early age, I read versions of *Ivanhoe*, *The Water Babies*, *Pilgrim's Progress* and *Uncle Tom's Cabin*. I shall never cease to be grateful to her for the intelligence she showed in this respect, encouraging me to nibble a little at a time, for in this way I never suffered from literary indigestion.

I am also much in debt to the various gentlemen who edited English textbooks in the early years of the century. They too were fearful of the dangers of literary indigestion. At least half of the English classics I have since enjoyed were fed to me piece-meal, in books like *Mother Tongue,* that offered carefully se-lected morsels calculated to whet the appetite, hors d'oeuvres served in the hope that some of us would acquire an appetite for the full course at the public library. I do not know whether this naïve but very effective method of teaching English literature is still employed in schools, but I sincerely hope it is. Without it, I feel certain, I would have never picked up, of my own free will, books like *The Mill on the Floss, The Vicar of Wakefield,* or even *Monte Cristo.* In all three instances, and in many others, I was coaxed into the orchard by small, judicious bites, repre-sented by the quarrel of Maggie and Tom over the apple, by the folly of Moses concerning the purchase of the green spectacles, and by that breathless passage in Dumas's masterpiece describing the escape of Dantes from the Château D'If.

One could retrace these steps along pleasant paths indefinitely, recapturing hours and hours of bliss spent in childhood and boy-hood, when a relaxed physical posture was not essential to the enjoyment of a book. I read hundreds of books hunched under the blankets with a ninepenny electric torch as my lantern, and hundreds of others standing upright against the school hot-water pipes on a blustery Exmoor plateau. Some of the titles I remem-ber but most of them I have forgotten, remembering only the pleasure and satisfaction I derived from them at the time, for literary taste is a wayward thing. No one person derives the same kind of pleasure from a specific book as does his wife, his dearest relative, or even his closest friend. Books bring different things to different people and one can never really say, with any author-ity, that one has *read* a book, for often something fresh and appealing emerges from a second, third or even a fourth reading.

There are a hundred books to which the bookworm returns

again and again, not so much to read but to browse in, and of that hundred there are, perhaps, half a dozen that are sources of lifelong comfort. If you were able to take a census of this select company among all the bookworms of the English-speaking peoples I doubt if the same titles would appear with tedious frequency in the findings. I have never, for instance, met anyone who regarded my own scaled-down selection as anything but eccentric, and this verdict has encouraged me to be tolerant with other people's favorites.

I carried five books in my kit bag through six years of war, and I am seldom to be found without at least two of them within easy reach. They are an odd and contrasting company and the only thing they have in common is their devotee, myself. They have shared every crisis point in my life, and because of this I shall try and make it my business to see that they are on hand when the lights go out. They are Stevenson's *Treasure Island*, the second volume of Carlyle's *French Revolution*, Mark Twain's *Huckleberry Finn*, Baron de Marbot's *Memoirs*, translated by A. J. Butler, and Helen Ashton's *Doctor Serecold*. I am partial to the Bible, to John Betjeman's collected verse, and to the *Oxford Book of English Verse*, but could, I feel, survive a year's isolation on a desert island without them. On the other hand I should feel very deprived without my standbys. I must have read each of these five books a score of times over the last thirty years.

I cannot hope to explain why, of all the books published since the fifteenth century, this chosen company should lay such a strong claim to my affection, but I can relate the circumstances of our original meeting so that someone wiser and more erudite than I may be able to deduce something relevant from the encounters. Dickens, Defoe, Swift, George Eliot and many, many others instilled into me the hope that, one day, I might earn a living by spinning yarns of one kind or another, but it was in the company of Robert Louis, Tom Carlyle, Mark Twain, De Marbot and Helen Ashton that this ambition submerged any others I had, or might have had. It is because of them that any other way of spending my days would seem bleak beyond the realm of thought. All, alas, are dead, and I shall never have the privilege of thanking any one of them personally for their traveling companionship. But I can still acknowledge it and, as it were, assure their shades that I will never forget their courage, gaiety and steadfastness.

I am exceptionally deep in Stevenson's debt. Not only have I derived countless hours of pleasure from his books (*Kidnapped* is a close runner-up to *Treasure Island*) but I have taken liberties with some of his characters, notably Ben Gunn. I feel sure, however, that he would have approved, for he loved children and it was for children I committed this form of plagiarism. It came about in this way.

A *Treasure Island* addict from the age of twelve, I naturally enlisted Jim Hawkins to help beguile my own children. The result was flattering to him and his creator. After three consecutive readings they clamored to know more about the background and the ultimate fates of Silver and Ben Gunn and, especially, the destinies of the three mutineers abandoned on the island. I did my best on Stevenson's behalf, supplying random answers to two streams of inquiry, one from Veronica, then aged nine, and one from Paul, aged seven. Veronica's questions were pious. Why, she wanted to know, was Silver such a bad hat when he obviously possessed so much potential? What *made* him bad? And what kind of man would he have been if he hadn't lost a leg? Paul's questions were more down to earth. Why did Flint bury the treasure instead of investing it in thousands of bottles of rum? How came it that there was a wreck in North Inlet upon which were "flowers a-blowing like a garding." And, above all, who was the skeleton pointing his upraised arms to the gold?

I hope I supplied reasonably honest answers, although privately I condemned Stevenson for leaving so many loose ends in such an absorbing tale. I told them that Silver's integrity had been blighted in early manhood, when he had lost ship and cargo to

Barbary Rovers; that Flint buried the treasure because his ship was crippled and overloaded; that the old wreck was another crippled vessel from Flint's fleet; and that Allardyce, the skeleton, had been the pirate's surgeon, the devil-may-care son of a Devon parson, who had enlisted with the buccaneers after a fatal quarrel with the Squire's son that sent him overseas to seek his fortune. Ben Gunn, according to my version, had been Allardyce's servant and was therefore never an unrepentant freebooter but a hanger-on from the day he fled his West Country village in his master's company.

The trouble was, of course, that these answers touched off many other questions, and soon I was filling in the blank years of every character in the book. It was Paul who saw commercial possibilities in this, pointing out that millions of *Treasure Island* enthusiasts would be interested to learn these facts in book form from me or from anyone else, and ultimately I took the idea to my publisher, then Michael Sadleir, of Constable's. Sadleir was outraged. "The Scots would come south and beat you to death with bagpipes!" he said; and it was not until after Sadleir's own death that I mentioned the idea to the firm of Hodder and Stoughton. The day I returned home there was a check from them and attached to the check a note reading, "If you ever do write the life story of Ben Gunn it's ours!" I had, at that time, no serious intention of writing the book, but fortunately for them and for me I owed a lot of income tax and used their check to keep the wolves at bay for a week or two. That meant, of course, that I had to write the book, and Paul at seven and a half, showed that he possessed more prescience than I or Michael Sadleir, for *The Adventures of Ben Gunn* is now in eleven languages. Incidentally, the Scots did not cross the border seeking my blood. Indeed, one of their newspapers paid me one of the nicest compliments I have ever received by addressing me as "A blood-and-thunder brother of Robert Louis Stevenson."

I read Carlyle's *French Revolution* when I was eighteen. I think the curious, present-tense style of this astonishing narrative appealed to me because at that time I was learning my trade as a reporter and Carlyle's prose was like reading an eyewitness account of the tumultuous happenings in France between 1789 and 1795. I think the reason why many people find the masterpiece difficult to read is that they approach it without doing their homework on the French Revolution. Carlyle, who was a strange, moody and apparently irascible man, took it for granted that anyone who opened his book was reasonably familiar with the background material and also assumed they had some knowledge of the topography of revolutionary Paris and the main outlines of current policies. His job, as he saw it, was to paint a huge, heroic canvas of the event as a whole, from the first rumblings of the underprivileged to the rise of Buonaparte, and how stupendously he achieves this, neglecting no single detail in unfolding the progress of the great drama day by day, hour by hour and, sometimes, minute by minute.

There has never been, and probably never will be again, a book dealing with a single historical process that has the thrust, the power and the compassion of Carlyle's *French Revolution;* but as a narrative it does not make its full impact until its author arrives at the stage where the Revolution is "eating its own children." His description of the fall of Robespierre, and the end of the Terror at the hands of the hesitant Thermidorians, is, to my mind, the finest piece of descriptive prose ever written in our language. It has a terrible lesson for all demagogues, all politicians, all who would set the world to rights at the cost of human suffering, and it was in these terms that I reread it in tent and billet when I found myself marginally involved in the final heave of the Allied armies to throw the Wehrmacht across the Rhine. It had for me—indeed it still has—a dreadful relevance. It is at once a sermon and a political tract of immense importance to subsequent generations.

How different a man is Mark Twain, and what a wealth of his own lovable personality went into his single masterpiece, *Huckleberry Finn,* a book that makes all his previous and subsequent writings seem the work of a hack with a gift for comic invention.

I first read *Huckleberry Finn* when I was thirteen, but it is not a book that can be appreciated to the full at this age. One is inclined to overlook the fact that the real hero of the story is the Mississippi, a river that had for Twain a mystique that made every human soul adrift on it its subject and its suitor. The adventures of Huck and Jim are exciting enough and would no doubt absorb the reader had they occurred on the Danube or the Thames, but what one discovers in a second and third reading of *Huckleberry Finn* is that here is a book about a civilization that disappeared forever in the battery smoke of Shiloh and Gettysburg. Every nuance of that civilization is reproduced here with truth and dash, as by an artist working at top speed against a fading light, but the chapters did not issue from Twain in that way. On his own admission he became hopelessly stuck halfway through and put the manuscript aside for a longish period, only taking it up again when he felt competent to finish it.

The book is crammed with river scenes that no one but a Mississippi pilot, who had spent his boyhood beside the stream, could re-create without resorting to purple passages. Some pages, such as those describing storms and floods, leap right out of the page and make a flash-bulb impact upon the imagination, and all the time, with the inevitability of the current bearing a steamboat down to New Orleans, the odyssey of runaway boy and runaway slave continues from Missouri to lower Arkansas, through hick towns, among a rich variety of scoundrels and charlatans, past feuding plantations, and finally to its surprise ending with the reappearance of Tom Sawyer. The story has, in fact, the breadth and smoothness of the river itself, and it has captured its moods too, and a philosophy that is content to hazard shy guesses at the meaning of existence but leave all the other questions unanswered.

My original copy of *Huckleberry Finn* fell to pieces in a Nissen hut in Oxfordshire, but although I had other copies at home I could not bring myself to throw this one away and brought it home in tatters. After all, one does not readily discard a friend who has rescued your sense of humor once a week over a period of several years.

The presence of Baron de Marbot's reminiscences in my kit bag was also due to reasons that go back to an adolescent enthusiasm. When I was sixteen I was in the habit of frequenting a second-hand bookshop kept by a courtly old gentleman called Appleby. Mr. Appleby loved his trade, and nothing pleased him more than to see a youth browsing among his stock. I did more than my share of browsing there and one morning I picked up a copy of Lockhart's *Life of Napoleon*, Napoleon having caught my imagination after I had been shown his Waterloo coach in Madame Tussaud's, a relic unfortunately destroyed in the great fire at that museum. I read on until lunchtime and was there again the next day. When I had followed the Emperor as far as the field of Austerlitz Mr. Appleby gently suggested that it might be a good idea if I bought the volume, and how could I disagree with him? It was, after all, marked down to sixpence. I took it home and from then on became absorbed in the story of the First Empire, the sixpenny Lockhart being the founder-volume of a Napoleonic library that now occupies three long shelves in my study. It was Sir Arthur Conan Doyle, however, who led me directly to Marbot, for in his *Exploits of Brigadier Gerard* (whose prototype was Marbot) he thoughtfully provides a list of personal memoirs of the period where he found material for his books. I finally found a copy published by Methuen, and the chasseur's account of his adventures between 1800 and 1815 made adventure fiction of the kind then provided by P. C. Wren and Sapper seem very anemic.

Marbot's memoirs, as a piece of autobiographical writing, are unique. Although they tell a series of hair-raising adventures from the Tagus to the Dwina, there is not a touch of bravado in the telling. Somehow, through the reek of embattled towns and the shock of battle that engulfed his entire youth, this remarkable man preserves not only his integrity but (what is surprising in any autobiography) his innate modesty, and he does not achieve this by self-deprecation. He thinks of himself as a good soldier and a brave man, and he does not mind telling you as much, but there is a curiously boyish charm about his accounts of deeds performed and missions accomplished that enlists the reader's sympathy from the first page, so that sometimes his adventures during his encounters with Italians, Spaniards, Englishmen, Portuguese, Prussians and Russians read like the autobiography of a man looking back on his early years at a tough public school.

The story begins when he is a sublieutenant and ends when he has become a full colonel. His devotion to the Emperor is simple and uncomplicated. He epitomizes the theirs-not-to-reason-why school of soldiering and, as his translator points out, "Few men of that age seem to have left a more creditable record."

The Memoirs of Baron de Marbot won its author a mention in Napoleon's will, and this surely provides proof that Napoleon was no bigot, for Marbot does not hesitate to criticize Imperial strategy and tactics when he feels mistakes were committed in the field. For the armchair strategist—indeed, for all who like blood and thunder secondhand—this book has everything. One can partake of every kind of adventure and narrow escape from death without moving from the fireside, and in the company of Marbot it is entirely possible to march and fight alongside the veterans of the Grande Armée throughout the period of fifteen years when they dominated the Western world. For anyone actually engaged in war it is a source of comfort and reassurance. No matter how tight the spot, or how demanding the circumstances, one can find a parallel by opening the book at random. With Marbot's book in my pocket I traveled over some of the same roads as those along which he had ridden in the company of men like Ney, Lannes and Masséna but thank God I was never called upon to face his personal risks, or exercise his daring or ingenuity. For all that he was a kind of patron saint for me when I crossed France and Belgium in the final stages of World War II, and I thought of him—indeed, I almost saw him in the flesh— when De Gaulle walked down the Champs Elysées, surrounded by cheering Parisians. How Marbot would have cherished that moment of liberation! And how proud he would have been of that section of the French nation that had kept its courage and will to resist during the German occupation.

The fifth book in my small selection has very little in common with the other four. It does not concern itself with pirates, Mississippi rivermen, revolutionaries, or professional soldiers. It is a simple story that deals with a single day in the life of an ageing local doctor called Luke Serecold and is, in fact, a page from his daybook, in October, 1929. Its pace is measured and its content reflective. As Serecold goes about his work, in a large inland market town that is somehow representative of any shire in provincial England, he looks back on more than forty years spent in that practice, so that Helen Ashton, the authoress, gives us a detailed and sometimes very touching account of a life dedicated to the service of others and the practice of a profession. Ponderous, deliberate, painstaking and sometimes gruff and forbidding, Doctor Serecold plods from visit to visit, linking past, present and future, and trying, not always with success, to equate his daily grind with a sense of achievement.

The story begins in the small hours when he is present at the deathbed of his aged partner. It ends about midnight, after he has helped his girl assistant to deliver a child in a stuffy, terrace bedroom, and that is the essence of this simple story, a matter of birth and death, with all manner of emotional crises, objectively viewed, between these two extremes. Almost without realizing it we learn how those forty years were spent, and everything important that happened to Serecold's patients, old, middle-aged and young, and also, what has happened during the period to Serecold himself in the pursuit of love, public health and personal duty. For Serecold, so unlike Marbot in most ways, has this much in common with the soldier. He also is a slave to duty, and one cannot but feel, at the end of the book, that the town where he practiced was singularly fortunate to have him within call.

Doctor Serecold is one of the most deeply satisfying novels I have ever read, and I am surprised and a little indignant that it is not acclaimed as a minor classic. For classic it certainly is in conception, development and economy of style.

In the secret places of our hearts many of us hope that some day we may catch up with the folk we have met between the covers of favorite books, perhaps at what Priestly, in his play *Johnson Over Jordan,* called The Inn at the End of the World, where his hero met his old English master and Don Quixote! If I am ever fortunate enough to cross the threshold of that inn I know the names I shall look for in the register. They will be R. L. Stevenson, Thomas Carlyle, Mark Twain, Baron de Marbot and, in the suite reserved for the created rather than the creative, my old friend Doctor Serecold.

Anatomy of a Comedy

Elsewhere I have referred to the myth of inspiration, claiming that ideas ultimately emerging as books and plays are, in nearly all cases, the product of a slow, smoldering bonfire in the lumber rooms of the author's mind. The R.A.F. comedy *Worm's Eye View* is a case in point. Its setting down on paper occupied less than a month. Its theme, characters and setting had been maturing for a period of four years and were not even recognizable as the raw material of a three-act play until more than thirty-six months of that period had elapsed.

For a broad comedy the *Worm* had unlikely foster parents, among them resentment and indignation. When it came before the public a few theater critics noticed this and commented upon it, but others, and the majority of the public, accepted it for what it was, a simple story about five airmen in a civilian billet in the winter of 1942–43, with a strong bias toward the more comic aspects of their ordeal. For, make no mistake, life in a civilian billet was an ordeal for most men in the armed forces, and herein lies the spring of resentment that drove me to set it down. This does not mean, of course, that I intended it to be anything but a broad comedy, but it does mean that in a sense it was an attempt to even the score.

It was not aimed specifically at landladies. I had good and bad billets, and one of the good ones was in Blackpool that everyone assumed (quite wrongly) was the setting for the play. *Worm's*

Eye View was broader-based, a wry comment on that section of the British public—a very large one it seemed to the services at the time—that stood aside between 1939 and 1945, and let things take their course, somehow managing to enjoy a tolerably comfortable war.

Public memory is notoriously short. A bumbling politician, given a few years' obscure retirement, can be almost certain of achieving the status of a father-figure under whose direction everything moved deftly and smoothly, and I sometimes think of this when I watch a film clip of Britain engaged in winning World War II. No one without personal recollection of those days would suppose that the strictures of total war against the greatest military power the world has ever seen did not embrace every man, woman and child living in these islands but this is very far from being true. At a guess only about fifty percent of the adult population actually involved themselves, and of the others a majority were incommoded—no more than that—while a minority waxed fat and prosperous in an era of universal shortage. This minority were the great uncommitted. They seemed to me at the time to have no animus against militant Fascism currently jackbooting its way across the free world. Indeed, to many of them the war came as a boon and even a reprieve. In the latter group were those who had found it irksome to compete in a free labor market that operated through most of the thirties under conditions of slump or near-slump. I remember being astonished, when I was demobilized in November, 1945, at the changed status of some of the men of my own generation who had contrived, in one way or another, to evade conscription. I had parted company with them six years before in circumstances where their economic future was, to say the least, uncertain. Some were unemployed and others were getting by on a few pounds a week. By Christmas 1945 they were not merely affluent but on familiar terms with affluence. They owned houses, sometimes several houses. Their tiny, faltering little businesses had become thriving concerns. They ran big cars. They sent their children to expensive schools. And not one of them volunteered information as to what, precisely, had brought about this change of fortune.

Now, I quarrel with this, but not violently. It happened on a much wider scale during the First World War, and it would happen again, no matter how many laws were passed to prevent it. It is part of the price that has to be paid for a free society and if, when one's entire way of life is threatened, a section of the community is more alert to the ping of the till bell than the uncertain trumpet this is something they must decide for themselves. Inside the forces I met hundreds of men and women who had made great personal sacrifices to do what they were doing and be where they were at that time, and when this question of opting out arose, as it often did in N.A.A.F.I. and billet discussions, it emerged that every one of them had a relative, sometimes a father, a brother or a sister, who did not accept the fact that this was his war and went right ahead making the best of it in the economic sense.

This does not mean to say that only those people in a uniform played a part in stopping Germany's attempt to put the clock back a thousand years. There were large numbers of civilians whose jobs were as vital, or more so, as the jobs of those enrolled in the Forces. At the top of this scale were elderly men and women who worked themselves into hospitals providing the means to fight and the food to sustain, and there were others, a million others, who performed prodigious deeds of valor and physical endurance in A.R.P., transport and other sectors. But there remained the uncommitted, a remarkably large minority in a country that was fighting for its life, and the uncommitted were the group that prompted me to write *Worm's Eye View*.

Among them were many landladies, but they were not exclusively landladies. There was the Midlands butcher who, in the winter of 1940, refused to accept service meat coupons issued to living-out personnel on the grounds that the services wasted food. There were grocers who practically lived under the counter. There were thousands of bureaucratic bullies who made a kind of hobby of persecuting men and women in the King's motley, and there were many insignificant and extremely tiresome little bastards who threw their weight about in bars, cinema queues, fish-and-chip saloons, and even omnibuses, people who would have proved invaluable to Hitler had he succeeded in getting a footing in the island. These were the minority who worked tirelessly at sapping public morale, hauling old ladies off to jail for showing a sliver of light through their blackout curtains, preventing soldiers and sailors burdened with kit from getting on a bus (sometimes with ironic witticisms, such as "Sorry, mate, war workers only"), landladies who wrung the last penny out of their billeting allocation at the expense of the billetee's rations, and proprietors of hotels who made a sick joke of Allied war aims by exhibiting "Officers Only" placards at the entrance of their bars. These people had no one face, were of all ages, and spoke with a hundred different accents but they had about them a common expression. The hostile stare they reserved for junior N.C.O.'s and rankers somehow reminded one of a face on a tarnished Roman coin.

There were pockets about the country where you seldom found such persons. In my experience Edinburgh was such a city, and Scotland generally had a hospitable reputation among servicemen. So did some of the small coastal towns that were being hammered in hit-and-run raids, and I met plenty of kindly folk in remote villages in the Pennines. Industrial cities were places to avoid if possible, for here, notwithstanding bombing attacks, the uncommitted swarmed, but they were also found in prosperous agricultural districts where the black market had moved into top gear, and in some of the prewar "pleasure" centers that were not on the Luftwaffe's visiting list. These last were particularly hostile to servicemen, for compulsory billeting at one pound and, subsequently, thirty shillings a man, limited the influx of free-spending holidaymakers.

It may seem strange to those who have no recollection of the years 1939–45 to learn that in certain areas seaside holidays and the British weekend continued uninterrupted throughout the war, but they did and many servicemen can vouch for it. In the early stages of the Battle of Britain I was senior man of a billet where we were set to work washing holidaymakers' dirty dishes when we came in off the square. I made a complaint about this and soon wished I hadn't, but later, more experienced in the channels of bureaucracy, I was instrumental in closing a billet where airmen were sleeping in rows on the floor while other rooms were let to civilians enjoying a seaside jaunt.

It might be argued that enlisted men and women should have been prepared to bed down on floors and eat hard tack, and so they were; it was not differential treatment that galled them so much as the obvious contempt in which they were held by the uncommitted. This, in World War II, was in contrast to the respect paid by most civilians to all servicemen in World War I, and perhaps, to a degree, it stemmed from the fact that every-body's life was at risk from air attack in the years 1940-44. But it does not explain or excuse the implication, so common at that time, that a man or a woman in uniform (officers excepted) must, of necessity, be an oaf or a slut, lacking the intelligence and education to be doing a significant job in wartime. I was conscious of this on many occasions, and so were many of the men and girls I met in the camps or abroad after they had emerged from British billets. Perhaps it had to do with inherited snobbery that is Britain's most repellent trait. I have never for-gotten the obsequious railway guard who punched my ticket on the way home from the Officers' Training Unit. I recognized him as a particularly boorish specimen who had always made me feel like a fugitive slave when I used his line as a corporal. A dramatic change in the attitude of the uncommitted was one of the first things you noticed after taking up a commission.

It would never have occurred to me to write *Worm's Eye View* had I not been acutely aware, throughout the first three years of the war, of these two Britains at war with each other. It was this conflict that offered itself as a theme for a play that seemed to me, at that time, worth writing, and I believe its ultimate success with audiences largely composed of recently demobilized service people was due to their awareness of this cleavage.

There were, however, other foster parents who contributed and the most important of these was the comradeship of the R.A.F. and the services in general.

2

For a long time I had been casting around for a means of expressing this compensatory element of all human catastrophes. Its presence throughout those years was like a rainbow arched across a landscape of desperate drabness, futility and boredom. I had always sensed the comfort that its permanent presence brought to the benighted and browned-off, but it was not until January, 1942, that conditions combined to give it a radiance that cried out to be captured and crystallized.

It was about 07.45 hours, and I was stumping across packed snow along one of those interminable Blackpool streets that seemed to have been designed by a municipal architect anxious to discover how much domestic ugliness the British can stand before returning to their Neolithic caves. It was very cold, but not as cold as it would be later on in the unheated, uncarpeted hotel we were using as Wing H.Q. The war, at that time, had reached a phase where it promised to continue for the rest of our lives. The excitement and challenge of the Battle of Britain and Dunkirk were a long way behind us, but the prospect of victory was even further ahead. For myself there seemed no future but to drift aimlessly about the beleaguered country carrying a mountain of kit and helping to absorb an ever-increasing stream of recruits into the machine. We had already multiplied our pre-war strength by twenty, and the air offensive was only just beginning. How long would it be before it looked like ending?

I was pondering this depressing prospect when I heard men's voices raised in chorus. This was not unusual in a recruit center, but in that setting, and at that time of day, the marching song sounded exceptionally strong and tuneful, and I realized why as soon as the column rounded the corner.

It was marching over hard-packed snow, a long blur of blue on white, the men pink-cheeked and cheerful-looking in the frosty air, the N.C.O.'s marching alongside like sheep dogs satisfied that the flock is under control and headed in the right direction. They were singing that ditty that attached itself to the R.A.F., a parody of "She'll be comin' round the mountain," and for some reason that still escapes me the sight and sound of that column was immensely cheering to anyone involved in what it represented. It reminded me of all the thousands of men and girls I had met during the preceding two years, and it seemed imperative that somehow, at some time, I must snare that comforting sense of collectivity and broadcast it for the benefit of the committed and the uncommitted.

I did nothing about it then or, indeed, for another twenty months. Most of that time I was on the move and camps and billets are not the best of places to do creative work of any kind. In late October, 1943, however, I was bogged down in what was then known as an O.T.U. (Operational Training Unit) on the Shropshire plain and had taken the camp bus into the little town of Wellington. I had, as I recall, a shilling in my pocket and I spent it on a pint of beer in a pub near the bus depot. At that particular time I wasn't thinking of an Air Force comedy or, indeed, any comedy. My mind was on higher things, a promised production of a Passion play I had written before the war, by Max Reinhardt, the well-known impresario. Suddenly, as I sipped the beer to make it last, I heard his name spoken by the nine o'clock news-bulletin announcer. He had died that same day in New York.

The news was shattering. I had never met Reinhardt and could have but moderate personal feelings about his death, but it meant that there would be no New York production of the play and that I was back to square one again. I went out into the street and along to the bus depot where the camp twenty-two-seater was filling up with airmen, W.A.A.F.'s and naval ratings from the adjoining camp. By the time I was aboard there were more than forty passengers on that bus. We sat on top of one another, a solid mass of greatcoated humanity with arms and legs extending in all directions. Most of us were wet, for heavy rain had fallen earlier in the evening and was falling again now. It was impossible to regret Max Reinhardt and the play under these conditions. When the bus started one's concentration centered upon the act of drawing breath and assisting, within one's limited powers, to extricate and shed three naval ratings who were very drunk and were threatening to be sick. We got rid of them at length, but when the bus stopped a dozen more climbed aboard so that we now sprawled in layers as the bus lurched through rain on quarter-headlights over unsurfaced roads. Not that the passengers resented their method of progression. They seemed, in that perverse way the British have of capitalizing on discomfort, to enjoy the experience, and soon they began to sing. They sang the same song, "She'll be comin' round the mountain," transposed as "She'll be flyin' in formation," and between lurches I experienced that same comforting surge of belonging that had registered itself in the Blackpool street. Here it was again, a feeling of collectivity that had to be matched against something to provide a conflict of some kind and broadcast throughout the country as the one compensating factor of all these years of sordid restlessness. Then I had it, and it seemed to me so obvious that I was amazed it had not occurred to me long ago. The opposition was there, a target waiting to be shot at. The conflict would be the busload versus the uncommitted, the people who had experienced this kind of thing opposed to the people who had not. It was all I needed. When the bus disgorged its load at the camp I went on up to the N.A.A.F.I. and there, in a matter of thirty minutes, I wrote a shorthand synopsis of *Worm's Eye View*. I deviated from it very little when, nine months later, I had a chance to translate the notes into a three-act comedy. So perhaps there is something in inspiration after all.

Anatomy of a Saga

Humphrey Bogart, one of the best actors Hollywood ever produced, was also one of the most forthright. He had a profound distrust of the script purporting to project a thesis and was fond of quoting, "If a writer has a message he should ring up Western Union." I agree with him. Artists are no more than incidental missionaries and ought never to forget this. The primary objective of a writer of fiction should be to entertain and divert. Anything else that emerges from his work is a bonus.

This is not to say, however, that a writer, particularly a novelist concerned with people rather than plot, with scene rather than structure, should place the slightest stricture on his characters saying anything they want to say, and if some of them are inclined to preach he should suffer them to do it and blue-pencil their outpourings in the galley-proof stage. Undisciplined characters are always the most rewarding, to the reader and to the writer, and when a character gets a bee in his bonnet it is often an excellent idea to indulge him.

I made this discovery during the years of desk work that went into two inordinately long English sagas, *The Avenue Story*, a book recording the daily life of a suburban community between 1919 and 1947, and *A Horseman Riding By*, a somewhat similar exercise based on the events taking place in a remote Devonshire valley, between 1902 and 1940. In both cases I set out to tell a straightforward story of a group of undistinguished British people—the only kind of people I really know. In both cases a specific theme emerged without conscious effort on my part.

The composition of a stage play or a film is largely a technical process. There are very definite limits set upon where your characters go, what they do, how they develop and even what they think. To write a play is to proceed from Point A to Point B, but the writing of a saga is a journey of infinite meandering. Some writers may find this tiresome, but I found it stimulating inasmuch as the main characters soon took hold of me and charted their own destinies.

In each case I began with a detailed map. I wanted to know the kind of neighborhood I was going to live in during the next year or so and in *The Avenue Story* I actually numbered the houses in Manor Park crescent, making each house the headquarters of a particular aspect of the British social scene during the period under review. Jazz and the cinema presided at No. 4, where dwelt a silent-picture pianist and her lodger, a bandleader. At No. 20, a few doors along, lived the Carver family, who provided a great deal of the action of the novel. Jim Carver, the father, carried the radical-socialist, and ultimately the patriotic banner, through three decades of changing political attitudes. Jim's buffer, whose opinions first opposed but finally merged with his, lived next door at No. 22; and across the road at No. 17 were the Friths, who stood for conventional suburban attitudes. So it went on up and down the road and it seemed to me, setting out on that interminable journey, that I was in full control of the team.

How wrong I was, and how confounded by the recklessly independent spirit of the Avenue-dwellers. Hardly one of them paid heed to the tug of the reins. Characters I had written down as thoroughly bad hats became pleasantly engaging, whereas others, destined to hold the lamp of virtue, degenerated into prigs. Most of them married the wrong partners and set the seal on their independence by making a success of it, so that it was sometimes necessary to call in the Luftwaffe to kill them off when the entire enterprise threatened to lose itself in a maze of irrelevancy. Tories inclined toward the Left, and pacifists became jingoes. Rascals made money and industrious little men lost all they had. Very few of the characters developed the way I had hoped and intended, but in the end I came to understand that the least of them were more specifically aware of their potentialities than I, so that the story that emerged at least possessed the merit of credibility.

In the process I discovered a good deal about myself and the subconscious springs that feed a writer's imagination, and some of these discoveries were sobering. One example will suffice. Archie Carver, grocer and black-marketeer, practiced the habit of falsifying his till rolls as soon as the shutters went up and concealing surplus silver in an oil drum under the floor. He busied himself thus until he had a small fortune down there in half-crowns and florins. It was not until I was directly asked (at a W.I. lecture) how I came by this quirk that I realized, with shattering finality, that it was something my miserly self had been longing to do for forty years!

I suppose the mutinies along the Avenue should have taught me something about my own fallibility, but they did not, or very little. When, ten years later, I drew up another map, this time of an entire landscape dotted with farms, woods, rivers, coves and second-class roads, I peopled this landscape with about a hundred characters whose names were plucked at random from the telephone directory. As theme-bearer for this rustic community I chose Paul Craddock, twenty-three-year-old Boer War veteran, who paid all he had for the Shallowford estate and the back-breaking privilege of squiring it over the locals. At least Paul was manageable in this field, for he held to his purpose—that of nursing the Valley back to prosperity through more than sixty years of turmoil, but his love life got out of hand in less than a hundred pages. He met and fell deeply in love with Grace, one of the century's New Women, and after a frustrating suit he married her. I did not heed her protests any more than he did. I saw them then growing old together, with a flock of children dedicated to the red soil of Devon, but alas, Grace found the life far too dull for her taste. Within a couple of years she had abandoned home and husband for the livelier joys of helping Mrs. Pankhurst to smash windows in Regent Street and plaster Cabinet ministers with soot and flour.

I felt so cheated at this betrayal of the future dynasty that I could have tossed the manuscript in the wastepaper basket, but a little of Paul Craddock's tenacity rubbed off on me after the door of Holloway had slammed on his wife, and I accompanied him back to the Valley to try again. We were both luckier than we deserved. Paul met a ripe, down-to-earth farmer's daughter called Claire Derwent and we both fell in love with her in a way that exposed the first marriage as an act of folly on his part and mine.

It is entirely possible for an author to fall hopelessly in love with his heroines. It had happened to me before, of course, but never quite like this, for there was something about Claire Derwent that combined all the physical and spiritual assets I most admire in women. She was pretty, buxom, possessed any amount of common sense, was impulsively generous, she loved the Valley and shared Paul's hatred of cities, and she was gloriously uninhibited whilst remaining feminine. I reveled in her. From the moment of her appearance on the scene the saga wrote itself, and her fertility passed to me who, at that juncture (page 400-odd) stood in desperate need of it. The book grew and grew until my publishers began to mutter darkly of *War and Peace* and *Gone With the Wind*, and talk of chopping the enormous manuscript in two and publishing it piecemeal. I managed to dissuade them from taking such a desperate course and ultimately *A Horseman Riding By* emerged under a single title but here's an odd thing. At least ninety-five percent of readers who have communicated their preferences to me are pro-Grace, thinking of poor Claire as a genial, complaisant cow!

A Horseman Riding By created its own theme as it went along, and in the end this theme dominated the story to an extent that belittled the individual characters, even the dramatis personae. The backdrop took over from the footlights, the acting areas from the actors. In the end I was not writing the story of one man's tussle with thirteen hundred acres, but of the acres themselves and everything that grew on them, tamed and untamed, and this was a rewarding process, because it led me into bypaths where all my life I have wanted to linger but have never had the time. I spent entire weeks wandering in Shallowford Woods and exploring the source of the Sorrel. I learned things about Devon flora and fauna that were more absorbing, and certainly more basic, than Grace Craddock's junketings with the suffragettes, or Paul Craddock's adventures on the Western Front. So that when I was asked to write a sequel and carry the story up to Churchill's funeral and the death of the Squire in 1965, I did not regard it as a chore but as a pleasing visit to stay among old friends for as long as I wished.

This book, incidentally, was finished before it had a title, and it acquired one in a curious way. I was addressing a group of senior boys on the making of a novel at my old school, and I happened to mention this deficiency after outlining the theme. A very obliging seventeen-year-old jumped up from the back and quoted the epitaph on the grave of the poet W. B. Yeats:

> Cast a cold eye
> On life on death,
> Horseman ride by.

It seemed to me applicable to Paul Craddock's rustic pilgrimage so I used it and later sent the volunteer the first copy off the press.

It seems to me, looking back, that I owe a great many people a great deal for their involuntary contributions to the day-by-day life of the Sorrel Valley over a period of thirty-eight years, ten of which expired before I was born. In writing a book of this size one is obliged to husband every scrap of basic material derived from one's own and one's contemporaries' human experience. For instance, one character, minesweeping in the North Sea in 1915, owed his life to the chivalrous conduct of a German

U-Boat commander. So did my elder brother, torpedoed off Falmouth in 1917. There are many manipulations of this kind but perhaps the most illustrative concerns Henry Pitts, the genial tenant farmer of Hermitage with the ineffaceable rubbery grin and a Devon burr that hums pleasantly across the Valley. I took a shameless liberty with Henry Pitts, for his name is that of an old school friend of mine, who possessed that identical grin, and whose expert simulation of the dialect in daily use by all the countrymen living within walking distance of school was a source of delight to us at the time. Whenever I wrote of Shallowford's Henry I could only visualize the real Henry. The two became so inseparable in my mind that there was soon no prospect of finding him another name. So I wrote to Henry and asked if he would condone such a license and being Henry he did, without demur. Perhaps this is why, after Claire, he became my favorite character.

2

When an author is living with characters for as long as I lived with the people of the Avenue, and the Devonians of the Sorrel Valley, they tend to become more real to him than the people he encounters in his daily life. Thus it is often a great wrench to say goodbye to them, and when one of them dies a little of the author accompanies him to the grave. Sometimes one is incapable of doing away with them. This was the case with the Carver twins in *The Avenue Story*, a roistering couple who kept me close company from their infancy to the day they set sail, as Commandos, for the Dieppe raid, in 1942.

I had intended Dieppe to provide the solution to a problem that had been engaging my attention ever since Bernie and Boxer were children. Boxer, the slower-witted, beefier twin, had relied upon Bernie, his brother, throughout their entire childhood, adolescence and early manhood, and if Boxer's character was to develop it was essential that he should at length stand on his own two feet and make his own decisions. This was why I determined a German mortar shell should dissolve the one-sided partnership by destroying Bernard but when the moment arrived I discovered that I was incapable of encompassing his death. I used up several pages in badly botched attempts, and finally I relented and Bernard survived, less his left arm. Happily the problem of development then solved itself for Boxer, as a prisoner of war, was obliged to make his own decisions and considerably enlarged himself in the process. The two brothers got together again after the war, and their reunion provided a happy day's writing.

I was more resolute when a flying bomb came down on the Avenue, in the summer of 1944. Until then only a few people I actively disliked had died in the Blitz, but it seemed to me a prime fault in construction to end the war with all the major characters intact. The flying bomb disposed of seventeen of them, and the detonation, believe it or not, left me in a state of shock.

It was otherwise with the death of Squire Craddock at the end of the *Horseman* sequel. His death had shape, for he was eighty-six, a widower with innumerable grandchildren and two great-grandchildren, and he died on his own acres. This is not to imply, however, that his death was easy to accomplish. In some ways, although artistically inevitable, it was as difficult as writing one's own epitaph.

I had been living with Craddock a very long time, sixty-three years of his lifetime and nearly four of mine. By then I had completely identified myself with him and by no means all an author thinks and feels concerning a character as close as this goes into print. I suppose barely one tenth of it does. But there it was, and it could not be evaded as I had evaded Bernie Carver's death. For years I had been looking at life through the eyes of one man and he had become very much a part of me. I shared his hopes and prejudices, his intensely felt love for the soil and his triumphs in preserving it from the jerrybuilders and bureaucrats. His friendships and his private feuds were mine, and because his second wife Claire had been a favorite of mine I had shared something

of the sensual pleasure she gave him and the grief that he brought
to her death ten years before his own. I knew all his children
well and some of his grandchildren fairly well. I had accompanied
him on his ritual rides on four successive horses through Shallowford Woods and down Coombe Bay High Street to the sea. We
had even dodged the same coal boxes on the Western Front
when he was rising forty and I was only six. And years later I
stood with him watching the splendid panoply of Churchill's
funeral and now he was taking the same road, this time alone. In
these circumstances I gave him the kind of death I would choose
for myself if one had any choice in the matter, high up on the
escarpment of French Wood overlooking the silver blade of the
Sorrel, on a drowsy summer afternoon with all the scents and
colors of the Valley advancing to meet him. It was a desperately
final parting but I like to think I did my utmost to make it har-
monize with his long tenure of the Shallowford Valley and with
the kind of departure he might have devised for me had our positions been reversed.

3

Do authors ever take pleasure in reading what they have written
when a book has gone out into the world to earn its living? Un-
happily no, and for a variety of reasons. In the first place, by that
time the book appears to them as featureless as the day-be-
fore-yesterday's newspaper. For another thing they are already
closely engaged with another set of characters and situations. But
the main reason why they look bewildered when the odd reader
refers to one of their books is that contemplation of spent characters is as profitless as charting the probable course of dead sons
and daughters, a matter, often enough, for profound regret and
awareness of one's rhapsodic carelessness at the time of creation.
The only cure for this is to spawn more children and hope they
will make a more spectacular success of their lives. "I should
hate," says Priestly, "to die over an unfinished book!" and I see

precisely what he means. To me the saddest thing in Dickens' life was that he left *Edwin Drood* incomplete, and perhaps, on this account, his soul is unquiet. But even Dickens, one of the most prolific writers who ever slaved at the job, had his favorite in David Copperfield, and I have mine in Claire Derwent. Squire Craddock kept me typing and scribbling for years, and I am beholden to him, for I always enjoyed his company, but his ripe and rosy-cheeked wife, replete with curves and *joie de vivre*, solaced many of those industrious hours without even him knowing it and I don't give a damn if Shallowford readers do find her cloying. I didn't invent her for public display and, as a matter of fact, I didn't invent her at all but—this has gone as far as it's going.

PART FIVE

The Uncertain Trumpet

Kitchener's Manic Stare

The one-story building, cramped between two modern office blocks, looked as if it had no business there. It was small, shabby and totally undistinguished. Some time, perhaps around the period Napoleon's invasion force assembled at Boulogne, it had been given its last coat of whitewash, possibly in readiness to house the balloon section of the Fencibles. Now it was being used as the recruiting center of the R.A.F. and above the barred window was a large notice board bearing a chalked legend that screamed, "R.A.F. Drivers *Urgently* Needed! A few vacancies in other trades."

Inside a sergeant sat at a trestle table covered with blank forms. The table and the chair he occupied were the only items of furniture in the room. It was very cold in there, colder and damper than standing in the queue outside, and the sergeant seemed aware of this. He had turned up the collar of his greatcoat, put on a pair of frayed mittens, and pulled down the Balaclava flaps of his forage cap, so that he looked like his great-great-grandfather huddling in a trench before Sebastopol. Thus far had the pointing figure of Kitchener directed me, a belated victim of hypnosis induced by the manic stare of the victor of Omdurman, in 1898.

The memory of the poster was very clear in my mind on that cold November morning, notwithstanding the fact that it had been stripped from the billboard twenty-one years ago. As a child I had been mesmerized by it, along with so many others, most of them to their ultimate ruin. The stern frown, the huge mustaches, the pitiless eyes and the accusing finger, combined to elevate the man to the status of God's Viceroy, so that I saw Kitchener, at that time, as the sternest of stern parents, the most merciless of birch-wielding schoolteachers, the He-Who-Must-Be-Obeyed.

So compelling was that frown and that finger that they could induce feelings of guilt in a six-year-old. Looking up at them I had a conviction I was shirking my duty by standing there alongside my mother in a butter queue. I should have been beating the charge on a parapet somewhere in Artois or Picardy, like the little drummer boys seen in battle scenes painted by Lady Butler.

Posters, of the kind used by big commercial houses to market famous products, had always fascinated me. They were the scenery of Central London, and many of them acquired the status of old friends, eagerly greeted at the junction of streets or as one approached a familiar railway arch. The gay, pajama-clad castaway, clinging to his huge bottle of Bovril; Grandma and granddaughter sipping Mazawattee Tea; the athletic old chap revitalized by a dose of Kruschen Salts and, as soon as I learned to read, the enigmatic Monkey Brand poster that announced, "Won't Wash Clothes," thus informing you what the product would not do but remaining obstinately silent on what it would achieve.

Kitchener's manic stare did not belong in this jocund company. It was at once a menace and a challenge. It did not so much as hint at glory but demanded the uncomplaining sacrifice of all personal ambitions. And after all these years it had drawn me here, to a room that looked like a dungeon cell in the castle farther up the hill and a single jailer, wearing a faded-blue uniform with blue fingertips to match.

2

The queue outside reached all the way to the High Street, about three or four hundred young men already seeing ourselves as latter-day Hell's Angels, rat-tat-tatting our way across Continental skies. And this in spite of persistent rumors that there were no vacancies for air crew and were unlikely to be for months ahead. Despite this the notice was encouraging. R.A.F. drivers were needed—*Urgently* needed. And there were vacancies in some other trades. The man immediately behind me, introducing himself as Hitchcock, had worked this one out having, it appeared, already gone into training for the R.A.F. by taking a crash course in the new service slang. "Got some gen," he muttered. "Don't think it's duff gen, either. Got to use the old loaf to slide into this outfit. A.G., that's my fancy. A.G.'s sit in the turret, and turrets roll away intact when a kite prangs. The rest of the crew fry, but the A.G. gets off with a shaking. Pukka gen," and he underlined his advice with a savage nod.

I was not prepared to accept his information concerning the survival prospects of air gunners, but he was right about having to exercise our wits in order to join the R.A.F. at that time. In the autumn of 1939, influence of some kind, or a stroke of luck, was needed to enlist in most arms of the forces, but one required exceptional persistence to infiltrate into the ranks of the R.A.F., as the queue outside the depot demonstrated. Hitchcock continued, in the same confidential undertone, "Back door approach, old boy. They're screaming for tradesmen, catch on? Drivers, flight-mechs., riggers, armorers, even cooks and butchers, Christ help us! You sign on and remuster soon as you've done your square bash. Stands to reason, doesn't it? I mean, there you are looking in from the inside, with the kites lined up waiting for you. Me? I'll take anything they offer even A.C.H./G.D. at a pinch." I did not know what A.C.H./G.D. meant, but I looked at Hitchcock with respect. Here was a man who had obviously done his homework. The rest of us had to rely on guesses and rumors. Logic was in short supply in the autumn of 1939, and there were a million unemployed to prove it.

As I say, Kitchener had done his part in getting me there, but it was difficult to equate his frown and finger with what occurred in that forbidding little room when, at length, Hitchcock, myself, and about a dozen others crossed the threshold and descended three steps into the subzero temperature. Elation ebbed from all but Hitchcock, sustained by his easy familiarity with R.A.F. slang and his pukka gen. The rest of us were not so fortunate and advanced with caution, not so much because of the penetrating cold but on account of the crestfallen expression on the faces of the steady stream of rejects. The squat, muffled sergeant at the desk worked by the book. He interviewed, if that is the word, each one of us under the swinging electric bulb but he did not accept a single man. He was like an impatient landlady in high season turning away good money, and one had the impression he would rise at any moment and hang a card reading, "Full. Try Seaview next door," at the window. Then he was confronted with Hitchcock and at once the scene assumed animation so that I forgot my purpose there and slipped into the role of observer. Suddenly it became terribly important to watch Hitchcock enlist. We saw him as the champion of democracy, taking on the forces of reaction and bureaucracy.

He said, gaily, "Put me down for heavy transport, Sarge— Queen Marys, crash tenders, fire engines, anything you like," and the sergeant raised his head, so that I saw him clearly for the first time.

He was a hard-bitten little man, small but thickset, overweight but not flabby. He had wary eyes and a ragged mustache that looked as though it had been gnawed a great deal, probably from frustration at having to redirect so much promising material to the nearest infantry depot. He said, blowing on his mittened fingers, "Full up. No drivers. Next," and I expected to see Hitchcock turn away with a grimace or a brave grin. He did not, however, but remained there, carefully extracting a packet of Player's from his pocket and offering it to the sergeant. The sergeant took a cigarette without thanks and lit it with a match struck on his thumbnail, in the manner of bad men in Westerns. "Okay, Sarge," Hitchcock said, "I'll settle for flight mech.," and he reached out to help himself to a form. The sergeant's hand got there first, pinning Hitchcock's to the table.

"Full up," he said. "Nex'."

Until then I had thought of Hitchcock as a bit of a blowhard. It goes to show that snap judgments should be made sparingly among the English, even during Phony Wars.

"You've got a notice outside," he said, obstinately, "a bloody great notice that's attracted a bloody great queue. Some of us have been out there an hour."

"You 'ave?"

"Yes, we have."

"I'm cryin' me eyes aht," said the sergeant. "Nex'."

"It's stupid," Hitchcock went on, as though reasoning with himself, "I mean, to have a bloody great notice up saying you want drivers when you don't."

"Bin thinkin' the same all week," the sergeant said. "Now bugger orf, mate, I'm busy." But Hitchcock did not bugger off. Instead he stood quite still, drawing on his cigarette, as though testing the theory of an irresistible force meeting an immovable object.

"Suppose," he said at length, "suppose you go out and scrub that notice?"

The sergeant's chin came up so sharply that it was as though the Invisible Man had struck it from between his cramped knees. He seemed to have some difficulty comprehending the full meaning of Hitchcock's suggestion, as though it had been spoken in a foreign tongue.

"*Scrub it?*" he repeated at last. "You mean *me?*"

"You or us," Hitchcock said. "It don't matter who does it so long as it's done."

The sergeant began to rock, not bodily exactly but from the shoulders upward. It was a rather curious movement and seemed to have been touched off by the impact of Hitchcock's words striking alternate blows on either ear. There was silence in the crowded room and a sense of terrible expectancy. We might have been watching a complicated high-wire act in which, farcically, but also tragically, only Hitchcock and the sergeant were involved. I don't think we saw it as a direct confrontation between the civilian mind and the service mind but the implication was there, and it was important to us all to see how it would resolve itself.

After what seemed a long time the rocking motion ceased and the sergeant spoke again.

He said, enunciating his words very clearly, "You mean *me* go out *there* and . . . and *rub* it off? Without orders? Without ser much as a chitty from S.H.Q.? On me own like?"

"Why not?" said Hitchcock, "it's wasting people's time, isn't it? Come to that it's holding up the war effort. No bloody future in a notice that doesn't mean what it says, is there?"

I saw then that Hitchcock was not so much a reckless man as an extremely insensitive one. Alone among the men crowded into that little room he was unaware of the enormity of his suggestion, of the sheer idiocy of applying the logic of a civilian to a man who must have sloughed it off years ago, when he was a contemporary of Lawrence of Arabia masquerading as Aircraftman Shaw at Uxbridge. Some instinct warned the rest of us of the impending explosion and we made what room we could for it, backing away from the trestle table and huddling together near the steps leading up to the street.

The sergeant half-projected himself out of his canvas-backed chair and lurched forward, supporting himself on spread hands. His body shook so much that the neatly stacked enlistment forms cascaded inward, burying his arms to the elbow. His complexion was that of a man in the throes of a seizure and I found myself looking at his mustache for specks of froth. He was obviously having the greatest difficulty in finding words adequate to the occasion, for his lips moved soundlessly as he fought to regain a measure of self-control. Then years of training reasserted themselves and he lowered himself slowly, as upon a bed of nails. One sensed that he had won a great victory over himself and that he owed it to those years on the square, when he had so often come within a hairsbreadth of falling upon some luckless recruit and beating him over the head with a rifle butt. Everybody, I think, was aware of this, that is to say, everybody but Hitchcock. He still looked relaxed and chipper, puffing away at his cigarette whilst awaiting formal sanction of his strange conceit. When it did not come, when the only sound in the room was the intake and expulsion of the sergeant's breath, he just had to press his luck. He was that type of man, the sort of man who would ask someone just acquitted of murder how he had administered the cyanide. He said, "Let's get weaving then. Where's the bloody duster?"

I have never seen a man move more swiftly or witnessed a room cleared at such speed. One moment we were all standing there, watching the confrontation, the next we were all in the street, striking the head of the queue in a body and driving it down the slope so that it lost all cohesion and eddied the width of the pavement. Hitchcock disappeared altogether, blasted from the face of the earth one assumed, but I caught a fleeting glimpse of the sergeant dancing a kind of clog dance immediately below the chalked notice, and a word or two of his self-accompaniment followed me as far as the High Street, phrases one had always associated with enraged drill sergeants.

A month later, when I returned to the little building, the notice was still there, but the sergeant had gone. In his place sat a corporal with steel-rimmed glasses and a schoolmistressy expression that discouraged me from seeking information concerning his predecessor. The corporal signed us on as Clerks G.D. and went through the ritual so impassively that it was ridiculous to identify him as the man to whom that pointing finger of Kitchener had directed us.

I never looked at a regular N.C.O. during the next six years without hoping to recognize that sergeant and buy him a beer, for somebody should have rewarded such scrupulous exactitude in the execution of orders. Soldiers have won medals for less, and a host of civil servants have harvested honors for doing precisely what he did as a matter of course. I never did meet him, however, and I never, as I half expected, saw Hitchcock swaggering round a perimeter in his flying boots distributing pukka gen. Perhaps, soon after their initial collision, they met and killed one another, but I think not. It is more likely that the sergeant had a stroke and that Hitchcock, troubled by the high rate of casualties among air gunners the following summer, entered the diplomatic service.

The Far Side of Glory

It ought to be obvious that anyone enlisting in the forces of the Crown sacrifices his individuality, but every generation has to rediscover this for itself. Just how complete this sacrifice is to an Englishman is not apparent until a day or so after he has taken the oath and donned the motley. He then discovers that it is far more absolute than joining a school or a secret society, or, indeed, entering into a marriage contract with a wealthy woman, for he is required not only to exchange his name for a number, and place himself wholly at the disposal of superiors (many of whom are semiliterate), but also to sign a book or possess himself of a little slip of paper if he wishes to remove himself from the camp for as much as ten consecutive seconds.

This yielding-up of personal liberty takes a good deal of getting used to, and an Englishman is less inclined to accept the strictures of his new situation than are his Continental neighbors. In countries across the Channel the male has been conditioned, over generations, to the straightjacket of conscription, whereas here a civilian at peace with the law rarely sees himself as a full-time soldier, sailor or airman, unless persuaded that his national existence is threatened.

Yet there are, for the observant and the moderately adaptable, certain compensations, apart from the glow of rectitude that comforts an enlisted man whenever he runs against a contemporary who had the sense to hang on to his individuality. Comradeship he takes for granted in a matter of days, one might almost say hours, and the Englishman is not much given to protestations of patriotism or the pursuit of glory. The real compensations, for my part, crept up on me during the first seven weeks of my service when I was square-bashing or hanging about waiting to square-bash, and although unobtrusive they were insistent in attracting my attention, giving me a gentle nudge every now and again and saying in effect, "Imagine that! You're shut up in a vast and extremely diverting lunatic-asylum-cum-jail. You haven't done anything, and you're not insane, but here you are, so make the most of it. Just look at that warder over there! He's far crazier than any of the inmates. Watch him and see what he does next. Is he going to pretend he's Napoleon?" Or, "What can be the real purpose of this bit of ritual? How did it originate? What kind of person thought it up and wrote it into a manual? He must have been further round the bend than the underlings he employs to teach it to newcomers!"

After a week or two this process of absorbing the impact of people and procedures becomes not merely engrossing but exhilarating, like a ride on a big dipper, followed by a visit to the hall of distorted mirrors. One does not know and cannot guess what will happen next. Or how it could possibly fit into the pattern of a war for national survival. It has, or seems to have, no possible relevance and no connection whatever with the apparatus of war, like tanks and dive bombers and machine guns. In a way it is like a waking dream that would soon develop into a nightmare were it not for the frequent bursts of laughter from all sides and an over-all sense of taking part in an unrehearsed comedy presented—one dare not say organized—on a gigantic scale.

I do not suppose for one moment that my experiences during that blazing spring and summer—surely the sunniest of the century—were any different, or more wildly extravagant, than those of anyone else who joined the forces in 1940. It was only that they seemed so, because for nearly twenty years I had been prospecting for material to be quarried from an English scene and taken home as raw material for books and plays and stories. Because of this, I imagine, my senses were exceptionally alert to the bizarre and the ridiculous, to the eccentric, the madly farcical and the pseudo-dramatic, so that although I was to remain in the R.A.F. for the better part of six years, it is the first six weeks of that period that are more deeply etched in the memory than any period that followed. I was not closely involved with any of the men I met at that time, and if I ever knew their names I have since forgotten them. The scene was changing all the time, and the moment we passed out as recruits the men with whom I shared those initial experiences were scattered to the ends of the earth. For all that, I see them clearly after nearly thirty years, in ones and twos and batches, in good humor and ill, in moments of vexation, frustration, consternation and speechless indignation, and to me, taken all round, this vision was worth the sacrifice of individuality.

I was sworn in at Uxbridge, the camp where Lawrence had buried himself at the height of his fame and subsequently described in his book *The Mint*, withheld from publication until long after his death.

At that time, for my draft at least, it was not a camp where one learned the rudiments of military life, that was attached to volunteers like a porter's stick-on label and subsequently replaced by another sticker identifying him as "R.A.F.-type." Uxbridge in May, 1940, was a huge reception center where a few hundred professionals, most of them promoted overnight to the rank of leading aircraftmen, corporal, sergeant and flight sergeant, were endeavoring, God help them, to absorb the hundreds of thousands of men who had volunteered for "the duration of the present emergency" (a subtly worded phrase this) into what had been a small, highly trained, extremely efficient service.

Regulars told me at that time what life had been like in prewar days, before the absorption of more than a million amateurs. Everyone knew his place in the hierarchy, every man was a master of his craft, and the R.A.F. functioned like a well-ordered Victorian household, all the way down from Air Marshal Papa, who read morning prayers, to A.C. Plonk, the scullery maid, who carried cans of hot water up four flights of stairs before she had rubbed sleep from her eyes. I believe this to be true. The framework still existed when I was swallowed by the monster, but even then, less than nine months after the outbreak of war, the prewar fabric had collapsed under the fearful strains placed upon it during the expansion period. Its victory that same summer, a victory that indubitably saved Europe from eighth-century barbarism, was more of a miracle than war historians would have us believe. Inside the R.A.F. it was generally assumed that the wartime expansion of the Luftwaffe was accompanied by even greater stresses, and that we kept far enough ahead to win the Battle of Britain by a whisker. I spent the first few days of my service life at Uxbridge before moving on to Cardington, where I shared a bell tent with nine others under the great hangar from which the airship R-101 set out on her fatal voyage to India in 1930.

Cardington at that time was like a large railway terminus, coping with half a dozen derailments, but Uxbridge was a veritable madhouse, where life alternated between short, crazy rushes and periods of bewildered idleness, shared by our N.C.O.'s. These last behaved exactly like a pack of half-trained sheep dogs coping with an unfamiliar flock of sheep. Whenever they heard a whistle they ran in, prancing and barking, but soon they decided that the whistle was a direction for other dogs away across the camp, whereupon they stopped short, crouched and hung on our flanks, panting and rolling their eyes.

The first of them, I recall, was a tubby little man with hastily tacked-on corporal's chevrons, who was required to swear us in and supervise our trade tests. I got the impression that both procedures were as new to him as they were to us. We shot about between marquees that contributed to the pervading Uxbridge smell, not unlike the West Buckland smell, inasmuch as it contained the same basic element of boiled greens but here it was laced with bruised grass, sweaty blankets and sunbleached canvas. The corporal lined us up and pressed tattered New Testaments into our right hands, squealing that we were to repeat after him the oath of allegiance binding us to "protect the king anishairs." We were uncertain as to what we were pledging ourselves to protect, but before we could discuss it we were deprived of our Testaments and hounded into a larger marquee, where, on a trestle table, there rested an Oliver typewriter and a book on ornithology open at a page devoted to chaffinches. Shorthand writers were then ordered to take down a dictated passage relating to chaffinches and type it on the Oliver typewriter. This was not difficult, for the corporal, having trouble with unfamiliar words, read very slowly, but when it came to typing it out the thing was quite impossible. The typewriter was so old and so clogged that Mr. Oliver himself would have had to borrow a Remington or a Smith's Premier in order to produce a legible typescript.

The corporal was aware of this and had, it seemed, insured against it. His job, as he saw it, was to produce qualified clerks at high speed and he did just this with commendable ingenuity. When the typewriter carriage stuck and the keys clubbed, he pointed helpfully at a wastepaper basket crammed with fairly legible transcripts of the same passage. "Take one of them an' 'and it to me," he ordered, and we did, wordlessly, sometimes using a test piece that the corporal had just returned to the basket. He then said, "Okay. Passed first class, all of yer. Congratulations, mates!" and we were herded out of the marquee at the double and into a pay tent, where we received eight and threepence apiece, representing three days' pay at two and ninepence per day. We went off to London and spent it at the Windmill Theatre, afterward repairing to the Union Jack Club in Waterloo Road.

At Cardington they were not quite so amiable. The tent lines under the hangar stretched away as far as the little railway halt and one of the N.C.O.'s placed in charge of our draft was another newly promoted corporal afflicted, poor chap, with a slightly twisted face as though, when a child, he had been confronted with some unimaginable horror, had blanched and had his features frozen in a singular expression. One of the less gentlemanly recruits in our tent said the corporal's face reminded him vividly of a cat's arse and after that we always thought of him as "Catsarse," not because we did not sympathize with his difficulties but because he seemed only to know two English words. They were "On p'ra-a-a-ade!"

He would appear two dozen times a day in the tent lines screaming "On p'ra-a-a-ade!" in a voice that would have rocked the airship R-101 at its moorings, but there was rarely any purpose in the order or the resultant scramble from the crowded tents. When we had assembled and numbered we would stand about in the broiling sun for upwards of twenty minutes and would then be dismissed, so that I readily fell in with the suggestion of a red-headed recruit, already far gone in disillusion, to hide under the blankets when Catsarse issued his next order to muster outside. It was an unfortunate decision. This time the others were away a long time and when they returned each was possessed of a couple of treasury notes. All Ginger and I had succeeded in doing was to dodge the initial pay parade and for me this resulted in complications that lasted until the following spring, when my name and number was finally added to the list in pay accounts.

My fellow conspirator on this occasion interested me, at least, his sense of disillusionment did. He was like a bride who had taken the greatest pleasure in the preparation for the wedding, in the actual ceremony, and the reception, but had recoiled from the moment of truth when she found herself between the sheets with a brutish husband.

Whenever he had gained the privacy of the tent he would begin to curse and mutter, his maledictions being shared between the R.A.F. and himself for being such a fool as to volunteer. Sometimes he would work himself up into a lather of self-reproach, searching madly for the hidden motives that had prompted him to commit such a monstrous folly and it was interesting to listen to him as he tossed and turned under his blanket, trying to find room for his legs without incommoding his comrades, or inadvertently striking the tent by dislodging the pole. He would mumble, like a deranged priest at his prayers, "Can't understand it . . . nobody pushed me . . . nobody twisted my arm. But here I am, trapped . . . finished . . . chivvied from arsehole-to-breakfast-time, and for what? That's what beats me. For what? For two and bloody ninepence a day!" Gloom finally got the better of him, his pessimism enlarging itself until it enfolded the entire nation and its present perils. "Point is we're going to lose," he would reflect aloud. "Nothing to stop that bugger now, that's for sure! We've had it, lads. We've really had it, you hear? He'll be over here in a week or so, paratroopers dropping right beside that hangar, and then what'll we do? Tell you what I'm going to do—run like hell!"

At this juncture in the war such wild talk was terrible to hear and began to alarm some of his tentmates. At first they reasoned with him, laying stress on our former triumphs, on the lamentable failures of Spain and France to invade us in 1588 and 1805, on the strength of the British Navy, on the possibility of a mass rising in Europe, but it was no use. He refused to be comforted and if ever there was a man seeking arrest under the new law prohibiting the spreading of alarm and despondency it was Ginger the Doomed. I often wondered what happened to him that winter, when the bombs were crashing down on British cities and the prospect of annihilation loomed large. Perhaps, like others whose patriotism overreached itself in the spring, he escaped from the service through one of the less conventional channels, such as loss of memory or persistent bedwetting, or perhaps he managed to persuade someone to reclaim him to industry. I cannot believe that he ever became converted to the war or to his part in it. His prejudice was too deep for that and all the more outstanding because, at that time, he was the only person I met who gave expression to a perfectly logical fear that we would be beaten in the short run. Perhaps he became a detainee under Regulation 18B and was given a comfortable cell alongside Sir Oswald Mosley. He would, I think, have adjusted to that. He could have sat out the war in Wormwood Scrubs, prophesying the collapse of the British Empire, whilst still probing into his own reasons for volunteering in 1940.

Before we left Cardington for Morecambe we discovered that we had misjudged Catsarse. He did possess a vocabulary larger than two words and exercised it for our especial benefit. It was the day we were bundled into stores and issued with our uniforms and were then so civilian-minded as to set up an exchange mart with the object of adapting them to our persons. Speed was so essential in those days that nobody bothered to measure our girth and we received greatcoats, tunics and trousers according to our height, ascertained by slamming each recruit against a wall and stunning him with a slide rule.

The results were extraordinary. Thin men, shrouded in voluminous garments, looked like carelessly assembled scarecrows, and fat men were unable to fasten more than the top button of any garment so that they wore tunic and greatcoats as cloaks, giving them the aspect of Corsican brigands. Glengarries were distributed with similar *sang-froid*. Some rested on biggish heads like blue tents pitched on a boulder. Others, flung at narrow-headed recruits, came halfway down the face, as though the wearer was preparing to rob a passing stagecoach. Realizing that we could not face the prospect of a long war in this sort of gear we began to swap and were well launched on the process when Catsarse appeared and demanded to know what was happening. His reaction was similar to that of the recruiting sergeant at the depot, when advised by Hitchcock to expunge the out-of-date notice. He saw the exchange not as a means of expediency but as a military crime that bordered on mutiny. He screamed and danced and ran about tearing garments from the backs of half-dressed men, and telling us at the top of his voice that we could each get a year in the glasshouse for taking such liberties with government property. It was useless to explain the reason behind the orgy of swapping. The harder we tried the more excited he became, so we spent the rest of the morning dodging about the tent lines in search of our original issue. Later on we did our swapping in private, but I never did manage to exchange my tunic, a very curious garment indeed composed of two entirely foreign halves, one designed for a man about six feet in height, the other for a shortish, rather plump man. I cannot imagine how it was ever sewn together in the first place and can only suppose that the tailor was blind and sewed by Braille. The left flap projected two and a half inches below its fellow, and the breast of the right half bulged, as though it had been cut for a busty W.A.A.F. Nor was this all. For some reason, that had to do with the fibers in the cloth, the ends of the vent stuck out at right angles like the feathers of an amorous duck. I wore it for three years and eight months and finally came to terms with it in the way a housewife will sometimes cherish a handleless kitchen knife, passed on by Mother, that she used to prepare the first meal after the honeymoon. I never succeeded in swapping my boots either, and they were a singular pair. They turned up at the toes and did not look like boots but more like a clumsy pair of Oriental slippers.

On our final day at Cardington we were mustered on the up platform of the railway halt, not for the purpose of entraining but in order to establish our identities beyond all doubt and have our names checked against a nominal roll. We looked directly across the line at Catsarse, who stood on the down platform alone, holding a sheaf of paper clipped to a board, and calling each name and number as his forefinger reached it in the column. As soon as his number was called the owner was required to jump off the platform and cross the line to the down platform, where he was at once dismissed, but as there were more than five hundred of us the process occupied most of the afternoon.

Little by little the ranks began to shrink until, at around 16.30 hours, I was alone on the up platform, wondering at my isolation, and beginning to think I was not properly enlisted. Then Catsarse tucked his board under his arm and glared across at me, inquiring, "You over there! Is your bleedin' name 'Daffodil'?" I told him it wasn't and explained who I was, but my words must have been carried away on the wind for, after re-examining his list, he said, "Number 925656?" and when I admitted to this, "Okay. Near enough. It's the number that cahnts. Dis-*miss*, A.C. Daffodil!" He then walked slowly away shaking his head, wondering perhaps if he was likely to encounter an A.C. Violet or Hyacinth in the incoming draft. Because of this I do not associate Cardington with hot summer days but with the promise of spring.

2

From Cardington we traveled by slow train to Morecambe, an eager, wisecracking, skylarking lot. We might have been excursionists getting our annual glimpse of the sea and secretly I marveled at our high spirits. The man next to me kept singing snatches of "Scatterbrain." In July, 1940, what, I wonder, did the English have to sing about? Was every man on that train exulting in his release from predictability?

We were billeted in one of the tall boardinghouses on the sea front. I was senior man of a group of twelve, wedged into three bedrooms, and we were not very welcome, because the landlady (the prototype of Mrs. Bounty, in *Worm's Eye View*) regarded high summer as her seasonal peak and all she received for billeting us was one pound per man per week.

What genuinely astonished me about Morecambe at that time was its neutrality, and in this respect the town was not unique. Blackpool, just along the coast, was no different in 1941, and some seaside resorts, far removed from the Channel coasts, managed to retain their resort status throughout the entire war. The week we arrived in Morecambe coincided with the opening stage of the Battle of Britain, but nobody would have imagined, passing along the sea front, or marching up and down the pier, that the nation was engaged in a war with a few hundred tribesmen in the Khyber Pass, much less the hordes of Panzers and Stormtroopers who had just taken Paris and the Channel ports. I don't know whether Wakes Weeks were on, but the town was crammed with holidaymakers wearing blazers and summer dresses, who gave us incurious looks as we stamped past their deckchairs, learning how to salute pilot officers to the front and flight lieutenants to the left. They were by no means hostile, and here and there one of them smiled, but they all seemed vaguely embarrassed by so much martial activity, and I got the impression they would have been relieved if we had been kept away from the sea and the parks. Our landlady, Devil take her, had civilian visitors in the first-floor rooms and we did their washing-up when we came in from the streets. We never succeeded in coming to terms with this. Nor did anyone ever persuade us that all those holidaymakers, licking their ice cream and nibbling their candy floss, were war workers enjoying a well-earned respite from factories in the North and Midlands. Neither were we successful in establishing friendly relations with our landlady, whose discipline was far more galling than that existing in any camp I occupied later in the war and who seemed, perhaps on account of lost lets, outraged by our presence. One of the bonuses of the nuclear bomb is that there can never be another war such as this, with one half of the nation under military discipline and the other living under a sign "Business as Usual."

From Morecambe, a month or so later, I moved down to Cosford, my first experience of a permanent Technical Training Camp that sat on the landscape like a vast town, northwest of Wolverhampton. Here I was set to work in an orderly room and soon came to realize that I should never have listened to that idiot Hitchcock about the prospects of remustering inside the service. At Cosford I found myself bogged down as a clerk, and it seemed to me extremely unlikely, short of a great stroke of luck, that I would be permitted to remuster to another trade as the war got into its stride.

The work was hard and very monotonous, a nonstop orgy of form filling and typing daily routine orders, nominal rolls, personnel occurrence reports, chits of every description and it entailed long spells of night duty, without a compensating day in the open. We were in Technical Training Command, one of the five commands existing in the R.A.F. at that time, and as always at this type of camp, where the intake of airmen taking specialized courses was continuous, the permanent staff was far too small to cope with basic requirements. Every so often armies of embryo flight mechanics and riggers descended on us, with their accumulated needs and complicated personal problems. Avalanches of paper poured into the orderly room and spilled into our trays. Telephones rang every few moments, and distant strangers asked us what they were to do with eighty-four flight mechanics stranded in Edinburgh, or sixty-three riggers left behind in Dover Castle.

The peacetime administration system, devised I was told, by experts from Gamages, Harrods and Woolworths, was already breaking down under the strains imposed upon it, not because it was ill-conceived but because it had been swamped and we newcomers had been given no opportunity to absorb it, but if we worked hard even more was demanded of the nucleus of regulars. In addition to coping with the enormous amount of paper work they had to find time to train us.

The office equipment was archaic. Elderly Oliver typewriters, of the kind I had used to take my trade test at Uxbridge, were totally inadequate for the tasks expected of them and went sick one after another, so that I sent home for my portable Remington and used it all the time I worked in orderly rooms. The regulars were a splendid lot, invariably kind and patient, and genuinely grateful for what little help we could give them, but as the pace of the war hotted up, and the administrative needs grew and grew with thousands of men arriving to be trained for manning the airfields of Fighter, Bomber and Coastal Commands, the desks could only be cleared by working round the clock, fortified every now and again by mugs of tea served from a bucket.

A popular legend has grown up concerning the undue emphasis placed on paper work in the armed forces during World War II. I have seen film shots of impatient squadron commanders of the Bader type, throwing files into the wastepaper basket as a gesture of contempt. I am sure Bader was far too good an officer to act in this way. He would have known that it took upwards of thirty ground staff to keep a single pilot aloft, and each one of those ground staff, "wingless wonders" as safely entrenched civilians came to call them, had to be trained and clothed and fed. They had to be supplied with stores, tools and equipment of every kind and their manifold personal problems had to be investigated by M.O.'s, padres, and legal and welfare officers. All these processes required detailed paper work and God knows, much as I hated it at the time, I soon realized that without that inflow and outflow of paper the R.A.F. could not have functioned for a week.

I was duty clerk at Wing H.Q. on Sunday, September 16, when we got the invasion alert and I don't think I ever did a longer or more complex stint in my whole life. I was on the job two days and one night without a break other than for meals, and only an occasional flash of that interval returns to me now. A gas-caped, tin-hatted flight sergeant, stumping into the orderly room and saying, casually, "Well, chum, the bastards are landing. This is it"; a warrant officer, demanding the keys of the decontamination center; a flying officer ringing from Crewe and demanding of me (with three months' experience) how he could get a trainload of flight mechanics to the camp when the regular rail service had been suspended. But above all, the quiet voice of a Spitfire pilot, ringing from Duxford, begging me to find his brother who was serving at the camp. "Things are pretty lively down here," he said, apologetically, "and I'd like to have a word with the kid before I take off again."

By early autumn, when some kind of rhythm had been established and I had been upgraded to leading aircraftman, I told myself that by any means short of desertion I must escape the claustrophobic atmosphere of that Nissen hut. For years now I had been free-ranging, making my own daily timetable and I found the immobility and repetitiveness of the job insufferable. I knew then that I had made a bad misjudgment and must start looking for a means to correct it, so I put in for a commission that necessitated volunteering for air crew. At that time only air-crew rejects were considered for commissioning in another branch and the prospect of being shot to pieces in the sky seemed infinitely preferable to drowning under an avalanche of forms.

There was a chance that I would be accepted as an air gunner, but although I passed the color test I was ultimately rejected on account of a defective right eye, and had to be content with the promise of the C.O. that he would put me forward for a commission as soon as I had completed a year in the service. That was too long to wait, so I tried to remuster to several other trades and at length took the desperate step of volunteering for their bomb-disposal squad, but here I ran down the true source of the trouble. Clerk/General Duties, was Group III, and it was a rule of the service that no one could remuster downward—that is to say, into Groups IV or V, embracing many of the trades practiced in the open. Apart from this, I was a shorthand writer, and we were in very short supply at that time. Stuck with clerking, I decided to relieve the monotony of the endless days and nights by organizing camp entertainments, starting with a revue and building up to a Christmas pantomime.

I have since met men in the entertainment industry who used camp entertainments as an escape hatch from routine work into an area where their talents were fully extended, but either I was unlucky or my talents were not sufficiently outstanding. The C.O., a blunt, ex-naval type, asked me how many acts pantomimes had and when I told him two he gave me two days off to write the script.

The pantomime, notwithstanding, was a success. It was expertly produced by a cheerful, fresh-faced bespectacled airman, who approached me one night and politely offered his services, telling me that he had played small parts in several British films. I accepted the offer gladly, and he made a splendid job of it. His name was Ken Annakin, familiar to a generation of postwar filmgoers as the director of *Those Wonderful Men in Their Flying Machines* and many other successful films, including one I was to write, *Value for Money*, with Diana Dors in the lead.

Incidentally, that pantomime, *Binbad the Airman*, was instrumental in saving the Birmingham Repertory Company part of its scenery. We borrowed a lorryload for the occasion and when we returned it the theater's New Street store was a smoldering ruin, having suffered a direct hit the night before.

In the late autumn the tedium of life in that scurrying place was relieved by the arrival of my wife and the issue of a living-out pass. It promised more than it offered. The only lodgings available to a couple living on an L.A.C.'s pay and a married allowance, together totaling about fifty shillings a week, was a small back room in a council house in a country town a few miles up the line, and rail journeys to and from the camp were complicated by endless delays caused by bombing. Another airman and his wife occupied the front room, the third bedroom being used by the landlady and her husband, a butcher who was dying of cancer of the stomach. His condition emphasized the hopelessness of that era, for us and for everyone around us. Each night, regular as clockwork, German bombers throbbed across the sky, showering the industrial Midlands with land mines, five-hundred-pound bombs and incendiaries. The landscape of the approaches to the cities changed day by day. At night the blackout regulations were made ludicrous by the numerous fires. Toward Christmas our landlord died. A few minutes before, he had asked me to lift him on to the commode, and when I saw that he was unlikely to last the night I telephoned his daughter. The doctor came, signed a certificate and shrugged his shoulders. What was one death among so many? Coventry, only a few miles away, was in ruins.

In the New Year I was posted to Bridgnorth, the first of many spot postings that were to contribute to the frustrations of that period. Trained men—and I now regarded myself as a trained man—were constantly being uprooted and sent off in dribs and drabs all over the British Isles, often to no purpose, for when they arrived nobody expected them. It usually required about a month to settle to a new routine, and that month was invariably wasted. Apart from this, these blind, individual postings had, I am certain, an adverse effect upon morale. Sailors and infantrymen learned to work together as a unit, sometimes serving through the entire war in one another's company, but every cross-country train in Britain at that time carried airmen encumbered with kit, making their solitary way to yet another camp. In the period between May, 1940, and December, 1943, I was booked in at thirteen.

Every now and again the mechanical grab at R.A.F. Ruislip reached out and snatched a shoal of men for overseas postings. On one occasion I got as far as the boat and was struck off the draft, having been promoted, in my absence, to the rank of corporal. It was a mixed blessing, carrying another two shillings a day but at the rank of corporal the buck, as the Americans say, stops. It cannot be passed any further and perhaps this explains Corporal Hitler's determination to initiate orders instead of acting as longstop. In the capacity of corporal I once found myself in the unenviable situation of having to select a required number of tradesmen to fill a draft for overseas. I did it by lottery.

In the late summer of 1941 prospects suddenly seemed a little brighter. I was posted to Blackpool, then seething with airmen; and May, who had been trekking round in my wake like a *vivandière*, found yet another back room in a seaside boarding-house.

We had visited Blackpool in the piping days of peace. I always thought of it in the context of *Hindle Wakes* and the intriguing query printed on the playbills wherever the piece was presented—"Should Fanny Marry Allan?" Fanny would have had plenty of alternatives in wartime Blackpool, where something like thirty thousand airmen were billeted in the town and all the principal hotels were used as wing headquarters. May got a job here on the local newspaper, and we then had sufficient money to eat if food could be found. One of the disadvantages of a living-out pass was that one was always hungry.

At Blackpool the curious schism of wartime Britain between serviceman and civilian was again evident. Town life was conducted on two levels. The resort was being used as a recruit-training center and all day long the voices of the drill instructors echoed in streets of late Victorian and Edwardian home-from-homes. But neither permanent staff nor recruits had much personal contact with the residents, who must surely have benefited from the enormous influx of service personnel. Bickerings between the two sectors were frequent and often acrimonious. It sometimes seemed to me that we were not in England at all but on neutral soil, Swedish perhaps, or Swiss. Later, in French and Belgian provinces, I felt much more at home.

It was at Blackpool that I became aware of the continuing failure on the part of the R.A.F. to adapt to the pressures of expansion, stressed earlier in this chapter. By now hundreds of thousands of conscripted men were joining us, called by regulars and volunteers, "the population of China," a term derived from their seven-letter service numbers and to anyone in a position to observe, the waste of manpower was appalling. Nowhere was this more apparent than in the hotel that housed the Non-Effective Pool, a place to which all the odds and sods gravitated.

Here were recruits whose initial period of training had been broken for one reason or another—through illness, accident, compassionate leave on account of bombed homes, recall to industry, and a dozen other reasons. By the autumn of 1941 the pool was a maelstrom and the N.C.O.'s in charge of it were overwhelmed by the resultant muddle. Nominal rolls of strays were pinned on the walls and senior N.C.O.'s running the pool were expected to keep track of every one of them. This was clearly impossible, for the names changed every hour as men came and went, were posted, deserted, or just went into hiding in cinemas and cafés. It was a sobering experience to stand and watch the poor devils at work, darting round rooms that had housed generations of Lancashire holidaymakers and scratching out names with stubs of pencil. I thought I had seen the ultimate in paper avalanches at Cosford, but work in that N.E. Pool was far more demanding than in an orderly room, and sometimes it seemed to me that the senior flight sergeant and his temporary staff were drowning under it and coming up for air every few seconds as a stream of runners appeared to wave more chits under their noses.

A more entertaining spectacle at Blackpool was to witness a swoop by military police on the known lairs of the scrimshankers, who were flushed out into the open like game and paraded in the street for a spot check of names and numbers, and an explanation of what they were doing watching a film at 1500 hours on a winter's afternoon. No amount of punitive action, however, could contain them. They were too many and far too well versed in the tactics of evasion. Even while their names were being called they would bolt down alleyways like rabbits, or drift away and merge with groups of men having their tea break. Because they all wore identical uniforms it was difficult to isolate them, and in the end the parade would shred away and the M.P.'s would go into action again, like a posse in a Western film.

It was all part of the national mood at that time, a kind of limbo between the backs-to-the-wall period of Dunkirk and the Battle of Britain, and the flood tide of hope that began with El Alamein and extended to D-Day two and a half years later. In the meantime, everybody I met seemed to put their faith in the Red Army, battling it out in Kharkov and Sebastopol. A heady wind of enthusiasm for Communism blew through the billets, and men began to refer to Stalin (as yet unmasked) as "Uncle Joe." I have always believed that the hangover of this brief love affair with the Russians had a good deal to do with Labour's unexpected victory in July, 1945.

In the meantime, however, the urgency had ebbed from the war. Fear of invasion had lifted. Hitler became a joke again, and service became a drudgery. A kind of disgruntled somnolence settled over the town, relieved only by newspaper reports of Russian heroism, and this uninspired mood was strengthened by news, flashed on the cinema screens in December, of the attack on Pearl Harbor. With that, Blackpool and its vast population of airmen seemed to settle down to wait for the invasion of Europe and the collapse of Germany.

Miss Colyer and the "Oh-Thems"

A good deal has been written, and even more shown on film, concerning the morale of the Londoner during the period of the authentic Blitz—that is to say, the nine months linking September, 1940, and May, 1941. Less well documented is the period between June, '44, and the early spring of '45, when a rain of flying bombs and rockets fell on the capital.

The two onslaughts have little in common, so little indeed that they might almost have been incidents in two separate wars. The first was conducted as an all-out terror campaign, with a sporting chance of gaining victory for the aggressor. The second was hardly more than a prolonged gesture of desperation on the part of Germany. Seen in retrospect it could never hope to do much more than confuse and dismay.

Its effect on the civilian population, however, was disproportionate, and several reasons account for this. It came at the end of a long period of strain and malnutrition, when Londoners were justified in assuming that their long ordeal was almost at an end. In addition it was a nonstop attack, without the daylight lulls that attended its predecessor. But, above all, its impact was psychological inasmuch as flying bombs could be seen approaching and seemed, indeed, to be making up their minds, as they bumbled across the summer sky, where to descend. Even the shortsighted were given a brief interval to decide which way to run and what cover to seek, but this was a mixed blessing. It put the responsibility of staying alive on you and not on the missile. It deprived you of the chilly comfort of fatalism.

By and large the authorities made light of its effect upon morale, trying to treat it as a kind of sustained nuisance, like the activities of an unpleasant neighbor, or the descent of a swarm of wasps at a picnic, but this was a deliberate policy on their part. Both they and the public were very much concerned with this form of attack, and at one time it looked as though the rain of flying bombs would achieve what the Blitz never did succeed in doing—compel evacuation of all but the essential services and population.

Authorities and public alike hated and feared the flying bomb and found the few moments between its appearance, cutout and ultimate dive, an interval of horrid suspense. In the early part of the attack, until the defenses had succeeded to a degree in containing it, hysteria was never far below the surface of the public mind in London and I saw little evidence of the we-can-take-it spirit that characterized the sustained bombing of '40–41. London was a weird place to live during that final summer of the war. A million and a quarter of its population had gone, and those who remained stalked rather than walked from point to point, showing in their expressions the effects of irritation, prolonged anxiety and loss of sleep. People were afraid, and ashamed of fear; by late July, when flying bombs seemed to be racketing in from the southeast at the rate of about one every five minutes, nerves were ragged and Blitz humor, the ultimate safety valve of the Cockney, had departed to the country with the third wave of evacuees.

Herein lies my deep respect for at least one Londoner, Miss Colyer, my Holland Park landlady, in whom resided all the good qualities of the British and all the characteristics that have made the Londoner, over centuries of good luck and bad, a byword for self-reliance and resilience. For Miss Colyer met the onslaught of the doodlebug with the same contempt and courage that she had deployed against every other weapon the enemy had used in attempts to confound her. I saw her then and I see her now as a justification for that delightfully insular line that appears in the verse of our national anthem. She had every intention of frustrating the knavish tricks of the King's enemies. Nothing the most fiendishly inventive among Continentals (whom she thought of, quite unconsciously, as a disreputable assortment of Dagoes, Wops, Squareheads and Frogs) could daunt or dismay her. Not for an instant. Not for the time it took a doodlebug to cut its motor and begin its long, swooping descent. For me, during that trying summer, she was far more than she appeared, a dignified, rather angular spinster, exercising a benevolent despotism over an assorted bunch of lodgers. She was the embodiment of a thousand years of London's history.

2

Notwithstanding the evacuations and the brief but lively February Blitz, it was difficult to find lodgings in London in 1944. Thousands of houses had been demolished or made untenable and thousands of landladies had gone into the country but hundreds of thousands of Allied servicemen and servicewomen were looking for digs situated within easy traveling distance of their Greater London bases.

I found Miss Colyer through one of those shopwindow advertisements, a grimy envelope gummed to a stationer's plate glass by its flap, announcing a room vacant at Number Seventeen, Clarendon Road, Holland Park, a twenty-minute bus ride from the Air Ministry. My room was on the first floor front of a tall, mid-Victorian building, of the kind the Forsytes built about 1850, perhaps on the site of an earlier dwelling. Its proprietor was very dignified but daunting until you got to know her, a tall, slim, extremely active woman in her late sixties, with clear uncompromising blue eyes and the complexion of a country girl in her teens. She looked much younger than she was, partly because of her complexion, but also on account of her upright carriage and the astounding but carefully conserved energy she showed ministering to her assorted lodgers, distributed about the three floors. She and her favorite lodger, known as "Mr. P" occupied the basement.

I never did discover how many people were assembled under that roof. Numbers seemed to vary. Sometimes about ten would assemble for breakfast round the mahogany dining table on the ground floor, but other times there would be only me, Vernon Noble, a fellow officer who joined me later, and an elderly woman I thought of as the Guru because she was devoted to Yoga and health foods. Mr. P, a genial man about Miss Colyer's age, did not breakfast with us and rarely appeared above stairs, but the nature of his relationship with Miss Colyer was carefully explained to me the first day I settled in. "Mr. P has been with me a long time," she said, holding my gaze with the unwinking steadiness of the Ancient Mariner, "and he lives in the basement front. *But there's nothing funny about it, you understand?*"

Of course I understood. There was not, there never had been and there never would be, anything "funny" about a single aspect of Miss Colyer's conduct, or her rigid adherence to the code of behavior prevalent when she was a girl in the eighteen-eighties, but I would not like to convey the impression that she was prudish, or even old-fashioned in her outlook. She was just Miss Colyer, of Clarendon Road, who kept a boardinghouse, stood on her own two feet, and was the most self-contained and fully integrated human being it has ever been my good fortune to meet. She was the British spinster at her best. You could picture her as the unmarried sister of a professional soldier, caught up in the siege of Lucknow and busying herself with the wounded in bombarded cellars, or as someone like Betsy Trotwood, who could be relied upon to mother David and Mr. Dick and keep the donkeys from her lawn. There were also elements about her that recalled Grace Darling, Florence Nightingale, Mrs. Pankhurst and Amy Johnson, any one of whom would have been improved by lodging with Miss Colyer.

She interested me from the beginning, a spare, tireless, indefatigable woman, reserved yet communicative, aloof but frigidly maternal, uncomplaining concerning the strictures of war and somehow managing to convey that what was happening across the Channel was a degrading street riot in which a few sober citizens, herself included, had become embroiled, and from which they would shortly succeed in extricating themselves.

Sometimes I would endeavor to draw her out about the war and extract from her conclusions about its impact upon a Londoner who had seen it through, as she had, from the beginning, but I was never very successful. She had fixed opinions regarding Hitler and Mussolini, whom she thought of as a couple of vulgarians, whose bottoms should have been tanned once a week throughout childhood, but she seemed to have no special animus for the German and Italian people, lumping them together with the French, the Spanish and the Russians, as interrelated families of coolies, whose lack of spirit had reduced them, perhaps deservedly, to the status of primitives in need of British missionaries to teach them hygiene and a few simple stories from the Old Testament.

Her approach to the Führer and the Duce was more personal and based upon deeply rooted prejudices. She said of them once, "What can you expect, Mr. D?" (she called all her lodgers by the first letter of their surnames), "what can you expect of two men of that sort? That Italian keeps a mistress, a Clara Someone, who looks old enough to know better, and that man Hitler bites carpets when he runs into a little setback. I don't believe all I read in the papers, but I believe that. I mean, people of that kind, keeping loose women, and biting carpets just because they can't get their own way, are bound to come a cropper sooner or later, aren't they?"

Her powers of understatement hypnotized me. Anyone who could refer, without irony, to Hitler's débâcle at Stalingrad as "a little setback," or see Germany's border states as put-upon neighbors in a suburban crescent, was unlikely, I thought, to be driven to cover by high explosive. And in this, as things turned out, I was right.

When the flying-bomb Blitz got into its stride, when the damned things began to crump down all around us at the rate of one every few minutes, I felt naked and exposed up in her first-floor front. Contemptuous of anything "those hooligans" could achieve, Miss Colyer had not even bothered to plaster her large window overlooking the street with adhesive tape and one night, convinced that it was my last, I took refuge with Mr. P in his basement two floors below. Together we weathered it out and were still there, dozing fitfully, when Miss Colyer marched in with our tea at seven-fifteen. Not a hair on her gray head was out of place. She looked fresh and vigorous and held herself as erect as a hollyhock stalk, so that we felt very sheepish in her presence and mumbled something about it being "a bit of a night." She looked surprised at this and said, addressing me, "Is *that* why you're here? Is that why you came down?" I could only admit shamefully that it was, and Mr. P spoke up gallantly, saying he had been glad of my company, whereupon Miss Colyer seemed at last to comprehend the reason for our disarray. "Oh, *them*," she said at length, "those buzz-things! Well, I wouldn't let *them* come between me and a good night's rest!" and she marched out to carry the Guru's tea tray up four flights of stairs.

One of the strange by-products of the doodlebug Blitz was the wanderlust it induced. Under the old Blitz conditions the besieged perfected a routine and adjusted to it jovially and almost happily over the months, but nothing like this occurred in the summer of 1944. For my part—and I know others who reacted similarly—I could only seek relief in roaming about from one end of London to the other, sometimes spending seven successive nights on seven different perches, as though seeking to confuse the mindless things and induce them to concentrate on worthwhile targets, like the Houses of Parliament and the Albert Memorial. Vernon Noble and I, in search of cover, spent one night under a billiard table at Highgate, and several nights in Air Ministry alcoves, where half a dozen stone floors interposed between us and the sky. After that I took refuge in the lighthouse-type home of the actor Walter Hudd, who kept blaming me, as a man enlisted in the Air Force, for the maddening persistence of the attack. Once I wandered out as far as Norbiton to stay with my friend Ken Annakin, and then back to Troy Court, in Kensington, that received a direct hit when I was on duty in Whitehall. But all the time one had a feeling of being hunted and in the end I crept back to Holland Park to shelter under the splendid indifference of Miss Colyer, who did not vary her domestic routine by a single second and moved among her shrinking band of lodgers like Queen Elizabeth reviewing poor-spirited troops at Tilbury.

You could not call her performance magnificent, because it wasn't a performance, merely a continuation of a placid, nonstop chore that had been the mainspring of her life ever since she put up her hair a year or so before Victoria's Golden Jubilee. And gradually, without being aware of it, we began to draw courage from her, and feed a little of it to each other, so that finally I settled for my first-floor front and lay there listening to regular explosions that slowly widened the plaster cracks in the ceiling. I was still uneasy but much comforted by the thought that no doodlebug, not even a demented one winged by ack-ack or fighter fire, or deflected by a balloon cable, would have the confounded impudence to single out a house where Miss Colyer was going about her business.

3

The extremely rapid deployment of British defenses against the flying-bomb attacks is an aspect of the war that has, I think, been overlooked by historians. When the onslaught was about ten days old I was sent down to the Sussex coast to report on the countermeasures, and I was very impressed by their imaginativeness and over-all efficiency.

The defense was organized in depth, with what amounted to four protective belts stretching in the path of the bombs from the Channel to the Downs. Along the coast, and just inland, was the gun belt, some of the guns being operated by mixed crews of men and girls, and immediately behind this the R.A.F. balloon barrage, with its crews tucked away in coppices and patches of gorse. Over the Channel and again, behind the barrage, fighter aircraft patrolled, so that a flying bomb had four gauntlets to run before it reached the southern perimeter of London.

The success of this system, moderate at first, increased as time went on. Between June 13, the date the attack opened, and the middle of July, two hundred and sixty-one were brought down by the gunners, nine hundred and twenty-four by fighter pilots and fifty-five by balloons, but enough got through to keep the Londoner on the jump. I witnessed several tragic incidents, but the only bomb that came close to killing me was the one that dived on the Royal Military Chapel at Wellington Barracks, soon after eleven on Sunday, June 18. I was on duty on the P.R. shelf under the glass roof when it glided down, and it seemed to pass within hailing distance a few seconds before impact, killing or seriously wounding seventy-eight civilians and one hundred and eleven service personnel attending morning service.

Down in the defense zone, where flying bombs were passing over or being shot down far more frequently, one felt much safer, probably owing to the openness of the ground, and the size of the target area. I lay on my back on Romney Marsh early one morning and watched a Tempest V fight a successful duel with one of them, and was on Biggin Hill Airfield when a winged doodlebug sent everyone diving for cover between cutout and impact. The course of damaged flying bombs was often erratic. I saw one hit by ack-ack fire a few hundred yards out to sea, between Eastbourne and Folkestone, but although it swerved it pressed on, passing over at about two hundred feet, heading due north. Servicemen, enjoying a bathe in the shallows, scrambled out of the water and fled up the beach but seconds after disappearing inland it reappeared still losing height, and finally exploded fifty yards south of the tideline. No one was hurt, but from then on one was apt to regard damaged missiles as more dangerous than those traveling on course at three hundred and forty m.p.h.

I spent an exciting and interesting week down here in the defense belts, but when I returned Miss Colyer was unimpressed. When I told her that the defenses were accounting for upwards of fifty percent of the bombs (this rose, in the last week of August, to eighty-three percent) she said, "Ah, so that's where you've been? Down at the seaside! Well, I hope you've been sleeping better down there than you did up here. Mr. P can't seem to get used to the noise at all. He's looking very peaky, and I've been telling him to see about a tonic. Iron. That's what he needs." It was the last thing, I reflected, that Miss Colyer would ever need. She had been born with a surfeit.

I grew so fond of her that when I went to France I made sure of retaining my room by paying her two months' rent in advance and promising to make up the balance if I was away longer. She accepted the money but said, querulously, "France? What are you going there for? Those hooligans won't last much longer. It's hardly worth the bother, is it?" I said I would like to be on hand when the hooligans were put down, but it was never the slightest good attempting to explain to Miss Colyer that war involved movement, apart from movement to and from the kitchen, and up and down all those stairs.

In the new year I was back again, with tales to tell of the liberation of France and Belgium, but Miss Colyer was dubious about the wisdom of using British taxpayers' money to push one tribe of barbarians from another tribe's territory. "All I can say is I hope they appreciate it," she said, glumly, "for if you ask me it's six of one and half a dozen of the other as regards foreigners. Somebody told me once we had to pay so much a mile to run hospital trains in France in that other war. Did you ever hear of such a thing?" I told her I too had heard of it and that it was true, but that it was unlikely to happen on this occasion because we were now broke and would be reduced to borrowing vast sums of money from the Americans.

"There's another lot," she said, emphatically, "shameless they are! Kissing girls in the street in broad daylight when I went out for the rations yesterday. Saw them at it!"

She perked up a little when the newspapers published those

revolting pictures of Mussolini and his mistress Clara, hanging upside down from a bracket in Milan. I thought the pictures would shock her, but they didn't. "You see what comes of keeping loose women," she said, piously, and then, "God bless my soul, what a way to go! I'm sorry for her, mind you!" "Her" was not, as one might have assumed, the erring Clara. Miss Colyer's sympathy was for Mrs. Mussolini.

She still had the power to surprise me. Soon after V–E Day, when things were reverting to normal, she appeared in my room one evening and asked me diffidently if I would come down and meet an old friend of hers. "She tells fortunes," she said, "and I want her to tell yours."

It seemed out of character somehow, Miss Colyer hovering with bird-bright eyes, whilst her friend peered into a tea cup, or gazed down at the Ace of Spades. I would have imagined that Miss Colyer would have regarded fortunetelling as a very frivolous occupation, of the kind practiced by Hungarian Gypsies and girls like Mussolini's mistress, but it was not so. She believed fervently in every prophecy her friend made, particularly the one concerning the trouble Mr. P was going to have with his leg, and the move the Guru was destined to make in the near future.

When it came to my turn the fortuneteller predicted a big success in the theater and when, jocularly, I told Miss Colyer that if the prophecy proved correct I would give her a present to commemorate our association, she spoke up very saucily and said, "You will? Very well, I'll have a portable wireless set. I've always wanted a portable wireless set. Don't you forget it, will you?" I said I wouldn't. She deserved something for all those early-morning cups of tea she had brought to my bedside while the hooligans were having their final fling.

You could never be quite sure how Miss Colyer would react to a given set of circumstances. She surprised me yet again that summer when I brought a friend home, a gunner from Devon, who had been flown back from a P.O.W. camp after five years of captivity. It was very late when I brought him in, so I made him a bed of cushions and rugs on the floor and Miss Colyer, appearing with the tea at seven-fifteen, only just avoided falling flat on her face when she opened the door.

Feeling some explanation was necessary, I told her the full circumstances, how my friend had been wandering the streets, and had begged me to put him up for the night before he could catch his train home. She said, sourly for her, "Disgusting! That's what it is, downright disgusting! Here you are, featherbedded up at that Air Ministry for a year or more, and that poor boy has been shut away with those hooligans, and where do you put him to sleep when he finally gets home? On the floor! Under my feet! And you snug between the sheets on a flock mattress!" She drove her point home by giving the gunner my tea.

I said goodbye to her when I was demobilized in November and never expected to see her again, but when the success her fortuneteller friend had predicted came with *Worm's Eye View*, I felt obliged to go out and buy her the portable radio she coveted. I had an uneasy suspicion that if I failed to keep a promise of that kind I would be classed, in her mind, with the hooligans, and she would come to equate me with Continentals who made a habit of welshing on promises.

I met her on the porch, carrying her string bag containing rations for the leftovers of her wartime clientele. It included Mr. P, who *was* having trouble with his leg, and the Guru, whose move had not yet materialized. She said, unsmilingly, "Ah, *there* you are Mr. D! Well, my friend saw it coming, didn't she? She read about you in the papers and was round here all out of breath the same night. What's that you've got? Is it the portable wireless set?"

I said it was and she thanked me gravely. "That'll come in handy just now," she said, "for Mr. P can't get about and he likes a bit of music to help the day along."

We went down into her basement kitchen and drank tea while Mr. P tuned in the set and got us a news bulletin that included items relating to measures the new government was setting in train concerning the Welfare State. Miss Colyer, of course, dismissed the entire experiment as an exercise in mollycoddling work-shy layabouts. " 'From the cradle to the grave,' " she quoted, scornfully. "Spoon-fed everyone is nowadays, and where will it end? That's what I'd like to ask that Cripps and that Bevan! They're no better than the hooligans! Well, I've work to do, I was in the middle of my spring-clean when you showed up . . ." And she marched out, erect as a beanpole, carrying her mop in one hand and a bucket of water in the other. She managed the ascent to the top landing without a pause.

I said to Mr. P, "She must be turned seventy. How long does she intend keeping this up?" and he said, grinning, "Not all that long. We're going to put together and buy a cottage in the country. She's always wanted a cottage in the country. Somewhere down your way, Wiltshire, Somerset or Devon."

They got their cottage, a year or so later, and lived out the remainder of their lives there, very peacefully I believe, right alongside the main railway line connecting London and the far west. They liked watching the trains and perhaps, when an express rushed by in the small hours, Miss Colyer would stir in her sleep and dream fleetingly of the whoosh of the "oh-thems" that had kept the population of London awake for nights on end but had never cost her a wink of the rest she needed to minister to all those lodgers and climb all those stairs. Over the past twenty-five years I have often listened to wiseacres advancing complicated theories as to why we won the war. If they had known Miss Colyer, TV viewers might have saved any amount of waffle.

Ambassador in Blue

You cannot always recognize a British ambassador. The traditional grand manner and Savile Row clothes are not obligatory. Neither is the ambassadorial purr and the Harrow tie. I know this because I traveled thousands of miles in the company of one of the best ambassadors Britain has ever sent across the Channel. He was called Johnny and his rank was Aircraftman Second Class.

On any R.A.F. camp in Britain he would have been pounced upon by the Warrant Officer, Discip. and put on a charge for scruffiness and the dumb insolence that accompanied complaints regarding his unsoldierly appearance. For all that, he was worth, in my estimation, two good-will missions, three squadrons of aircraft, and any amount of overseas aid from the Treasury. I accompanied him on Continental journeys totaling a distance of seven thousand miles and I never saw him put a foot wrong. In towns and villages from Hasselt in the north to Toulouse in the south, the name of Winston Churchill is doubtless still revered, but by now it will have been forgotten in certain isolated communities where Johnny is remembered with affection, for he was, as I say, the best advertisement the British nation ever sent abroad.

His age was difficult to judge. It might have been anything from twenty-three to thirty. He was of medium build, with a florid complexion, friendly brown eyes, reddish-brown hair and plenty of it. Unremarkable features, one might say, but they added up to something engaging that is very difficult to define, a kind of over-all optimism and hopeful expectancy, like those of a naughty boy awaiting the explosion of a harmless practical joke, a jack-in-the-box concealed in teacher's desk perhaps, or the dis-

covery of a dead rat under the floorboards. It was this hint of
fun ahead that vanquished the prejudice and suspicion of those
who had formed the habit of avoiding any personal contact with
the military, and I for one never undervalued Johnny's contribution toward the resettlement and pacification of Europe.
France, in the winter of 1944–45, was a cheerless place and to
wander in it, short of food, petrol and cigarettes, was a cheerless
and depressing business. It was like crossing central Europe after
the Thirty Years' War. Many towns visited were in ruins. Every
river you had to cross had no bridge. The railways had been
blasted from the face of the earth. The roads were pitted and
scarred by the constant passage of armies. There was very little
to eat and nothing to buy. A farmer's wife who watched me
drop one of her saucers burst into tears at witnessing so grievous
a loss. Whole departments were emerging from the nightmare of
four years' enemy occupation, like sleepwalkers caught halfway
down the stairs. They had great difficulty in comprehending
what had happened and had to be coaxed to part with a saucepan
for heating our K rations. And all the time it rained. To have
Johnny along in these circumstances was to struggle ashore half-
dead from a wreck and find a Crusoe waiting on the tideline.

When he was first allocated to me as driver he looked rather
like Crusoe, a Crusoe who, for some obscure reason, had dyed
his goatskins blue. His forage cap had no affinity with the neatly
perched, angled caps I had seen on so many airfields in Britain. It
was more like a medieval peasant's hood, its Balaclava flaps enclosing red ears and tufts of hair some three inches in excess of
regulation length. His tunic was even more unconventional. Instead of gleaming buttons, or even tarnished buttons, it was se-
cured by a row of safety pins. I later learned that Johnny, in his
role as ambassador, had cut off the buttons in various towns he
had liberated and distributed them as a form of largesse to the
populace. So far he had not indented for replacements.

He was a tireless if erratic driver, and he had a pleasing baritone
voice. As we drove along monotonous roads, from the Dutch
border to the Pyrenees, he sang songs of home, and whenever

we stopped, in town, village or hamlet, he went to work on the promotion of the Entente, greeting locals in a curious hybrid language that was singularly original, a compound of West Middlesex and classroom French. I had never heard anything at all like it. Most Englishmen, stuck for a verb or a noun in an unfamiliar language, will either revert to the "Er . . . er . . ." technique, invite help, or dry up altogether and fall back on pseudo-Gallic gesticulation. Johnny said what he had to say without fumbling, interchanging English and French words as he went along and playing the conversation by ear. The first time I heard him employ this means of communication was when admonishing a pedestrian who only just avoided being run down in Courtrai. He braked the van, leaned from the cabin, beamed at the offender, and said, "Now, now, *m'sieu! Allez à la* bloody *trottoir!*" It was a perfectly phrased statement of reproof and the pedestrian was so beguiled by it that he forgot his fright and beamed in acknowledgment.

More or less the same thing happened when we were crossing the Oise on a raft operated by an aged ferryman and his middle-aged son. The raft, a ponderous affair, had a kind of drawbridge operated by a wooden lever, and Johnny, anxious to reach dry land before our vehicle lurched into the flood, jumped out of the van and threw his weight on the drawbridge lever. He was, of course, unfamiliar with the vagaries of the apparatus and chose the wrong moment. The heavy drop-plank struck a half-submerged pile, rebounded and threw the hand lever into the "up" position. Unfortunately for the ferryman he happened at that moment to be bending over the crank and the heavy lever struck him a telling blow on the point of the jaw, laying him senseless at our feet.

His son thought he was dead and began to lament as the raft spun in slow circles, nudging the bank. He made such a terrible outcry that knots of Frenchmen on the far bank began to prance and gesticulate in sympathy. Johnny was solicitous, but no more than that. He knelt over the ferryman and laved his face with the waters of the Oise so that presently the man stirred and groaned, whereupon Johnny flashed a smile at the son and said, "*C'est triste, m'sieu! C'est très triste, mais* he's *seulement* wounded, not *mort!*" The announcement went all the way toward relieving the younger ferryman's fears and also reassuring his anxious compatriots on the banks.

There was something about Johnny that solaced everybody we encountered on that interminable winter journey. He could always find the way, or recruit mechanics, or get us a *logement militaire* when there seemed no prospect of finding anyone alive, much less helpful, in all that desolate landscape. He would disappear and return with a gendarme in tow, and the gendarme was always billing and cooing as they conversed, God alone knew how, upon the subject of short cuts, the possibility of finding petrol, the probable fate of Laval, or the precise whereabouts of the *Mairie*. The part I played in these encounters was insignificant. By the time the guides had reached me they were thoroughly softened up and beguiled by Johnny's ambassadorial tact. They approached me as if I was a very important person indeed who had done them immense honor by stopping at their poor village. We were right down into Anjou before I discovered that he always told them, in whispered asides, that I was Winston Churchill's favorite nephew.

He drank enormous quantities of pernod and cognac, which was usually all the inhabitants had to offer, but he was never the worse for drink. The liquor reddened his ears but never slurred his speech or interfered with the verbal juggling that his form of address demanded. I always sent him into farms and houses to borrow cooking utensils, and his embassies in this field were always successful and often ended in our being invited into the kitchen, where the family would gather round Johnny and demand to know Le Capitaine Churchill's pleasure. He had long since run out of buttons, but he would generally find something to give them—a crumpled Lucky Strike, a thin sliver of Sunlight soap, an autograph, or even a Gallic embrace. The deference paid me on his account was tremendous, and in the absence of money or goods we both used it as currency.

All this, however, was by way of being a curtain-raiser to the dramatic exposure of the kind of person he really was. It was not until Christmas Eve, when we stopped at an isolated farmhouse just beyond the Gascon town of Agen, that I recognized him as a man who had, in addition to everything else, the power to perform apostolic miracles of the kind performed by the early Fathers of the Church. I would not have believed it if I had not witnessed it, attentive and stone sober, and I do not blame anyone who thinks, on reading this, that I am romanticizing on Johnny's behalf. But it happened for all that, and for me it still has a spiritual significance that I have never found among bishops.

We had halted, as usual, to heat our miserable K rations and the farmhouse we entered was occupied by a teen-age girl who spoke English, the inevitable aged relative who is found in every French chimney corner and the girl's mother, a middle-aged woman nursing a very inflamed whitlow on the index finger of her right hand. The whitlow that she held up for inspection and sympathy was loosely covered by a dirty bandage. We had obviously called at an inopportune moment. The woman was in considerable pain, and it was not easy to relieve pain in France at that time. Doctors were grossly overworked and most drugs were unobtainable, and for once it seemed as if Johnny's charm was not going to work. The woman and the aged grandfather held themselves aloof, the one rocking to and fro with her left hand clasped over her bandaged right, the old gaffer mumbling and whistling as he contemplated a fire of green twigs. The daughter was more hospitable and lent us a saucepan, but it was clear that the family classified us not as allies or even enemies but merely *les soldats*, a species of uniformed tormentors of no particular nationality who, from Roman times, had surged to and fro across their land making all kinds of demands and causing all kinds of difficulties. This hostility to anyone wearing a uniform was not uncommon in most corners of Europe at that time, and the only thing to do was to let it wash over one's head and move on. But it had never happened to me in Johnny's company and because of this I was troubled.

When we had finished our meal and thanked the girl for the loan of the saucepan, she stepped up to us and asked in a quiet, level voice, if either of us was of the Catholic faith. To my astonishment Johnny admitted that he was. Up to that time he had not given evidence of holding any religious beliefs and I had assumed that, like most of us, he wore identity discs stamped "C. of E." On hearing he was a co-religionist, however, the girl's attitude changed and even the woman suddenly stopped rocking and looked across at him hopefully. The girl went back to her mother and for a while they conversed in low tones. Then she returned to Johnny and asked, in carefully enunciated English, if he would sing a healing hymn over her mother's whitlow. "Because of Christmas," she added apologetically.

Johnny said that it would be a pleasure and I watched, secretly spellbound, when he stood up, raised his hand as one administering a blessing and began to intone in Latin.

The scene imprinted itself upon the mind with the clarity and detail of a painting by someone like Vermeer, and it has remained in my memory ever since, every detail carefully etched so that nothing enclosed in that big stone room was missed or forgotten. There was an unnatural stillness present. The only things that moved were Johnny's lips and the slow spiral of the burning twigs. The woman, the gaffer, the girl and myself sat perfectly still, our eyes on Johnny, and momentarily he had hypnotized us. His deep voice boomed across the room with tremendous authority, and his cadences reached us from another age, when pilgrims sought the benediction of their priest before embarking on a hazardous journey in search of grace. At that moment neither he nor any one of us was part of the twentieth century. We were transported, by his voice and bearing, back to the twelfth century, when every living soul in the West acknowledged the majesty of an Old Testament Deity and his Son, the Saviour. Then, having concluded, Johnny picked up his cap and went out, and I followed in embarrassed silence. Without comment we got into the van and drove off. Neither of us referred to the incident during the drive down to Toulouse.

We did not stay in the city long. The day after Boxing Day our work down there was finished and we drove back along the same route. By chance it took us past the same farmhouse, and again without comment Johnny stopped, got down, and went in. I followed more slowly and I watched the woman and her daughter welcome him into the house. They greeted him as an old and respected friend, and to me they displayed the deference that Johnny had won for me all the way from Brabant. While we were eating and the family were bustling round us, I glanced at the woman's right hand. It was unbandaged and there was no sign of the whitlow, or, indeed, of any area of inflammation. The skin around the tip of the index finger was clean and whole. The ambassadorial touch, it would seem, had enlarged itself.

An Auster Odyssey

It was now clear that the war in Europe would last through the coming winter and probably the summer of 1945. Hopes of an earlier collapse on the part of Germany, encouraged by the near-success of the July bomb plot, faded when Montgomery's plan for a direct drive on the Reich was dropped in favor of Eisenhower's broad-front approach, so that someone down on the Second Corridor came up with the eccentric idea that the bomb tonnage required to flatten Germany could be worked out (presumably to the last half-ounce) by a review and assessment of the damage to French and Belgian targets prior to the D-Day assault in June.

The originator of this scheme, whoever he was, must have substituted clairvoyance for arithmetic. The object of the R.A.F. air onslaught on France, in the period between January and June, 1944, had two specific objects. The first and most important was to isolate the Normandy coastline. The secondary and subsequent object was to strike at the launching sites of the flying bombs and rockets. For years now the air attacks on German cities had been mounted with the object of reducing her war potential and there was absolutely no way, at that time, of assessing their effectiveness with any degree of accuracy. However, the Second Corridor wanted that set of facts and figures, and possibly my report on Le Havre encouraged Dudley Barker to name me as the man to collect them, not as a lone observer, with a single ground-to-ground photographer, but as C.O. of a small flight made up of three pilots flying Austers, a P.R. photographer with experience of air-to-ground photography, a motion-picture cameraman, a driver and a fifteen-hundredweight van.

Briefing was sketchy. I was to command whilst the flight was on the ground and the senior pilot was in charge once we were in the air. I was given fifty-six major targets in France and Belgium and was told to visit them all, collect detailed information on the effectiveness of the bombing, secure corroborative film and pictures, and send back the data as I assembled it. My secondary instructions were to contact and interview people of the Resistance movement who had promoted the escapes of large numbers of R.A.F. personnel during the last four years, to look out for propaganda angles with an R.A.F. slant, and generally show the flag in all the places I visited where the British had not yet penetrated.

When I raised the vulgar question as to how I was to keep the team fed in areas remote from Allied bases they said, gaily, "Oh, you live on the country, old boy," and gave me an impressive-looking pass signed by Eisenhower and expressing his earnest wish that, as one of his investigators, I "would be given aid and comfort by all." I was very flattered to represent the Supremo in all the areas of by-passed territory, and I liked the phrase "live on the country." Somehow it smacked of a Napoleonic advance down the valley of the Danube in the year of Austerlitz and Trafalgar. I was less sanguine, however, about extracting aid and comfort from the civilians I had seen during my recent trip to Le Havre.

The senior pilot and I went out to have a look at the aircraft set aside for our use. They were Mark I Austers, and I said they reminded me of the flying machine Blériot used on his epoch-making cross-Channel trip in 1909. The pilot, an Ulsterman, was more forthright. He flatly refused to fly the aircraft and demanded Mark III Austers. Fortunately for all of us he got them, and whilst we were awaiting their delivery I visited various underground headquarters in A.M. to examine the reports of Lancaster and Halifax crews who had struck at one or other of my fifty-six targets during the last few months. The tonnage of bombs dropped was impressive, and all the attacks looked as though they had been pressed home, but there was no real evidence available of what had been accomplished in terms of destruction.

We set out from Hawkinge one gray October afternoon and came down at Ghent to find out where we were. There was little, we had been told, to fear from enemy aircraft. The R.A.F. and the Ninth U.S. Army Air Force had now obtained complete mastery of the sky over the Continent. "If you should meet a stray enemy fighter," one well-wisher told me, "you're on a good wicket! Those Austers can only do a hundred and ten m.p.h. flat out, so all you have to do is keep turning and hedge-hopping, and the slowest fighter plane in operation will over-shoot you." I was to ponder this when we were cruising a lonely course over the old battlefields of the First World War, and to recall Dudley Barker's cheerful parting remark concerning our sole armament. "Look after my revolver, won't you, Del?" he had said. "And remember, it's never been fired in anger!"

A group captain we met some time later was horrified by the setup. Not, I gathered, because we were flying unarmed, but because we had flown Austers over water. "Dammit," he said, "any fool can crash-land an Auster on the ground but you wouldn't stand a dog's chance if you ditched one. Besides, they haven't even issued you with Mae Wests!"

I was never a man to stick my neck out, and had already gone to some pains to ensure surviving the war, but the elements of risk attending the expedition did not bother me then, as they did when we were home and dry and I could view it in retrospect. At the time I was tremendously exhilarated with the prospect of having the freedom of Western Europe, with no one to shackle me with orders and advice. In a way, it was a welcome return to the old, free-ranging days on the *Chronicle*, with enough stories lying around to satisfy the greediest reporter. I liked my senior photographer, a stocky Flying Officer called Bernard Bridge, who had been a photographer on the *Blackpool Gazette* after opting out of his father's funeral furnishing business. Berni was a cheerful, uncomplicated soul, who had been present, in his official capacity, at both Sicily and D-Day landings, and was sometimes prepared to take foolish risks to get good pictures. He was madly devoted to the ballads of Robert Service and was fond of quoting Yukon verses at uncomprehending Frenchmen. I came to like one of the pilots too, a phlegmatic Canadian boy called Huck, and generally flew in his aircraft, learning how to chart our progress as we moved from section to section on the maps. We flew low over the battlefields of innumerable Continental wars, all the way from Zutphen to Passchendaele, cruising at ninety m.p.h., but the Auster tanks held only about ten gallons and our hops were necessarily brief. Often enough we were almost dry when we came down in a field or on a strip of heath, for it was never easy to find a safe landing ground within reach of target areas. For one thing the Germans had staked all the likely fields and the obstacles had not been removed. For another, much of the available ground was being used to graze cattle and, to make things worse, whenever French or Belgian civilians saw an R.A.F. aircraft on the point of touching down, they would converge on it from all directions. It was attempting to avoid some scampering children that caused our first crash at Mons. The Auster was a write-off and the ciné-cameraman was badly cut about the nose. From then on we worked with two aircraft.

It took a little time to evolve effective methods of gathering the material Air Ministry was seeking. Officers attached to Second Tactical Air Force gave us some useful, large-scale maps, and we began covering centers like Louvain, Courtrai and Malines whilst based on Brussels. In areas like this the main bombing attacks had been concentrated on the railway stations and goods yards and the wrecked station was usually the first port of call. I spoke French indifferently, my principal trouble (apart from tenses) being a strong and apparently guttural accent that led me, on two occasions, to be mistaken for a Luftwaffe officer on the run. Our uniforms were not dissimilar, and an old lady, watching a friendly railway official take me firmly by the arm, cackled with glee and said something that embarrassed my guide. Pressed to interpret he said, with a smile, "She said, 'I see you've captured another of the swine. Are you going to shoot him?' " Something similar occurred at a country hamlet much further south. Seeing me step from van to farmyard two venturesome farmworkers leaped down from the loft aperture, shouting abuse and brandishing pitchforks, and this despite Dudley Barker's revolver that had never been fired in anger. On that occasion I discovered that I could speak French fluently, and once I had identified myself we all three shared the joke over a glass of Pernod.

The Belgian railways were in ruins. At Malines locomotives and rolling stock were piled in pyramids of twisted steel and splintered woodwork. Turntables and repair shops were shattered, but nestling in the heart of one pyramid of wreckage was a tiny engine displaying a plaque saying it had been made in Britain in 1835 and sent to Belgium as the pioneer locomotive of the State railway.

At Mons everyone hastened to remind us of the British links with the town, beginning with the Expeditionary Force's first battle, in August, 1914, and ending with the recapture of the town in November, 1918. The Belgians, it seemed, could not distinguish between airmen and infantrymen, and always called us Tommies. One mountainous old dame nudged me slyly and said, with a wink, "Ah, Tommee! How good I knew your father!"

I soon arrived at two conclusions. One was the deadly accuracy of R.A.F. bombing, resulting in very little damage to civilian houses and almost no civilian casualties. American bombing, carried out mostly by daylight, and usually from a great height, was less accurate, but the French civilians libeled both of us. "When the French aviator bombs," they said, "he hits the target. When the British bomb they hit the town. When the Americans bomb they hit the department." The other conclusion concerned the heroism of a sizable minority of the people who had lived under the Nazis since 1940. Many of them had performed prodigies of valor. Railwaymen, who carried special passes that enabled them to move about at night, were obvious recruits for the Resistance movement and once the Allies had landed in Normandy the local saboteurs, always enterprising, redoubled their efforts to harass the enemy. Near Louvain a German ammunition train was driven a mile out of the station and deliberately wrecked in collision. Another was driven through the station at ninety m.p.h. and deliberately overturned. Forged railway passes were issued to a network of skilled saboteurs in order to beat the curfew. Food, rifles and money were stolen from stationary transport, and sixty pounds of dynamite was used to blow up a third train in this area. It was at Mons St.-Ghislien, however, within a hundred yards of the spot where the Old Contemptibles inflicted so many casualties on Von Kluck's legions in 1914, that the most dramatic incident occurred. Here a German supply train was held up by masked highwaymen at the station, driven a mile down the track and then headed into a prepared gap caused by a dismantled bridge over a sunken road. It was still there when we arrived, a locomotive and tender upended in a chasm between two embankments, and a pile of shattered wagons blocking the track behind.

The Belgians paid a high price for these courageous acts. On All Souls' Day I visited the Tir National in Brussels, the building where Nurse Cavell was shot in 1915. It was used as a place of execution for Belgian civilians who were shot in the rifle range. In the gardens behind, close to the desecrated memorial to Nurse Cavell, were rows of graves, each with a rain-sodden photograph of the victim attached to the cross, and all that afternoon parents, widows and orphans paraded past, many of them in tears. I saw one woman throw herself face foremost on a grave and I think of her, and others like her, whenever a stream of advice concerning how Britain should shape its destiny reaches us from Bonn.

As the days passed, and the weather worsened, the work sorted itself into a pattern. The first, and pre-eminent priority was to keep the flight mobile in areas where there were no depots from which we could draw rations and petrol. We had very little money, and no prospect of getting any, and sometimes it was very difficult to keep the aircraft and the van in service. We

347

found billets on the *logement militaire* system, seeking out the mayor at every place we visited, and demanding beds on the strength of our passes. As for food, we lived mostly on American K rations, tins of self-heating soup and canned vegetables cadged from stray U.S. units, and cooked in utensils loaned to us by cottagers.

Then there was the investigation itself that soon resolved itself into a standard procedure, beginning with introductions, and a series of bewildering interviews with stationmasters, factory managers and civil officials concerning the effect of raids on specific dates, and ending with a clip of ground-to-ground, air-to-ground and film sequences of the havoc caused by the bombs. This was interesting but exhausting, partly on account of the Continentals' propensity to talk and gesticulate in chorus. Very few of the people I interviewed spoke English and often they violently disagreed with one another concerning important factors of the attack, so that acrimonious arguments would sometimes ensue with me as the referee. A more absorbing aspect of the job was my inquiries into Resistance activities and interviews with families who had lived under Nazi rule for four years. It was then that one began to get a real understanding of what the occupation had meant in terms of oppression, and what it would have meant to the British if Hitler had launched a successful invasion in 1940.

People approached me shyly, pressing little notes into my hand addressed to airmen whom they had hidden and passed on to the Underground between Holland, in the northeast, and the Pyrenees, in the southwest. One young man I met in a town called Joigny, had concealed two British airmen in the back bedroom of his house whilst German officers had been billeted in the front room. At night, when the Germans retired, they would knock on his door and wish him good night. He finally organized an escape by dressing the airmen as railwaymen and sending them down the track to join a repair party, after which they were "claimed," redirected, and passed on to the local distributing center. The young man's nerves were still ragged and all the time he talked his hands shook. His mother, an elderly woman, was bedridden as a result of a visit by the Gestapo.

I met another young man, thin as a wand, who crept out of some bushes near a flying-bomb site in the Forest of Nieppe. He handed me a letter addressed to a flight sergeant who lived at Harrow, whom he had dragged from a wrecked fighter plane in 1941 and hidden for several days in a woodshed. The airman got away safely but suspicion attached itself to his rescuer and he spent a long period in a prison camp at Lille. A third man, in Arras, told me that he owed his life to an R.A.F. attack that had wrecked telephonic communications and prevented a check on his forged papers the night following his arrest. In the subsequent confusion he was released with a caution.

I met several families who described to me wholesale arrests and random executions of hostages and farther south, in the Limoges area, I questioned the photographer who took the first pictures of the Oradour-sur-Glane outrage, where the entire population of the village was shot or burned in the church on June 10, four days after the Normandy landings. Years later I had the satisfaction of reading that some of the perpetrators of this French Lidice had been traced and executed. The French told me that the Vichy police were more to be feared than the Gestapo, and most of the people I talked to expressed a fervent hope that Laval would be caught and shot, as indeed he was as soon as the Third Reich collapsed.

As we moved about the Flanders plain, and down into the central areas of France, I was constantly reminded of older wars in which the English had been engaged. Flying over Vimy Ridge at about five hundred feet one clear, autumn morning, I saw the zigzag lines of the Western Front trenches in the patterns of discolored earth. The same patterns showed on the surface of filled-in shell holes. Nearer the coast, just visible on the northern skyline, was a forest of crosses, marking one of the many British war cemeteries.

In the Loire area it was of feudal wars one thought, for here, unmarked by bombs, were châteaux stormed and occupied by the armies of the Plantagenets, and something of the freebooting past remained in the attitude of isolated farmers with whom we sought lodging for the night. Down here we were neither friends nor enemies but *les soldats*. One got the impression that a long line of the farmer's ancestors, reaching as far back as Caesar's Gallic campaigns, had been forced at sword's point to entertain detachments of military adventurers passing through the locality, and that one war had merged with its successor into a complex of quarrels that was no concern of farmers, who had more important work on hand.

I remember one such family near Blaye, where we sipped thin potato soup while huge hams, reserved for the market, hung from the roof beams. The family retired to bed at seven P.M., to rise at four and go about their work on the farm. The sons slept in a hayloft. Living with the family was the inevitable French grandmother, a frail little woman trailing clouds of black serge. She spent all her time making pieces of blackened toast on an oil-stove, telling us they were *pour le malade. Le malade* was her husband, who had died years before. War or no war these people lived frugally, as frugally as medieval peasants. In the morning, when we were filling the petrol tank of the van from a jerry-can, a few drops were spilled by a gust of wind. With a shout of joy the patron threw himself in the snow and crawled under the van to catch the trickle in a cup.

Perhaps the most surprising feature of this long haul into the central provinces was the discovery of stray English women, who invariably wept when they heard an English voice and would go to extraordinary lengths to be of service to us, offering to wash our shirts and socks, and making a tremendous fuss when we accepted their hospitality.

The first I met was in the Breton village of Sable-sur-Sarthe, where we stayed a night with the widow of a King's Messenger, who had spent the first part of the war in an internment camp but had been released, despite her refusal to surrender her British nationality. Her elegantly furnished drawing room was lined with bookshelves containing works by George Eliot, Seton Merriman and other English authors, and she told us that she had billeted German officers until the arrival of the first U.S. troops in the area. They too, it seemed, had behaved "correctly," and one lodger had carried her bag to the station on one occasion. When she complimented him on his gallantry, however, he said, with Teutonic candor, "We have been instructed to behave correctly, madame. If we had been instructed to cut your throats we should do that!"

We met another Englishwoman in Bordeaux, the wife of a French aristocrat serving with the Artillery in the war that was still going on between the Free French and pockets of Germans holding out in Biscayan ports. She had some hard things to say about the panic of 1940, when she had made her way down to Pau from the far northeast. Water, she said, had been sold to thirst-maddened refugees at two francs a glass. She told us something of the black market, without which most of the French would have starved. Toward the end of the war prices for necessities were astronomical. Her husband told me that he had spent four hundred thousand francs on food alone since the collapse of France.

The most touching encounter I had with an expatriot was in Saumur, on the Loire, where we took the first photographs of the extremely successful attack on the main railway line, including the Saumur tunnel, demolished by the famous Dambuster Squadron with the first of the R.A.F. "earthquake" bombs. One bomb had penetrated right through to the line, leaving an immense crater, and this raid was instrumental in stopping the arrival of a Panzer division en route for Normandy.

We walked out of the tunnel and straight into a wedding reception in the town, our arrival resulting in my most embarrassing moment of the war. The guests at once joined hands and formed a ring around me, singing "Tipperary," a song that many French think of as our national anthem. Afterward the bride advanced into the center of the ring to embrace me. The guests then drank my health and gave three cheers for King George VI and three more for General de Gaulle. A young French ambulance driver, who spoke very good English, volunteered to be my interpreter during our stay and that same night she offered to take me to the home of an Englishwoman who had been stranded in Saumur since 1940. I went to an apartment near the Loire bridge and advanced to shake hands with a middle-aged woman standing near the fireplace. Hearing my voice she at once burst into tears and was unable to control herself for several minutes. She said, at length, "That was stupid of me, but yours is the first English voice I have heard in four and a half years." She asked me where I lived and when I told her in Exmouth she began to cry again. She had been born and raised in Sidmouth, nine miles along the coast, and we had many mutual acquaintances.

By no means all the good will extended to us was from stranded English people. Some of the French people in the remote provinces were exceptionally kind and helpful, and all were generous with the little they had at their disposal. A watchmaker at Poitiers went to a great deal of trouble to obtain an egg for my supper and later the following day, when I happened to reach into my valise, I found another. Written on the shell was "Long live the R.A.F." This man, incidentally, had listened to BBC bulletins throughout the entire war, using a homemade wireless set about the size of a cigarette packet, that he kept hidden in his cellar. At Angoulême, a little farther south, I experienced another instance of the French Provençal's enthusiasm for the R.A.F. Trying to make one drink last the evening in a café on Christmas Eve I was presented with an excellent bottle of wine from an anonymous donor. A note attached said, "From an old Free Frenchman. Happy Christmas to you, Englishmen."

By then we had worked our way down into the southwest, hundreds of miles from the nearest Allied supply depots, and were living on our wits. It was bitterly cold and one of our Austers iced up and became unserviceable, so we had to abandon it and push on with one aircraft and one pilot, plus a van with a dead-beat battery. Every morning when we set out I would recruit a team of French civilians to push the van a hundred yards in order to get it started, so that our departures were always an occasion for civic clamor. These were matched by our arrival in the next area so far unvisited by the Allies. As soon as the van or aircraft appeared the entire community would stop work and run toward us, embracing us, shaking our hands, and demanding autographs. Huck, the Canadian boy, was unimpressed by these demonstrations. "Guess I could do with less flap and more grub," he would say, for rarely, in any of these out-of-the-way places, was there a bite to eat, except a little goat's-milk cheese and a few slices of salami. There was usually, however, plenty to drink and occasionally one or other of us was a little the worse for wear after breaking new territory.

At Bordeaux we were accorded the honor of liberating the Mouton wine cellars, owned by the Rothschild family, and were persuaded to sample vintages as venerable as our guide. The sergeant and I were down in that cellar several hours and our emergence into the street coincided with the march-past of a column of French troops, on their way to invest the German naval brigade, still holding out at the tip of the Gironde peninsula. Seen through a rosy haze of alcohol it was an impressive scene, detachments of troops, including Colonials and units of the Foreign Legion, swinging along under the command of a white-haired old colonel sitting a huge, unclipped gray. The colonel saluted us gravely, and we returned his salute, steadying ourselves against the wall of the vaults. We were obliged to remain there, propped at attention, until the long column had disappeared.

Life was rarely as convivial as this. Down in Toulouse, where we spent Christmas, we went hungry until I managed to sell my boots for five hundred francs and buy one small tin of turkey and one tinned Christmas pudding on the black market. The two tins did not do much to satisfy five sharp-set men and by noon on Boxing Day we were on the prowl again, having pooled a couple of hundred francs to pay for a communal meal if one could be found. In the late afternoon we found a downtown café, of the kind used in film sets dealing with French low life, and the woman in charge said she could provide us with a rabbit stew if we were prepared to wait whilst she cooked it. We waited. We would have waited all night, and eventually a large tureen appeared, holding enough stew to satisfy all five of us. It was highly flavored with garlic and rather sweet to the taste, but we enjoyed it and congratulated ourselves on having found the café. I went into the kitchen, screened by a heavy curtain, to pay the bill and here, on a chopping block, lay half a terrier. The front half.

There is something revolting about eating a dog, even if it does taste like rabbit, and I wilted at the thought of those bowls of stew we had just emptied. The woman, however, was not abashed. She stared at me unflinchingly, holding out her hand for the money, and having recovered somewhat I tottered back into the café to unload my secret on the others.

It was interesting watching their reactions. Huck, after sitting still for a moment, gripped the edge of the table and said "Jesus!" uttering the name softly and reverently. The photographer and the sergeant clapped handkerchiefs to their mouths and ran into the street without a word. Johnny, the driver, mused for a moment, sniffed the half-empty stew pot and began to bark.

The next day Johnny and I had better luck. In search of information we drove southwest of the city and found an abandoned camp, with its gates open and its sentry boxes unoccupied. A spiral of smoke rose from the cookhouse and scenting food we drove there, to find a lonely R.A.F. corporal making tea over a petrol stove. He was the only inhabitant of the place and I never did discover what he was doing there, or how long he had been isolated from his unit. He was waiting, he said, to be collected by some Americans, had been in France since D-Day, and had since been so mobile that he had not had a chance to write to his mother. There was no food in the camp apart from tea, tinned milk and a sack of brown sugar, so we sat with him all that afternoon brewing pot after pot of black, syrupy tea. Just before we left he asked us if we wanted cigarettes and we told him we could take as many as he could supply, cigarettes being currency all over Europe that could produce anything from a liter of petrol to the services of a harlot. He unlocked a cupboard and exposed shelves stacked with cartons of Chesterfields and Lucky Strikes. "Guess they won't miss four hundred," he said, casually, and presented us with a carton apiece. We were so grateful that we asked him to name a favor we could do him in return. He said, thoughtfully, "You'll get home before I will. Here's my mum's address in Highgate. Give her a tinkle and tell her I'm okay." About a month later, when I was back in London, I phoned his mother, describing the circumstances of our meeting, and how grateful we had been for her son's tea and cigarettes. "Ah, that's our Ken," she said. "Give his soul away, Ken would."

We had another interesting encounter down here that Christmas. One evening a Resistance fighter arrived with a priest and a car and asked us if we would care to dine at a remote convent in the Pyrenean foothills. We agreed very readily. We would have accepted an invitation to dinner from Goering and Goebbels at that juncture. We drove south in the teeth of the mistral until we stopped outside a fortresslike building standing on a rocky ridge in complete isolation.

It was not a convent, we learned, but a château being used as one, and the Mother Superior was a Scotswoman who had settled on the Continent in 1930 and refugeed southeast in the great exodus of May, 1940. Since then the château had been a staging post for fugitives crossing into Spain by underground routes and among the men who took refuge here were Allied airmen and F.F.I. intelligence officers on the run from the Vichy police. The Germans often raided the place but caught only a single English agent, who was taken to Toulouse and died under torture, without revealing the names or whereabouts of his colleagues. She did not know his name and could only describe him as a very gallant man. His body, she thought, had been thrown down a well in the locality. A large number of civil and military fugitives, she said, had escaped over the Pyrenees into Spain at this point. The Germans and their Vichy allies could not watch every pass and among their ranks was a spy who kept the organization informed as regards which routes were to be watched on a particular night.

One of the most interesting observations the Mother Superior made that night concerned the fears she and her friends had entertained regarding the possibility of an invasion of England, in September, 1940. She asked me to describe the mood of Britain at that time and I told her that there had been no panic on the part of the public and that most people found the idea of a successful landing in Kent or Sussex unacceptable in view of our naval strength. "Then we were more afraid than you," she said, with a smile, "for to us an invasion seemed perfectly feasible and the continued resistance of Britain was our sole hope of a future." I added her name, the name of the priest, and that of the F.F.I. officer who had brought us here, to my list of people I felt should be thanked officially for their contribution to the Allied cause and on my return I handed in the list with a suggestion to this effect. I never heard whether or not they were contacted by the services. Perhaps they did not look for acknowledgment, facing the risks of a firing party, or transference to a concentration camp, in the knowledge that they were making the only contribution available to them of defeating Hitler. They came from all walks of life. Among them were men and women of wealth and social position, who could have come to terms with Vichy, and lived lives of moderate comfort throughout the war. There were others, a majority, who had nothing to gain by loyalty to the Allies but stood to sacrifice their lives if they came under suspicion of helping a fugitive airman or cutting a telephone wire on a moonless night. I have never seen any official figures of the strength of the Belgian and French Resistance movements at any one time, but it must surely have amounted to hundreds of thousands who played a greater or lesser part in campaigns of sabotage in one form or another. I talked to a hundred of them and also a few of the men they had smuggled back to Britain. I think of them now as the most courageous people I have ever met.

Their spirit, perhaps, is epitomized by the women of the village of Wizernes, a rocket site in the Pas de Calais area. A British bomber had crashed here, plowing into the woods just short of the village, and all five of its crew were killed and buried in the local churchyard. The women of the village came to lay flowers on the graves but were driven off by German troops. They returned shortly afterward, broke through the cordon and placed the wreaths. The graves were still covered with fresh flowers when I arrived in the area.

Snow fell as we worked our way northward to Bergerac and Limoges. At Bergerac a frantic husband called on me and told me his wife was running a high fever after childbirth. She was, he said, a niece of General de Gaulle, and her doctor was in desperate need of penicillin. There was no penicillin to be obtained in Bergerac so he begged me to drive over to Bordeaux and see whether I could obtain some. We were desperately short of petrol, and the countryside was flooded, but I did not have the heart to refuse him, and Johnny and I set out, the journey taking a full day. Authorities on whom I called spent hours telephoning Paris and asking for a supply of penicillin to be sent south, but I never found out whether they were successful. It was a wretched experience to have to return to the husband empty-handed.

Stage by stage we moved back into the Paris area, the job almost completed, and only a few of the target areas on my list remaining to be covered. To the north-east the Battle of the Bulge was raging and we had been lucky to miss the Luftwaffe's swoop on several of the airfields we had used. Good photography, in the weather conditions obtaining, was impossible, so we crossed off four targets in the east and one in the west. The western one was a factory or port installation on the coast, Air Ministry having omitted to tell me that it was still in German hands. I should have paid a call on them had it not been for the watchfulness of a sixteen-year-old F.F.I. sentry, concealed in a hedgerow outside Pauillac. He jumped out and flagged us as we approached a crossroads and stood there shouting and waving his arms, a wild, piratical figure, dressed like a Corsican bandit, with billowing cloak and a belt stuffed with weapons. I have often wondered since whether the German garrison would have surrendered to a single R.A.F. officer prepared to bluff it out. It would have been pleasant to return home to Dudley and Geoffrey with a thousand Nazi prisoners in my train, but the boy who stopped me said the road ahead was swept by machine-gun fire, so I took his word for it and reversed.

I met many German prisoners during my travels about France and Belgium that winter and was always impressed by their punctilious respect, and their general desire to please. In an American P.O.W. camp at Compiègne I was about to lift a mug of coffee to my mouth when a young German stepped forward, saluted smartly, and warned me that the coffee was too hot to drink. The incident seemed at odds with the arrogance of these men at the time of their easy conquest of Europe.

One of the last places I visited was the French Military Academy at St.-Cyr, near Versailles. It had been almost completely destroyed, and anyone who knew anything of the French military tradition could not but feel despondent at picking over the ruins and treading underfoot photographs of groups of cadets of pre-1914 classes who must have died, almost to a man, at the Marne and Verdun. Near the gate I stumbled over what I thought was a boulder. It was the decapitated stone head of General Kléber, the man who took command of Napoleon's army in Egypt when Bonaparte returned to France soon after the battle of the Nile. I would very much liked to have taken Kléber's head home as a souvenir, but it weighed a hundred-weight. Every barrack block around the central courtyard was a charred shell half-filled with debris, but the magnificent equestrian statue of General Marceau, who led the armies of the First Republic, was unscathed. A bomb, however, had smashed through the chapel floor and opened the grave of Madame de Maintenon, the favorite of Louis XIV who persuaded him to expel the Huguenots, among them my own ancestors.

Years later, when revisiting Versailles, I heard a guide describing the British destruction of St.-Cyr as an act of vandalism. I am not given to arguing with professional guides, a very unrewarding occupation, but I did challenge this one, telling him that St.-Cyr, at that time, was being used as a German radar station.

Near Périgueux I came across an example of the terrible tensions an occupying army produces among civilians and how that tension persists after the conquerors have departed. Approaching an isolated farm to borrow a saucepan I noticed that the door showed signs of having been battered, probably by rifle butts. When I went into the kitchen a young woman and an old man stared at me with expressions of terror, as though I had walked in flourishing Dudley's revolver, and the old man's agitation continued, even after I explained that I was British and came in peace. Suddenly the poor old fellow began to quake and tears streamed down his face, and so he continued all the time we were there, despite gifts of cigarettes and a slice of Sunlight soap. His daughter told me that, not long before, a skirmish had taken place close by between Germans and Resistance men and the farm had been searched by the enemy, who smashed in the door and interrogated the old man concerning his nonexistent associations with saboteurs. His nerves were shattered by the experience so that the mere sight of a man in uniform was sufficient to reduce him to a state of gibbering terror.

By mid-January I had done all that could be done and sent our sole remaining Auster on to Brussels, where it ultimately collided with a balloon-barrage cable. The chief pilot survived to push on into Denmark and receive the surrender of the German troops stationed there in May. Berni, the Blackpool photographer who had accompanied me on most of the trip, had been withdrawn by then and posted, much to his indignation, to the Far East. I shared his disgust. He was older than me, had survived a hard war, and would have been due for early demobilization shortly after the German surrender. As it was he was killed when his Dakota ran into a violent storm over the Indian Ocean. He is one of the many old friends I recall with affection when idealistic young people of a succeeding generation dismiss the Second World War as one more instance of their fathers' muddle-headedness. If I learned anything during that seven-thousand-mile journey across Europe it was that this particular war was a just war on the part of all who opposed German fascism. Wars may be unfashionable, and undoubtedly most of them in the past have been unnecessary, but World War II is a clear example of the necessity to fight to the last gasp under a given set of circumstances. The victory that came a few weeks after my return to Britain does not seem to have brought us much beyond a succession of almost insoluble economic and social problems, but this is beside the point. Defeat would have reduced us to a state of wretchedness beyond the realm of thought.

Bull's-eye: Or, Don't Ring Us, We'll Ring You

The old town looked smaller and shabbier than I remembered, and very still behind a veil of violet autumn mist, draping the leafless chestnuts and elms where the road climbed east to the frontier of The Curry, otherwise known as Budleigh Salterton. Lower down the hill that glimpse of the estuary I had always looked for, linking two parallel blocks of Georgian houses, would be just visible in the half-light, a steel sword laid across a blur of woods on the Haldon shore, but the over-all stillness of the place surprised me a little. It was the day before Guy Fawkes Day, and in the twenties and thirties impatient little boys set fire to one another's hoarded bonfires and then discharged a rip-rap or two to celebrate on the fourth or rather the fifth of November.

I humped my valise and the large cardboard carton full of free-issue civvies down the station approach and took the road for home. That evening was all of twenty-five years ago, but I can remember what I thought. "Catch me north of Bideford or west of Taunton from here on and you can shoot me!" Something on those lines.

It had been a day for new beginnings, or so H. E. Bates declared as he pranced about the demob center at Wembley in his squadron leader's uniform, topped by a loud coster-type civvy

cap, and looking as incongruous as a pantomime comedian in
Ascot rig. Bates and I had been two of the first P.R. men in the
queue, scoring heavily on the points system that controlled demobilization. He was forty and I was thirty-three, with five and
a half years' service, so we said our farewells and bundled down
the spiral staircase to the lift, schoolboys on the last day of term.
On the way out somebody stole my flying boots, the legacy of
a pilot killed near Vanderville.

We had passed our medical check a day or so earlier, standing
behind a pilot with a half-healed back injury that threatened to
delay his return to Civvy Street while he convalesced. The M.O.
pointed out that any pension claim on his part would be jeopar-
dized by precipitate demobilization, and that if medical advice
was set aside the pilot would have to sign papers absolving the
Board from responsibility. The pilot's voice rose an octave as he
shouted, "I'll sign anything, *anything!* Just let me *out!*" I knew
just how he felt. For the past month now a sense of panic that
threatened to develop into hysteria followed me wherever I went.
The war in the East was over, and even the blackout curtains
had been burned, but I felt more nervous and insecure than at
any time during the last five years. Something, I felt sure, would
come between me and demobilization at the last minute.

The feeling of unease left me at Wembley Stadium, where
they fitted us (with rather more care than they had demonstrated on enlistment) for our civilian issue. Bates was so cock-a-
hoop that he decided to make an occasion of it. Exchanging his
coster cap for a trilby, he drove me back to Soho and stood me
lunch in one of our favorite cafés. He was, by then, well established as a novelist, one of the best short-story writers in Europe,
and by far the most authentic and gripping of his generation in
aerial-warfare topics. He spent that lunch, I recall, giving me
good advice concerning subject matter, but I discovered that a
good deal of the itch for success had gone, now that I had my
ticket. It no longer seemed very important to have my name on a
gilded board outside a theater in Shaftesbury Avenue. I was prepared to settle for less, a good deal less. There was home and

there was the weekly paper, jogging along all this time under the shiftless eye of temporary reporters and unpaid subscribers. Sometimes they sent me copies, but I soon gave up reading them. It irritated me to see so many wrong initials and misspelled place names, and the strict paper rationing enforced at that time gave the *Chronicle* a wan, anemic look. Its information was stuffy and lacked punch. No sense of fitness was apparent in the relative space allocated to funerals in the residential section and funerals in terrace-house blocks. Wedding reports omitted to devote a single line to the dress worn by the bride's mother. Accounts of sales-of-work and the local dramatic society's productions were scamped.

2

There was a light over the door and May was waiting on the step. Veronica, eighteen months now, was awake and stared up at me unwinkingly. I shut the door, remembering as I did that there was no seven- or nine-day limit on the time I would spend here now, and that I carried no pass with a date stamped on it. It was like being born again.

The feeling soon passed. In a week or two it seemed as though the last six years belonged to the period of early childhood. I made the same calls, went the same rounds, asked the same questions and used the same typewriter to reduce the answers into paragraphs. I saw the same faces and identified them with the same causes—the British Legion, the Bowling Club, the National British Women's Total Abstinence Union, the Caged Bird Society. A great part of Europe was in ruins and the dead lay in shallow graves from the Caucasus to the Pyrenees, but down here, despite the odd gap torn by a hit-and-run raider, Councillors continued to debate the relative advantages of a new rockery or a parking ground. The names on the stored-away beach huts were unchanged—"Upsidonia," "Farenuff," "Restawhile," and "Yrtiz"—but I did not quarrel with this. It seemed to me just as it should be. After all, that was what the war had been about, the right of people in small communities to live their lives in a way that suited them. But for me things were not the same and never would be again. Within seven weeks of my demobilization the first of my stray chickens came home to lay an egg on the doorstep I had recrossed so thankfully. Before the new year was a month old *Worm's Eye View* was a smash hit.

It came out of a clear sky so suddenly and dramatically that I had to rethink the entire structure of my future, all but overlooked in the excitement of the Auster odyssey, the furore of the peace, the July election, and the weeks leading up to the day of demobilization. I don't know why I should have been so surprised. The summer that had passed, from a professional viewpoint, had been promising. Basil Thomas, of the Wolverhampton Repertory Company, had staged *Worm's Eye View* in October, 1944, when I was in France, and it had been bought by a Midlands industrialist called Barlow, who sent it out on tour the following spring. It played six dates and at three of them attracted packed houses; but when the tour ended, all hopes of bringing it into London faded. It proved impossible to book a theater, the company dispersed, and I had resigned myself, philosophically, to the passage of another false dawn. I returned the R.A.F. uniforms and props to store and reposed what hopes I had of a West End production in another play, dealing with the post-Crimean life of Florence Nightingale. It was called *The Spinster of South Street*, and I had written the first draft in Blackpool billets and the second in my room at Cranwell. Since then it had featured in the York Drama Festival, with Jean Forbes-Robertson in the lead, and Flora Robson had shown some interest in it. From time to time I had letters about it, but so many promises regarding plushy productions had been made to me through the post and over the telephone during the last thirteen years that I was not in the least surprised when this proved another nonrunner. I had a third play almost completed, a Cockney comedy, concerning a family split by evacuation, entitled *Peace Comes to Peckham,* but now I wrote largely from habit, like an energetic, town-bred terrier enlarging a rabbit warren from which the rabbits had long since moved away. I had a wife, a child, a secondhand Ford and a job I enjoyed. It was enough to get on with, more than many of my wartime contemporaries had, once their gratuities had been spent. I was happy to sit back and await my postwar credits. They would come in handy for a holiday in the nineteen-seventies.

But, as Ernest Raymond says, you never can tell what a piece of writing is doing out there in the dark. Tony Bazell, the actor who had played "Duke" in the tour, mentioned the play to Tony Hawtry, then running the Embassy Theatre at Hampstead. By Christmas it was on, and Beverley Nichols had written of it, "This play made my ribs ache." By January it had transferred to the Whitehall, wartime home of Phyllis Dixey, whose curves I had admired every time I walked past the Horse Guards to Trafalgar Square. By February it was packing them in and netting me more than five times the salary I earned as a journalist. I gave it a run of several months and Ronnie Shiner, who had always shown unshakeable faith in the play, gave it a year. We were both pessimistic. Its run, after beating the current record set by *Chu Chin Chow,* lasted five and a half years.

I remember reading an article written by R. C. Sherriff, the author of *Journey's End,* on the subject of how a man adjusts to success in the theater. He said the general view that an author was buried up to his neck in money was a mistaken one. It never happened this way. The money came in dribs and drabs, subject to all kinds of deductions and penal taxation. For every shilling grossed, eightpence slipped between the floor boards. In my case there was ten percent for the agent, ten percent for the Wolverhampton initiators, a backlog of outlay to be recovered by the promoter, and several expensive trips to town to attend to various matters arising out of the production. All the same it was far more money than I had ever thought to earn, and I set about spending it. Before the run was two months old we adopted an-

other child, this time a week-old boy. We bought a better car
and began attending country house sales and replacing all our
furniture with antiques.

I knew very little about antiques at that time, my interests in
that field being confined to arms and armor and pre-Raphaelite
paintings, but May had a tremendous flair for the business and
what she did not know she soon learned from books. Our three-
bedroomed house on the outskirts of the town was soon crammed
with French commodes, porcelain figures, clocks, oil paintings,
eighteenth-century English pieces, prints and hundreds of books
that made it difficult to enter the tiny room where I had worked
before the war. We began to give parties, usually for old friends
who were filtering back into the town from the services, and
that summer we bought a secondhand Daimler that gave us both
a sensation of trundling in the wake of film stars who owned
houses with swimming-baths. One day, feeling madly reckless, I
put a pound each way on the Cambridgeshire. My highest stake
up to that time had been half a crown on the Derby. When the
horse won at fifty to one I almost ran to the Post Office Savings
Bank with my winnings.

In the autumn we bought a detached house on the cliffs at Budleigh and commissioned builders to do extensive repairs to it, the
Americans having occupied it during the war and burned doors
and banisters to keep themselves warm. Cautiously our lives as
well as our possessions began to expand.

We enjoyed it all immensely but success, and the relative affluence it brought, had disturbing undercurrents. I never had
felt and never learned to feel at ease with theater folk, except
when interviewing them as a journalist. I did not see them as real
people. To become one of them enlisted me, against my will, in
a band of gypsies, who lived from hand to mouth, selling their
skills like clothes pegs and painting their faces in anticipation of
riotous assembly round the campfire. In habits of thought, and
standards of social conduct, they were foreign to all the people I
had known and consorted with over the years. Their gaiety was
as brittle as their promises, and I saw their frequent bouts of
melancholy as unconscious rehearsals for parts they might be

called upon to play later on. Their comradeship was lightly bestowed and as lightly discarded. Above all, I had learned the hard way not to believe a single word they uttered, even when they were sober.

This was one thing, but another was more fundamental and had to do with our future habitat. Were we to up stakes and go and live among the gypsies? Or would we be better advised to do what Warwick Deeping and his wife did when the overnight success of *Sorrell and Son* engulfed him in the twenties; that is, sit down and pretend that it had never happened?

For it was in these terms that I began to see myself, not as a creative artist, with some undefined role to play in the theater, but as a stay-at-home entertainer, someone who turned out three-and one-act plays much as a cabinet maker makes something practical from a stock of seasoned timber. I saw playwriting as a kind of extended journalism, better-paid certainly, but not nearly so interesting or so vital, because it was contrived and made to fit a pattern imposed on it by custom and fashion. I had always thought of everything I wrote as worth the passing attention of an audience but I had not (and still have not) an urge to compose moral symphonies, or to project fashionable or political themes over the footlights. I have never had much sympathy with the notion that the theater should be used for any means other than diverting people, and this is not to say that I was obsessed with comedy. A play, to me, was a prolonged charade. If one sought enlightenment or mental enlargement then one went to a book and turned the pages slowly, pondering the wisdom therein. It was this detached approach to the stage that determined my course from 1946 onward. I stayed where I was, among the people I knew and liked and trusted, and on terrain with which I was thoroughly familiar, continuing to write plays—a whole spate of them—but never letting them engage more than the surface of the mind and thinking of them, always, as a means of livelihood and nothing else.

It is not surprising that this attitude soon brought me into conflict with dedicated professional associates, none of whom could ever understand why I shied away from rehearsals and set my face against rewrites and the turmoil that surrounds each new production. In the chapter, "The Even Sadder Truth About Me and the Footlights," I wrote lightly of my disenchantment with the stage, confining myself to the more amusing aspects of the situation in which I found myself after the success of *Worm's Eye View*. In fact, it went much deeper than that, the pull of divided loyalties wrenching me this way and that, sometimes so violently that I do not look back on that decade with much pleasure or satisfaction. Professionally that is, for my private and personal life was full of interest and excitement. The two children were growing up and more than compensating us for the disappointments we had suffered in the past. I learned to ride and rediscovered the Devon countryside from the saddle. May succeeded in teaching me a degree of discrimination concerning antique furniture, and although I worked regular hours, and sat at a desk six hours a day, I still seemed to have as much leisure time as I needed.

One of the more amusing aspects of this period in my life was that of looking at local functions through the reverse end of the telescope. For eleven years preceding the war, and for a period of fifteen months after it, I had watched the world from the press table, but now, to my continuing surprise, and sometimes to my embarrassment, I had stepped forward to take my place beside the mandarins. I found myself crowning carnival queens and addressing Rotary Clubs and Women's Institutes. I judged fancy-dress parades and opened bazaars. And sometimes, hearing myself utter familiar clichés, I would glance uneasily at the press table, where a group of old friends would be scribbling into notebooks, and then my presence on the dais would seem quite absurd, as though I was mounting a practical joke at my own expense.

From time to time people I hardly knew staged plays I had written in London and the provinces, and although none was as successful as *Worm's Eye View*, they all paid off, either on tour at home and abroad, or in the repertory circuits, or among the amateurs, and sometimes in all three of these areas. In the late forties I had plays running at the Whitehall, the Princes and the Playhouse, but I stayed away from them whenever possible. I could never listen to them without thinking how easily they could have been improved. I wrote an occasional film script and found this exercise extraordinarily dull and when television became popular, in the early nineteen-fifties, I sometimes wrote a play for that medium, having already written a number of pieces for radio. I preferred radio work to TV writing. It is more interesting, from a creative point of view, to tell a story by sound only, and I have a theory concerning the surprising lack of impact made by a majority of television plays. It revolves around the enormous number of options open to the originator. The limitations of a radio play are severe and this, I think, demands a great deal more thought and selectivity on the part of writer, cast and director.

I did many other things apart from writing. For more than two years I ran a small farm, learning how to milk cows and rear pigs, fowls and ducks. May became an expert at making Devonshire cream and butter, and we ultimately acquired a T.T. license from the Ministry of Agriculture. Later on I ran a brace of antique shops, but all these activities, I soon realized, were no more than field work in preparation for what I really wanted to do. On January 1, 1956, almost exactly ten years from the time *Worm's Eye View* began its run, I cut the painter and did it, settling down to write the first section of *The Avenue Story*, a long saga that aimed at projecting the English way of life in a London suburb from the end of World War One to the reconstruction period of the late nineteen-forties.

The abrupt change of direction involved us in considerable financial readjustments. I had published three or four books by then but the theater had claimed by far the greater part of my time. In that first year as a novelist my income dropped seventy percent, but so did my expenses, and once the backlog of taxation was paid off I was no worse off. Although my standard of living fell, and we moved from house to cottage, I enjoyed a sense of liberation that had evaded me since the day H. E. Bates and I drew our civvy kit at the demob center. At last I could write what I wanted to write, and not what fashion and the advice of professional actors dictated.

In the next decade I completed three two-volume sagas, four

histories of aspects of the Napoleonic Empire, and half a dozen shorter novels. The three plays I wrote during this period were historical dramas, specially written for Pitlochry Festivals. Everything I knew and felt and had experienced over the past forty-odd years went into the characters I created and came to life as they grew from a few sentences on a blank sheet into three-dimensional, flesh-and-blood men and women. In most cases I used the West Country backdrop, where the sky and seascape are never the same for more than ten minutes and the landscape, apparently unchanging, puts on a brand-new costume for each of the four seasons. From going to London once a fortnight I went there about twice a year, and after half a dozen brief and very depressing expeditions to the Continent, I threw the travel brochures in the wastepaper basket and settled for more familiar scenes, the Welsh hills, the Lakes, the moorland country of the North Riding, the Cheviots, and, above all, the pine, bracken and granite outcrop country of the West. I can never be absent from Britain for more than twelve hours before I begin to suffer the pangs of homesickness, and the older I grow the more mulishly insular I become. One of the postwar trends that continue to amaze me is the annual summer trek to countries like Spain and Italy where, as I see it, a majority of people are still grappling with social and political problems solved by British liberal governments in the late nineteenth century. They may have more sun, and they may be temporarily solvent, but they are amateurs in the essentials of democratic practice, particularly those of maintaining public order and sharing what there is to be shared. Some day I hope history will acknowledge this.

Which brings me, more or less, up to date, a balding, unrepentant, stay-at-home, content to sit here weaving home-grown garments, at peace with most people (except gibbering enthusiasts who strap men and monkeys into capsules and send them spinning round space), and content to accept at its face value the farewell tag stage directors toss at young actresses after an unsuccessful audition—"Don't ring us. We'll ring you!"

Over There

No aspect of late-twentieth-century life (save, possibly, that of public enthusiasm at a professional football match) causes me more genuine astonishment than the annual, biennial and sometimes triennial expeditions of the British to the Continent.

Sometimes I pause to watch them gathering at the aerial assembly point, loaded down with baggage and sporty impedimenta of every description, awaiting what strikes me as a parody of the Last Trump, a rehearsal for the moment when relatives stand whispering beside the bed, when the defeated physician shakes his head, and the fingers of the dying fidget with rumpled sheets —"Passengers for Flaight 105 to Barcelona, will you *please* go to gate seven . . . ," "Passengers for Flaight 209 to Rome, please collect your hend-luggage and go to gate nane. . . ." For me it is a summons to the ferry of the Styx. To them it is routine, as ordinary and banal as the whistle of the guard and the slamming of doors on the departure platform of their suburban station. Nobody seems bothered. Nobody takes a last, lingering look at a familiar background, or wipes the perspiration from his forehead. They are about to embark on a journey that would have thrown Marco Polo and Columbus into screaming fits. They look as if they were drifting down the garden path to make sure the garage is locked. Their *sang-froid* and fortitude amaze me, but even the inexperienced among them seem hardly aware of anything more than a tremor in the rhythm of their workaday lives. They are flying sunward or skiward, to walk among strangers in strange lands, to subsist on strange, indigestible diets . . . yet they show less agitation than they might en route to the office toilet. I turn away, shaking my head at my own insularity and at the astounding adaptability of the island race, grandsons and granddaughters of men who rarely set foot in the adjoining county. I feel like a time-machine traveler whose cogs jammed the night Prince Albert died.

There had been talk of a promotional visit to America for quite some time, but I had never taken it seriously. For six years, between 1940 and 1945, I lived in a kit bag and was posted about Western Europe like an illegibly addressed parcel, and I was fond of saying, in those far-off days, that if, after the war, you caught me the wrong side of the Channel, you were at liberty to shoot me. By and large, I kept my isolationist vows, and whenever I broke them I regretted it. But sometimes a man's destiny gets between him and his inclination, and thus it was, on the Monday following hijack Sunday in September, 1970, that I actually found myself among those blank-faced airport dawdlers, headed, not for the Costa del Sol or Salzburg or anywhere relatively handy, but for New York and beyond. I was stunned by my own hardihood.

By courtesy of a solicitous West End hotel manager, aware of my isolationist prejudices, I was also stunned by a bottle of his best champagne, so that I submitted to the curious antics of Heathrow dispatchers with equanimity, even when they began frisking me for hand grenades. The haze lasted long enough to keep me indifferent until I was airborne in a West-bound Qantas jet, but it began to disperse about the time we flew over the long, jutting peninsula where I had spent most of my life and to which it now seemed probable I would never return. For a man who, reckless with managerial champagne, embarks upon a promotional tour of the United States is not, to my mind, tempting Providence. He is tacitly inviting his solicitors below to blow the dust from his deed box and begin to calculate to what extent the Chancellor will benefit by his abrupt departure.

The effects of the champagne lingered, however, long enough to enable me to make a kind of inventory of what I knew, or thought I knew, of America and the Americans.

It was a long and varied inventory, going all the way back to the day I was born, February 12, 1912, for February 12 is Lincoln's Birthday, and it seems my arrival caused something of a stir in the family, my father, a fanatical radical, revering Abe Lincoln as the Skipper-next-to-God. It was a fortunate day on which to be born in our house. Busts and pictures of Abe occupied all corners of the house, and every bookcase was stuffed with Civil War memoirs. Perhaps this circumstance alone was responsible for what I can only regard as a special relationship with America, for I never did see it as a foreign country, in the sense that France, Switzerland and even Australia are repellently alien. It was a vibrant, romantic land, where anything could happen and most things did, to the immense profit of the Hollywood dream spinners and their generations of dupes, of whom I became one at the age of eight. Yet my awe for America was not wholly enclosed in celluloid. A little of it seeped out into the open every now and again, so that I can remember very vividly the first two Americans I ever met, and what imprinted them upon my memory.

One was a boy with whom I went swimming in 1925, a visitor paying a brief visit to our small seaside town. I remember him because his shirt buttoned up the front. I had no doubt at all, as I pulled my own shirt over my head and watched him unbutton his, that my suspicions concerning the Arabian Nights quality of America were solidly based. For here was proof of it—a shirt that you put on and took off just as though it were a pajama jacket. The fact that these shirts are now commonplace in Europe today is also proof that everything, given time, flows eastward.

Not long after that, an American boy joined our school, a friendly, uninhibited chap called B. O. Lisle, who received many

373

tuck parcels and invited me to share his transatlantic bounty—
peanut butter and maple syrup. He was a generous boy and
spread them very thickly on my school scrape, persuading me
that over there it was considered a rare treat. How I swallowed
it, every last mouthful, without affronting him, I shall never
know, but I did. It must have had something to do with *noblesse
oblige*, and the knowledge that the Americans were a proud,
trigger-happy people.

I survived Lisle's peanut butter and maple syrup, to witness all
the gangster films of the early talkie era, sitting rigid in my sixpenny seat throughout successive showings of open touring cars
screaming around South Side corners, squealers slumping behind
the splintered glass of telephone booths, and an endless succession
of lethal confrontations between two groups of cornered underlings wearing snap-brimmed hats. The overlords never died in
these preliminary engagements. They expired a reel or so later,
on glistening pavements, croaking a final wisecrack into the ear
of a solicitous priest or a plainclothes cop.

It might strike the modern American as very odd that my conception of his country in those days was based upon such trivia,
but it was so. Even when I read the British newspapers, the headlines as likely as not were given over to Capone, O'Banion, Dil-
linger and Prohibition. There were also the dance hits that
washed our shores year after year from Tin Pan Alley, so that
our very romances were, so to speak, set to transatlantic rhythms.
I wholly approved of this. Those songs helped me through my
adolescence. Many were the bobbed heads I cradled on my breast
as we crooned of moons waxing and waning over every state in
the Union. And how many times did I summon Swanee River
and the Mississippi to my aid when I was making with a brunette
and a four-and-sixpenny ukulele?

There was Hollywood, there was Tin Pan Alley, and there
was Mark Twain. And later on there were *Oklahoma, Annie Get
Your Gun,* and Steinbeck. And, further back, as a kind of beginner's course, there were Louisa M. Alcott and Harriet Beecher
Stowe. Is it any wonder I was ill prepared for the avalanche of

honest-to-God Americans that in 1942 enveloped every shire of my native land?

How they startled us, those shiploads of GI's, spilling in green-gray waves on embattled, blacked-out, browned-off Britain. Hollywood, Tin Pan Alley, Louisa M. Alcott, Mark Twain, and even Steinbeck, had done nothing to prepare us for anything of this kind. The animal high spirits of the very earliest arrivals rocked us on our heels. For it was "Hiya!" and "Howdy!" as the siren wailed the Alert and All Clear. "Birming'm" became "Birming-*ham*" overnight, and the civic tyranny of the blackout failed to mask all those scuffling embraces in doorways, all those shameless, stay-with-me-baby kisses at local bus stops. And this in a land where, before the war, policemen growled "Move along there" to lovers holding hands in the park!

We have never recovered from it. The Permissive Age is allegedly a British export, but that is hogwash. I have been watching the British carefully for half a century, and I know very well that permissiveness is as much an American import as the It girl, chewing gum, and the Charleston.

And after the GI's came the postwar tourists. Singly. In pairs. In camera-clicking coachloads. A strange breed this, with very little in common with the stay-at-home American. "Elmer, I *told* yew to git a taxi! . . . Don't stand there, Elmer, git a taxi, honey! . . ." Or: "We were through Stratford-*upon*-Avon yesterday. Kinda cute, Stratford-*upon*-Avon. But this is a package tour. We're doo in Edinburgh by sundown. . . ."

And after the tourists the TV coverage, dedicated almost exclusively to an America seething with street riots and with demonstrations so unlike our own, where policemen walk sedately beside sheepish banner-carrying demonstrators, and a brass band up ahead plays "Colonel Bogey."

Not much of a playing-in course for a first-ever visit to the States, you might say, and brother, would you be right! For years and years and years I had been listening at all the wrong keyholes.

I was aware of this almost as soon as we touched down. A blanket of solicitude enfolded me, disguised as a charming air hostess, gathering me up like a lost child and piloting me swiftly through customs. The customs officer did not so much as glance at my baggage, but he did say, "Have yourself a good time, sir!" No customs officer in the world had ever been that expansive.

The air hostess handed me on to a girl with a Cadillac. The Cadillac was twice as big as Capone's armor-plated sedan, the one that toured our fairgrounds. The girl was the girl one dreams about when, at nineteen, one is hopelessly vulnerable to perfumed femininity. She purred, "So glad you got here. We were worried, though. We thought you might have been diverted to Cuba. . . ." We glided over the Queensboro Bridge and into the concrete canyons. At the hotel were three gift-wrapped bottles of cognac. I remembered what happened to Dylan Thomas, read the notes and ordered pineapple juice.

People gathered. Urbane, soft-spoken men and young ladies who in my heyday, around 1930, would have been absorbed en masse into the Ziegfeld chorus. Slowly and effortlessly The Skedule took over—literary parties, press interviews, radio slots, TV confrontations, and every aspect of The Skedule succeeded in surprising me. It was played on such a low key, insistent certainly but never strident; it was faultlessly timed, smoothly oiled, expertly manipulated. It made me feel a little like a bubble being passed carefully and conscientiously from fingertip to fingertip. No noise and no hustle. The machine took over, and all that was required of me was to act like the end product.

American journalists, I discovered, are all specialists of one sort or another, so that talk strayed far from the book, touching on areas closer, alas, to the interviewer's heart. With one it was canals. With another it was Raymond Chandler's Gomorrah beside the Pacific. With a third it was, believe it or not, our very own Wars of the Roses. With all of them, given time, it led to Shiloh, Chancellorsville, Antietam and Leonidas Polk, last of the warrior bishops. Just as the customs man advised, we all had ourselves a good time. For these, in the main, were topics close to my heart. It was very different with the radio and TV interviewers. One and all, they had done their homework, but they didn't let it show until we were actually on the air. I had forbidding memories of BBC interviews. At Television Centre, London, they have a way of making you feel you are there seeking an audience with an exclusive mortician about what is to be done with Uncle Harry's remains. That, or waiting in the antechamber of some great English aristocrat, whose patronage you crave for the publication of a dictionary and the post of chamberpot emptier. It was so different here. They greeted one in shirtsleeves, called me Ronnie, and gave me endless cups of coffee in paper cups. It was much more like the sergeant's mess and the better for it, at least until they asked about an obscure character in the book before last, someone you had long since forgotten. For all that, I was disconcerted only once, and that had nothing to do with my recollection of characters I had sent out to earn their bread and salt and promptly forgotten, like a reckless philanderer who sires bastards twice a week.

I forget where it was exactly. Interviews tended to become blurred as time passed and crisp new Skedules were left with my hotel clerk. All I recall is that we were having an earnest discussion on Lord Shaftesbury, the nineteenth-century reformer who freed the children from the mines and factories and sometimes succeeded in reducing their servitude to a ten-hour stint. My host knew a great deal about Lord Shaftesbury—far more than I—and I was learning fast, but suddenly an acolyte entered and handed him a slip of pink paper, so that I thought idly; "They aren't infallible, then. It's gone wrong. The mike's dead." There was nothing wrong with the mike. The Shaftesbury buff shifted his seat slightly and said, into another mike, "Have you ever tried Windberg's table wines? But you must! They grow on you. Like Mr. Delderfield's sagas. . . ." He was not gone for good, however. In a flash he was facing me again and saying with the same note of earnestness, "They tell me Charles Kingsley's *Water Babies* stirred the public conscience on chimney sweeps. How do you rate Kingsley, Mr. Delderfield?" I didn't rate him highly at that particular moment. I was too busy promising myself a private binge on Windberg's table wines.

I had expected the parties to be wild Bacchanalian affairs, but they were among the most decorous I have ever attended. Either folk could hold their liquor over here or it had got around that I was on tomato and pineapple juice. The librarian ladies fascinated me. They seemed to set great store on saga authors and were handy with all kinds of flattering statistics. It seemed I was filling some kind of gap in their shelves between, say Gibbon's *Decline and Fall* and *Everything You Want to Know about Turkish Sex;* and their polite enthusiasm gave me a solidity that I hadn't had when I touched down at Kennedy. It gave me a spurious respectability too, of the kind withheld from professional scribblers since the trial of *Lady Chatterley*, when authors went into the bracket of bawds. The librarian ladies put me through a crash course on the tastes of Middle America, and it made me feel, not significant exactly, but humored, like a man who has missed first prize at the marrow show but come away with a "highly commended." Only the male Russian librarian (white and bearded) bothered me, asking repeatedly who, among Tolstoy, Gorki, Dostoevsky and Lermontov, had breathed the hardest down my neck. Eventually the lady librarians gave him a long drink and shooed him away, continuing their helpful talk on the literary tastes of Middle America.

There were times, of course, when I wasn't working, when I would be taken in tow by someone in the book world and driven away to sample Middle America's hospitality. It was only then that I fully understood how shamefully I had been hoaxed over the years, how willfully I had been misled and had misled myself on the American character and the American scene. By then, of course, I had stopped expecting to be mugged every time I stepped out of the hotel and had even taken to talking to strangers in elevators. The forty bucks I had hidden in my socks on arrival were still there. You don't need money among the Middle Americans. The one aspect of the transatlantic legend that has substance is the hospitality you can expect among Americans at home. I never did succeed in paying for a drink, a meal, a taxi ride, or even admission to a cinema. The Middle Americans took care of all that between showing me where to wash and brush up, running me to and from airports in rush-hour traffic, finding places where I could get a real English pot of tea, and talking wistfully of Britannia, whom they seemed to reverence as a matriarch of incredible age and enormous dignity, with the right —nay, the duty—to chide hordes of quarrelsome great-grand-children scattered about the world and currently not behaving so well.

It shamed me, this kind of talk. Maybe, once upon a time, Britannia had qualified for that splendid role, but not since I was halfway through my adolescence. I thought of places like Carnaby Street, and the dropout center at Piccadilly Circus, and then of all the libels I had read and slanders I had heard about my gentle hosts. It was like living a lie so big and so outrageous that it belonged in the repertoire of the late Doctor Goebbels.

Toward the end of my stay I did ask myself if I wasn't being conned all over again. After all, I reasoned, I was a guest, moving mostly among people with a common interest in books and writers, and to add to that, of course, I was an incurable romantic and a relative innocent concerning the lives and characters of foreigners. But here I had to acknowledge a conclusion that had been taking root in me ever since touchdown. I wasn't among foreigners at all. I was having half-hourly reencounters with the kind of folk who were once thick on the ground in any British seaside resort or market town, but who seemed to have folded their tents and stolen away about the time they invented the computer and country lanes became four-lane highways. In a way it was like stepping back into a time when people talked to one another in trains, when the water cart was still seen on the street,

when suburban rose growers gave little boys a penny a pail for
horse manure, and all the children of the suburbs collected
cigarette cards and played conkers. It was a very cozy, reassuring
feeling. The only thing wrong about it was that it had absolutely
nothing in common with all I had been told or had imagined
about the America of today.

I have wondered since, in my new role as an Americophile,
whether I could have been horribly mistaken, whether, in fact,
I got the kid-glove treatment from start to finish, encouraging
me to shy away from that aspect of America fitfully revealed to
me in the undeniable schism between the haves and the have-nots,
the doves and the hawks and, above all, between the Kids and an
Establishment forsworn to a philosophy of laissez-faire material-
ism. It is possible, I suppose, and the prophets of doom one meets
everywhere outside America, those who seem persuaded that the
North American civilization is hell-bent on self-destruction and
wholly dedicated to public and private violence, can produce
formidable statistics and any amount of evidence on film. I can
only reiterate, however, that it did not strike me as so, and that
the Americans I met were, almost without exception, decent,
homely, self-respecting folk; slightly troubled, certainly, but far
from despairing, and nothing like as cynical as the average
European, who has long since ceased to examine his conscience
and is inclined to regard anyone who does as impossibly naïve.

I have thought of something else, too, since my return, and
here it is, naïve or not. A nation that, in the space of less than
two centuries, explored and tamed a trackless wilderness three
thousand miles across, opened its doors to millions of the home-
less, the dispossessed and the persecuted, survived a fratricidal war
lasting four tormented years, and after that an economic blizzard
on the scale of the Wall Street Slump, yet still rallied twice in a
single generation to the defense of human dignity, is certainly
equipped to search out men and women of stature who will, in
time, set about solving all the major social problems of the seven-

ties and eighties. It might even do more. It might, conceivably, emerge with an impressive credit balance in the books of the human heart.

This is a guess, and certainly it is an earnest hope, the very best available to Europeans in this day and age, for I am not among those who fail to acknowledge free Europe's enormous debt to America between 1917 and 1971. For my part, to give the claim relevance, I can only add that on my return home I felt obliged to clear my desk of accumulated work and write over a hundred bread-and-butter letters, of the kind I was taught to write as a child after being given hospitality by a relative or friend. I do not recall an urge to write a single bread-and-butter letter after a stay in any other country I have visited since the dust settled over the Third Reich.